The 1984–86 famine relief operatio[n] ... peacetime mobilisation of the internati[onal] ... seven million people faced starvatio[n] ...

The relief operation, spearheaded by the United Nations, shipped and distributed $1 billion of food aid to the region in a few months.

This book investigates why such a potential disaster was allowed to develop. Forewarning of imminent famine was available from many sources early in 1984. Yet a complex web of factors prevented more than a trickle of aid from reaching Ethiopia.

An international outcry following the screening of a BBC documentary film on the famine prompted the United Nations to launch a massive relief programme.

Here is the story of that programme, written by the man who master-minded it. The impressive achievements of this operation are detailed. Yet many faults and shortcomings are also acknowledged. A frank and honest portrait emerges which does not shrink from addressing the difficult questions.

The problem of rebel-held areas in Tigray and Eritrea, the Ethiopian Government's controversial resettlement programme, accusations of corruption, inefficiency and food diversion are all dealt with in a critical manner.

Jansson argues that despite some shortcomings, the UN system led to a largely effective operation which saved millions of lives.

Harris and Penrose provide essential background to this and show conclusively that the eleventh hour intervention could have been avoided if the warning signals had been heeded.

They also look to the future and warn that the crisis is not yet over. The post-famine feeding operation presents many problems, and Western aid agencies still have much to learn.

Kurt Jansson was Head of the UN Relief Operation in Ethiopia, December 1984 to January 1986. He has been a member of the UN Secretariat since 1952 and has administered UN programmes in the Lebanon, Pakistan, Nigeria and Kampuchea.

Michael Harris was Overseas Operations Director of Oxfam, 1970–1984, and now acts as a consultant for a number of international relief and development organisations.

Angela Penrose is a writer, researcher and lecturer who has worked in Africa for many years.

Note from the Publishers

The authors of *The Ethiopian Famine* initially approached Zed Books quite independently of each other, but almost simultaneously — Kurt Jansson with his graphic and immediate account of the UN relief operation, written from the very helm of that endeavour, and Michael Harris with the background story to famines in Ethiopia and the prospects for current rehabilitation programmes, researched principally by himself and written by Angela Penrose.

We took the view that here were two manuscripts which, while complete in themselves, were looking for each other; each seemed to illuminate and enlarge the other. Accordingly, we proposed to the authors that the two should be published as a single volume. They agreed readily, and the book went into production without further ado.

We have, therefore, an unusual book — neither an edited volume, nor a collaborative piece in the usual sense of the word. Neither author was required to revise his or her own work in the light of the other's, nor to intervene in any way upon the other's work. Each section of the book stands alone, although they belong side by side.

The Ethiopian Famine

Kurt Jansson
Michael Harris
Angela Penrose

Zed Books Ltd.
London and New Jersey

The Ethiopian Famine was first published by Zed Books Ltd.,
57 Caledonian Road, London N1 9BU, UK,
and 171 First Avenue, Atlantic Highlands,
New Jersey 07716, USA, in 1987.

Cover designed by Adrian Yeeles/Artworkers.
Cover photograph by Hugh Goyder/Oxfam.
Typeset by EMS Photosetters, Rochford, Essex.
Printed in the United Kingdom
by Biddles Ltd., Guildford and Kings Lynn.

British Library Cataloguing in Publication Data
Jansson, Kurt
    The Ethiopian famine : the story of the
    emergency relief operation.
    1. Famines —— Ethiopia
    I. Title   II. Harris, Michael
    III. Penrose, Angela
    363.3'492   HC845.Z9F3
    ISBN 0-86232-744-X
    ISBN 0-86232-745-8 Pbk

Contents

Maps

Photograph appears on page xxiv

Abbreviations

AMC	Agricultural Marketing Board
CELU	Confederation of Ethiopian Labour Unions
COPWE	Commission to Organise the Party of the Working People of Ethiopia
CRDA	Christian Relief Development Association
CRC	Christian Relief Committee
CRS	Catholic Relief Services
CSO	Central Statistical Office
ECA	Economic Commission for Africa (of the United Nations)
ECMY	Evangelical Church Mekane Yesus
ECTA	Ethiopian Transport Construction Authority
EDU	Ethiopian Democratic Union
ELF	Eritrean Liberation Front
EPLF	Eritrean Peoples' Liberation Front
EPRP	Ethiopian Peoples' Revolutionary Party
EWPSD	Early Warning Planning Services Department
EWS	Early Warning System
ESUE	Ethiopian Students Union in Europe
ESUNA	Ethiopian Students Union in North America
ERCS	Ethiopian Red Cross Society
ENI	Ethiopian Nutrition Institute
FAO	Food and Agriculture Organisation (of the United Nations)
HSIU	Haile Selassie I University
ICRC	International Committee of the Red Cross
ME'ISON	All Ethiopian Socialist Movement
MoD	Ministry of Defence
NGO	Non-governmental organisation
NMSA	National Meterological Services Agency
OAU	Organisation of African Unity
ODA	Overseas Development Administration (of the UK government)
OEOA	Office of Emergency Operations in Africa (of the United Nations)
PA	Peasant Association
PMAC	Provisional Military Administrative Council
REST	Relief Society of Tigray
RRC	Relief and Rehabilitation Commission (of Ethiopia)

SCF	Save the Children Fund
TPLF	Tigrean Peoples' Liberation Front
UNDP	United Nations Development Programme
UNDRO	United Nations Disaster Relief Organisation
UNHCR	United Nations High Commissioner for Refugees
UNICEF	United Nations Childrens' Fund
USAID	United States Agency for International Development
WHO	World Health Organisation
WFP	World Food Programme

Glossary

arata: loan
awraja: sub-division of a province
belg: short rains (spring)
Birr: Ethiopian currency unit; 2.07 Birr = US$1
dega: high, temperate zone
deha: poor farmer
degazza and *deyri*: (crop-destroying pests, grasshoppers & army worm)
gult: a fief granted by the emperor incorporating the rights to tribute and labour from peasants on a certain piece of land
habtam: rich farmer
kebele: urban dwellers association
keremt: main rainy season
maskal: Feast of the True Cross, 27th September
malba/welba/weland: further stages of land reform involving greater degrees of collectivisation
meher: main harvest, November, December; currently used to refer to main rainy season leading to main harvest
mulatch deha: very poor farmer
quola: low-lying, hot area
rist: hereditary right to piece of land
tschikashum: village headman
woreda: sub-division of an awraja
woyna-dega: intermediate zone
zemecha: campaign

Maps

Map of Ethiopia and Population
(approximate figures)

	POPULATION (1984 CENSUS)	DROUGHT-AFFECTED PEOPLE 1985	1986
Eritrea	2,615,000	830,000	650,000
Gonder	2,905,000	365,000	135,000
Tigray	2,410,000	1,430,000	1,000,000
Welo	3,610,000	2,590,000	1,455,000
Shewa	8,090,000	850,000	630,000
Sidamo	3,790,000	535,000	445,000
Harerge	4,150,000	875,000	1,200,00
others	- -	525,000	400,000
Total		8,000,000	5,915,000

(estimates of drought-affected people based on RRC figures)

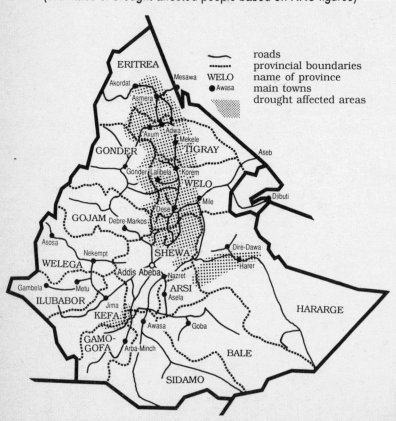

Major NGO's and Their Main Places (Province) of Activities, 1984 - 1985

CARE   American NGO
CDAA   a pool of American NGO's
CONCERN   Irish NGO
CRDA   Christian Relief and Development Association:
          the pool for the smaller NGO's
CRS   Catholic Relief Service
ECS   Ethiopian Catholic Secretariat
EOC   Ethiopian Orthodox Church
ICRC   International Committee of the Red Cross (Swiss)
IMT   Italian Medical Team (Italian Government)
LRCS   League of the Red Cross Societies
LWF   Lutheran World Federation
MSF   Medecines sans Frontieres (French and Belgian)
OXFAM   English NGO
SCF   Save the Children Fund (English and American)
WUSC   World University Service of Canada
WV   World Vision International (American)

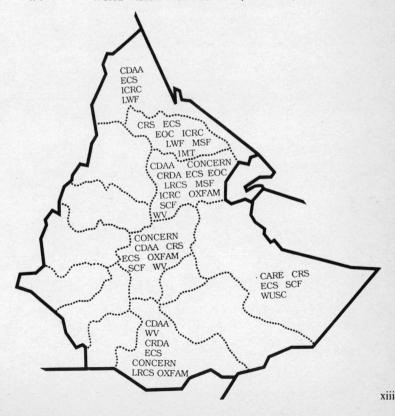

Security Situation 1985

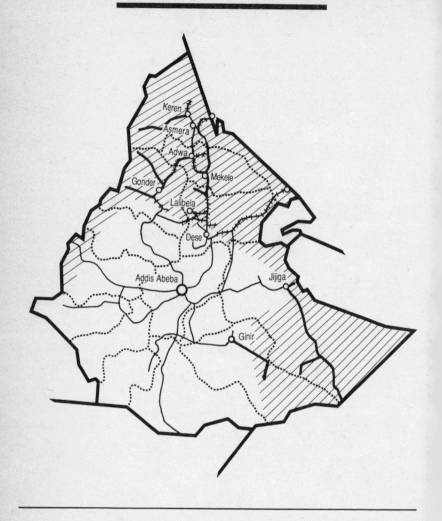

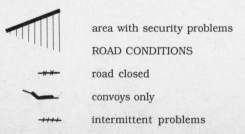

area with security problems

ROAD CONDITIONS

✗✗ road closed

convoys only

✦✦✦✦ intermittent problems

Major Distribution Points with Regular Supply

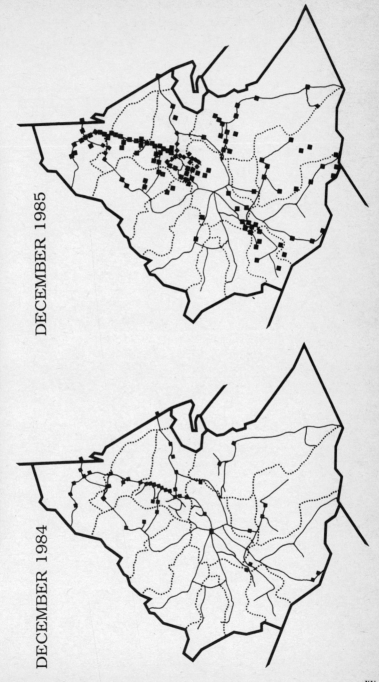

DECEMBER 1984

DECEMBER 1985

Relative Importance of Road and Air Transport, 1985

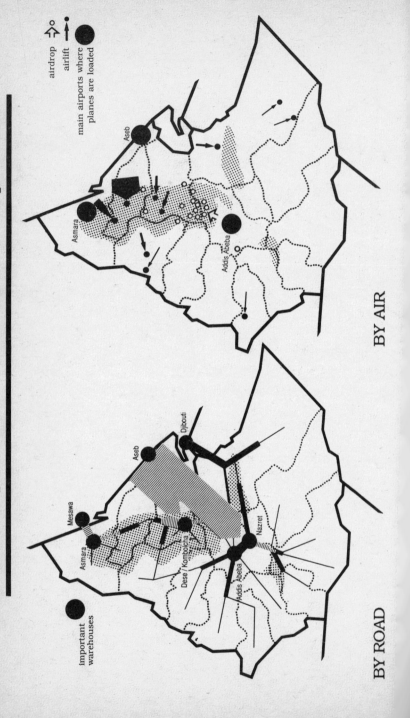

Number of People in and around Shelters and Displaced Population

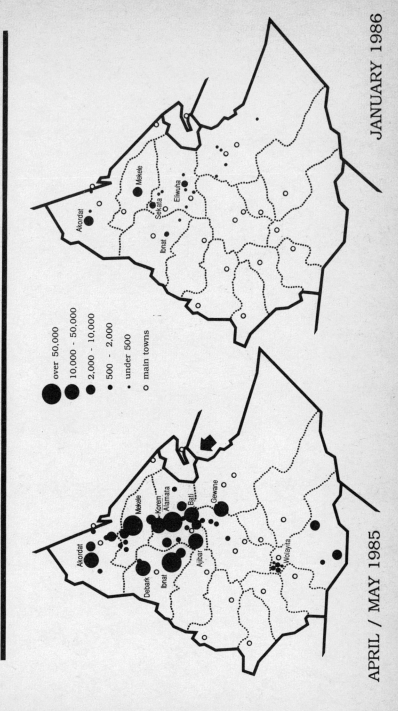

JANUARY 1986

APRIL / MAY 1985

over 50,000
10,000 - 50,000
2,000 - 10,000
· 500 - 2,000
· under 500
o main towns

Akordat
Mekele
Sekota
Elwuha
Ibnat

Akordat
Debark
Ibnat
Mekele
Korem
Alamata
Bati
Ajibar
Gewane
Wolayita

Resettlement 1985 - 1986

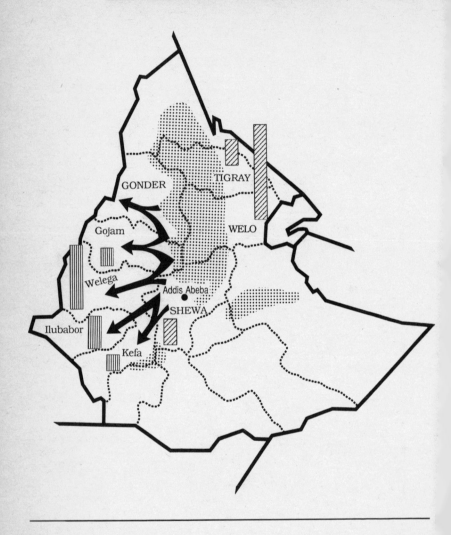

main drought affected areas
(courtesy Dr. H. Hurni)

number of people by
province of origin

new province

number of people

300,000

100,000
50,000
0

Introduction

by
Michael Harris

Introduction

This is a book in two parts, both written by people with detailed knowledge of Ethiopia.

Kurt Jansson had a long and successful career in the United Nations Development Programme (UNDP) and after retirement was brought back by Perez de Cuellar, Secretary General of the United Nations, into surely the most tragic situation of the decade — tragic because it need not have happened. In 1980 Kurt had been appointed to a similar role in Kampuchea so already had experience in trying to bring some order into a situation involving governments, UN agencies, voluntary agencies and the representatives of the media. In both Kampuchea and Ethiopia, he had to concern himself with the conflicts of the great powers, the conflicting interests of the UN agencies and the often uncoordinated efforts of the voluntary agencies.

Kurt Jansson's calm leadership, honest neutrality, and understanding of the political nuances enabled the UN system to coordinate a largely effective operation that saved millions of lives. Parallel to the UN operations were the non-governmental organisation (NGO) activities, which I shall refer to later. But the vastly increasing and influential roles of the voluntary agencies, following Kampuchea and then Ethiopia, have brought a new perspective to both emergency and development aid.

Kurt Jansson's inside view of the whole Ethiopian famine relief operation is not only of interest, but of considerable value to all those who, sadly, will be involved in future disasters. In describing the reactions to the Ethiopian situation, that were often defined as 'too little and too late', the question must be asked 'Will it happen again?' As things are at the moment it appears only too likely, and for this reason Kurt Jansson's account is essential reading for those who will be involved in similar emergency situations in the future.

Apart from its intrinsic interest, Kurt Jansson's contribution provides proof that given the right leadership, both the UN and the voluntary agencies can together perform a remarkably successful operation. The UN comes in for much criticism which on occasions during the early stages of the famine is justifiable, but it is good to see the later effectiveness and splendid work of the Office for the Emergency Operations in Ethiopia, of which Kurt Jansson was the Director.

Angela Penrose's contribution, in the second part of this book, provides the background to the whole Ethiopia scene and, what is equally important, possibilities for future action. As I have said, the possibilities of future food shortages in the Sahel, including Ethiopia, are very real. Every effort must, therefore, be made to correct some of the causes responsible for the tragedy of 1984/85. When I was in Ethiopia during the 1974 famine, we never believed there would be a repetition, even more terrible, a mere 10 years later. In 1975, the new Revolutionary government commissioned a team to investigate the causes of that earlier disaster. One finding was:

> The primary cause of the famine was not a drought of unprecedented severity, but a combination of long continued bad land use and steadily and increasing human and stock population over decades, rendering a greater number of people and their animals vulnerable when the drought struck. Insecure and inequitable land tenure systems, communal or tenancy, were another primary cause of the disaster. Soil erosion and massive deforestation added to the deterioration.

Has the situation changed? Is development going forward fast enough to allow the massive increase of food production by the small farmers that is so necessary? A comprehensive study of the social, economic and political background and future development is needed to complement Kurt Jansson's story.

Angela Penrose is well-equipped to provide this. She worked at the National University in Addis Ababa in 1973/74, and when it was closed owing to student action, she became the administrator of the University Relief and Rehabilitation organisation. This was one of the few indigenous organisations in Ethiopia at the time and she gained unique experience during that famine. Since then she has been able to keep closely in touch with events in Ethiopia and visited the country in February 1987 in order to update and finalise her contribution to this book.

During 1985 and 1986 many books, of varying qualities and depths, were written about Africa; those listed in the bibliography are among the best. The majority are by journalists and describe the situations in Ethiopia, Sudan or Mozambique. I think this book offers something that others lack — Kurt Janssons's inside story. It tells of his personal contacts with Chairman Mengistu Haile Mariam but, above all, is a revealing account of the aid programme over the most critical time of Ethiopia's famine. No two books or articles written about this period entirely agree on facts or figures; this can be explained by failure of research, the crisis mentality, always present in times of stress, but sadly much information has been influenced by political gerrymandering and biased and discriminatory opinion. This particularly applies to the media reporting; Kurt Jansson deals at length with this.

Angela Penrose's contribution provides a background to the crisis and concentrates on the historical aspect, the causes of the famine and the part played by the international agencies; and perhaps most importantly, the future and what is being done in the whole field of development. It must be understood that without development in its wider interpretation, a series of future famines is unavoidable. By development I refer to the whole field of rural development, from support for the small farmer, credit facilities, land tenure, environmental control, population theories, price control of basic commodities and, above all, security. It is in these areas that foreign aid can offer assistance and this applies particularly to the non-governmental agencies.

Numerous NGOs have worked in Ethiopia for many years, some arrived during the 1974 crisis and stayed, and a multitude of others arrived in 1984. What is the future for those still there? How can they best offer their aid? Are they welcome, and can they really become involved in long-term work that may possibly help prevent future famines? It was in an attempt to answer some of these questions that an American NGO, Feed the Hungry, through its affiliate group the International Institute for Relief and Development, under its President Dr Tetsunao Yamamori, asked me to set up a small group of experts to help it find some answers. This group includes such luminaries as Robert Chambers from the Institute for Development Studies at the University of Sussex, Hakan Landelius of Rädda Barnen, and Kurt Jansson himself. We believe that one of the problems is the need for more basic information about the country and its government. The lack of information forthcoming from the government makes it in many ways its own worst enemy. It is felt, therefore, that as a start a number of papers should be prepared covering such matters as the economy, the contribution of foreign aid, the Ten Year Plan, the structure of government and its methods of operation, and the policies guiding resettlement and villagisation. These latter two subjects are the cause of much criticism and accusation. From all reports and personal accounts it is clear that much has been at fault in the methods of implementing these controversial activities, but too little is known of the policies behind them and how and why the guidelines and methods of operations were established. Angela Penrose's document is an attempt to provide some of what we believe is the type of information that will be of assistance to those committed to work in Ethiopia. Some eight papers are planned, the majority to be written by Ethiopians, as it is felt very strongly that this must basically be an Ethiopian undertaking. These papers will be freely available to all interested parties.

It is impossible to discuss the Ethiopian famine or development or any aspect of work by foreign or international agencies and ignore the politics of the situation. Our involvement and what we write will doubtless be criticised and challenged because it appears to avoid, and even ignore, the politics that dominate every aspect of life in Ethiopia, especially foreign aid; this particularly refers to the peoples of Eritrea and Tigray. The sufferings of those two war-torn provinces is as great, if not greater, than in the rest of the country. It is not often realised that many relief organisations based in Addis Ababa use Sudan as a base for their operations in Eritrea and Tigray.

It is my strong opinion, and I speak with the authority of involvement in overseas aid for more than 25 years, that poverty and suffering resulting from an emergency is almost all man-made and therefore political. Wars and civil disturbances, refugee situations, the denial of human rights, and the poverty that causes the deaths of unknown millions of children throughout what is termed the Third World are the results of political decisions and political mismanagement. In this situation the North is rarely blameless.

This situation of man-made disaster and its political cause must always be understood — acquiescence is another matter — and how to face it must be a matter of judgement. The overriding reason why aid by international agencies is offered must be basically humanitarian, to assist those in the greatest need or for those who cannot help themselves. Whether we approve or disapprove of the politics of a country that requests aid, it is always the needs of the people that dictate the work. Merely to condemn the situation in Eritrea and Tigray and denounce the causes is not a solution. How development, as opposed to emergency relief, is tackled is the answer. Salvation lies in projects that give people the authority and an understanding and wherewithal to tackle their own problems. To rant and rave at conditions we believe to be intolerable may only make matters worse. From the projects we support comes the knowledge of how to proceed. The fight against discrimination, corruption, abuse of human rights, violence and injustice must continue, but how this is done calls for sensitive approaches and great care; and must not reflect adversely on those in need. Because this book deals with operations based in Addis Ababa it must not be thought that the people in the northern areas were forgotten. Nobody fought harder than Kurt Jansson to obtain approval for food to enter those areas.

A recent article in *Le Monde Diplomatique* asked how we can avoid the problems of the starving child in a Marxist state and pointed out the need for tolerance. Certain donor countries are prepared to support such countries as Ethiopia and Vietnam with emergency aid, but not development. This surely is a specious policy. Lack of development hastens the return of an emergency. We saw, however, the contortions needed to obtain food from certain Western donors. Food aid can be used as a political weapon and can be denied to those whose governments are not in accord with the richer and more powerful donor.

One of the striking results of the Ethiopian crisis was the wave of public sympathy that followed TV reports; more than £100m was raised from the British public alone. This had a direct bearing on the actions of donor governments; they could not claim that support for government funding was lacking. Public conscience and an understanding of what was happening in Africa was reflected in strong support given to NGOs.

For the past few years governments and UN agencies have increasingly supported and encouraged NGOs. Although many think that praise and recognition of their activities is justified, it has at times been embarrassing. Why? Is it because of their success as opposed to the failures by others who should know better? Possibly it is their understanding of basic problems of poverty based on their grassroots experience. Again, NGOs have the freedom to work with the people who are in need and, unlike official agencies, they do not have to channel their funds through governments.

Such recognition, whilst pleasant, has its dangers; official expectations have to be met, a high profile is expected, flexibility and independence may be sacrificed and, if things go wrong, the NGO may become the official scapegoat. However, as Peter Gill puts it in his excellent book *A Year in the Death of Africa*, there is recognition that Small is now Beautiful and the large and unsuitable projects known as 'white elephants' that roamed the African bush are now extinct. Long may this last. Despite all this, however, the voluntary agencies, who until recently referred to themselves as charities, now have a role to play unimagineable to their founders of

40 years ago. I think it is a pity that charities have become NGOs, the word charity should be a constant reminder of their role, however large they may become.

Concentration on the voluntary organisations should not detract from the work of the UN agencies in Ethiopia. The success of the Office for Emergency Operations in Ethiopia cannot and must not be denied. Provided future catastrophies can be dealt with by someone with capabilities comparable to Kurt Jansson's, many difficulties will be overcome. There is no doubt, however, that in normal times and in the absence of a focal point or supreme commander, both UN agencies and voluntary organisations would benefit enormously from better coordination and sharing of information amongst themselves and between each other. This is the great need; if such cooperation had been in operation before the disaster, much time could have been saved and procrastination prevented. Even lives might have been saved. I hope not only that this book will help those in authority to understand the need for sharing information but that action will be taken to bring it about.

Finally, what of the future? Can further catastrophies such as the Ethiopian famine be prevented? Will advantage be taken of the lessons learned? Few will forgive us, certainly not the dead, if we fail.

Michael Harris
Oxford
February 1987

SECTION 1

The Emergency Relief Operation –
The Inside View

by
Kurt Jansson

For my wife Eeva,
my sternest critic and my staunchest supporter.

Acknowledgements

In writing this account I was fortunate in receiving enthusiastic cooperation from my former colleagues in the UN Emergency Office in Addis Ababa. I am particularly grateful to Suman Dhar who spent a month with my wife and me in France and whose efficient collaboration made this book possible. I also very much appreciate the cooperation of Roman Roos and Martin Büechi who visited us for some days going over facts and figures particularly about distribution and transport. Tom Franklin and Paavo Pitkanen provided very useful material, the former on the role of the NGOs and the latter on the air transport operation.

Without the help of these colleagues it would have been difficult to sort out the mass of information and figures that I assembled in Ethiopia.

My wife acted as an unofficial editor applying her realism and common sense to the task. I hope it shows in the text.

To the Reader

The famine in Ethiopia shook the world in 1984–85. Few events after World War II have caused more politics around a human tragedy, more discussions and recriminations or more misinterpretations and outright distortion of facts. But the famine also unleashed a tremendous surge of compassion and generosity which helped to save millions of lives.

The intention of the following chapters is to tell what really happened in Ethiopia during the critical period in 1984–85 when the vast emergency operation reached its peak. My aim is to put on record the facts about the famine relief action for the benefit of the countless people who contributed to the resources needed or whose governments responded with generosity to the emergency.

Kurt Jansson

L to R: Chairman Mengistu of Ethiopia; interpreter; the UN Assistant Secretary General for Emergency Operations in Ethiopia, Kurt Jansson.

1. Prologue

A few days after a dramatic BBC newsreel on the famine in Ethiopia was shown on TV on 23 October 1984, the telephone rang in my home in the South of France. James P. Grant, Executive Director of UNICEF, with whom I had worked on many previous occasions, asked me on behalf of the United Nations Secretary General, Mr Perez de Cuellar, if I would be ready to go to Ethiopia to coordinate an international emergency relief operation. He told me that he and James Ingram, Executive Director of the World Food Programme, had taken the initiative of proposing to the Secretary General that a special office for emergency operations be established immediately in Ethiopia and that they wanted me to take charge of this office. I agreed, and on 6 November 1984 I was appointed UN Assistant Secretary General for Emergency Operations in Ethiopia. This was fast action and a record hard to break in the UN system or any other inter-governmental organisation. From the end of November 1984, the office in Addis Ababa was operational with a skeleton staff in space quickly made available by the United Nations Economic Commission for Africa (ECA).

Much has been written and said about the slowness of international response to appeals for assistance for famine victims in Ethiopia. Warnings and appeals had in fact been issued by the Food and Agriculture Organisation (FAO), World Food Programme (WFP), United Nations Disaster Relief Organisation (UNDRO), and United Nations Children's Fund (UNICEF) since 1983 and the matter had been discussed in the United Nations Economic and Social Council (ECOSOC) and the General Assembly. Since 1983, among the UN agencies UNICEF had been particularly active in mobilising assistance to drought victims through health, nutrition, sanitation and water projects in Ethiopia. A number of non-governmental organisations which had been working in Ethiopia for many years had alerted their headquarters to the approaching crisis. The embassies of donor countries kept their governments informed of the situation. Without any doubt governments and international organisations knew about the impending crisis.

A number of explanations have been advanced as to why the international community reacted only after the news media, particularly television, focused attention on the human suffering caused by the famine. Blame has been apportioned by politicians, writers and officials of international organisations. It seems clear to me that every part of the international community, whether governments, United Nations agencies or private organisations, bears a share of the

1

responsibility. I see no reason to concern myself in this context with these events which took place prior to my appointment. Those interested in the subject can consult a number of sources including FAO, WFP, UNDRO and UNICEF reports. A recent book, *A Year in the Death of Africa* by Peter Gill, provides an accurate account by a neutral observer of the political, bureaucratic and financial factors that played a role in this sad chapter of the Ethiopian drama.

The establishment of a special office in Addis Ababa at the level of Assistant Secretary General was an unusual move in the United Nations. Normally the task of coordinating disaster relief at the country level is in the hands of the senior United Nations Development Programme (UNDP) official designated in most countries as the UN Resident Coordinator and Resident Representative of the UNDP. The aim of the Secretary General's decision was to pull the relief operation out of the usual UN structure, which is not suited for emergency operations on a large scale requiring quick decisions and rapid practical action. Operational agencies in the UN system are geared to medium and long-term development objectives, although most of them have a small unit for emergency work. The notable exceptions to this general pattern are UNICEF and the WFP which, although not intended for emergency operations, have adjusted their machinery to be able to respond quickly and effectively to emergency situations. They are also headed by two of the most dynamic top officials in the UN system, James P. Grant and James Ingram. Grant, Executive Director of UNICEF, is a true human dynamo with an inexhaustible capacity for initiatives, quick action and willingness to bend rules if they serve a purpose he considers essential.

His single-mindedness, his enthusiasm for new ideas and his disdain for bureaucracy irritate many people but he certainly gets things done; I wish the UN system had more of his formidable dynamism. James Ingram, head of WFP, has a different personality. He has none of Jim Grant's exuberance and "bulldozer approach" but a lot of drive and is just as ready to take initiatives, overcome bureaucratic obstacles and adjust rules and regulations to meet emergency situations where ordinary UN approaches would not work. James Ingram established a WFP Africa Task Force which was given unusual authority, within reasonable limits, to take operational decisions, a mechanism which proved very useful.

UNDRO, the organisation in the UN system specially established for disaster relief, is geared primarily towards mobilising international assistance when disaster strikes. UNDRO was not established to handle operational activities in disaster areas and does not have the resources to do this. Field operations should normally be done by UN agencies with established offices throughout the developing world. In fact, UNDRO is represented *ex officio* in each country by the UN Resident Coordinator or the Resident Representative of UNDP. UNDRO has established close contacts with donors, particularly the EEC and European countries in general. I found UNDRO extremely helpful in mobilising resources for the relief programme. The area officer for Ethiopia, Frank Verhagen, a lively Dutchman, was very much "on the ball".

The initiative taken by James Grant and James Ingram would have failed if the usual lengthy procedure of consultations among the UN agencies concerned had been undertaken. A decision had to be made in an exceptional way. In this Jim Grant is a master. If something important has to be done quickly, he brushes aside inter-agency objections and reservations. Grant and Ingram persuaded the Secretary General to dispense with the usual inter-agency consultations; arrangements with the cooperating agencies could be made later. This was bound to result in strong objections from some agencies which had not been consulted. Bradford Morse, Administrator of the UNDP, was particularly upset that he had not been involved, although the decision meant that the normal responsibility of the Resident Coordinator in disaster relief was taken over by another official appointed from outside of the UNDP. This was understandable because the Ethiopian crisis received a great deal of attention in the press and among governments and the implication that the UNDP was unable to handle the crisis in this case was unavoidable. I knew Bradford Morse well and I had no doubt he would accept the arrangement in due course. The extent to which the Secretary General's decision created uneasiness in the UNDP was illustrated by the fact that Bradford Morse sent one of his senior officials to Addis Ababa to work out a written understanding of the division of responsibility between Kenneth King, the Resident Coordinator, and myself. I found Kenneth King, a former Minister in the Government of Guyana, a very reasonable person and we had no difficulties agreeing on the working arrangements between us. Briefly, I was to handle the emergency operation and Kenneth King would be responsible for activities related to rehabilitation or reconstruction work and to assist the government "in coming to grips with the causes of the emergency or lessen the likelihood of its recurrence". The draft paper was submitted for endorsement to Jean Ripert, UN Director General for Development and International Economic Cooperation who, on 21 November 1984, transmitted it to Bradford Morse. In this letter Mr Ripert stated that "it was felt as a result of the growing complexity and magnitude of the situation in Ethiopia and the increasing problems of internal distribution, that it would be useful to appoint a senior official who could devote his full-time attention to enhance operational coordination and planning with regard to the crisis".

The other UN organisation with strong reservations about setting up the special office was the FAO, which has a central role in assessing emergency needs and mobilising assistance. The Director General, Mr Edouard Saouma, had not been consulted and was known to be very protective of his "turf". When he was informed of the Secretary General's decision, Mr Saouma cabled for the opinion of the FAO Country Representative, Hans Dall, a relaxed Dane with an excellent reputation in FAO. Dall answered that he had no problems with the arrangements and that he would extend to me his fullest cooperation. This settled the matter and FAO was a willing partner in the relief effort. The same was true of the World Health Organisation which, on its own initiative, assigned a public health specialist to my office.

Despite the initial internal disagreements and reservations in the UN system, in Ethiopia there was full and wholehearted cooperation among them. Coordination of the UN agencies was never a problem. The major agency, the World Food Programme (WFP), was placed immediately under my direction as far as the emergency was concerned. UNICEF, which had a major role in matters of health,

3

water supply, sanitation and supplementary feeding, worked very effectively with my office. During a visit to Ethiopia in November 1984 Jim Grant made clear at a UNICEF staff meeting that he expected the local UNICEF office to work with me as closely as it had previously in Kampuchea.

At my request UNICEF handled the administrative work of my office and acted as the paying agent under the budget. The latter was established at the level of US$500,000 for the initial year with the understanding that it would be financed by UNICEF and the WFP with a contribution from UNDP, at its own insistence, and the United Nations itself. In the end UNICEF footed most of the bill. The budget was composed of basic administrative expenses and allocations for small emergency procurements that could not wait for donor country action, such as expenses for rebagging grain for the airdrop and a token contribution to the fuel costs for this operation.

My intention was to get going very quickly with the minimum staff necessary; only three UN staff members were assigned to my office. Three local secretaries and drivers were hired on temporary appointments through the UNICEF office in Addis Ababa. My experience in Kampuchea had shown that to maintain the confidence of donors and help the authorities in distribution and logistics, a group of field monitors was essential. I asked UNDRO to contact donor countries to request them to provide young men or women with previous field experience, if possible, who could do this work without cost to the UN. UNDRO acted very efficiently and within a short time we had four monitors who were joined later by seven others. I made a point of not accepting any staff on direct secondment by governments — the monitors had to be UN staff members. Secondments could have entailed political interference and perhaps created distrust among the Western donor governments. The monitors had UN contracts arranged by UNDRO and in most cases sponsoring governments provided a vehicle for each of them.

I first arrived in Ethiopia on 8 November 1984 as part of a group accompanying the Secretary General on his visit there. The Secretary General was extremely alarmed by what he saw. He assured me of very strong support for the emergency operation and asked me to report directly to him. He had established an Operations Support Task Force at UN Headquarters consisting of representatives of the UN agencies concerned with disaster relief, chaired by Mr Abdulrahim A. Farah, Under Secretary General for Special Political Questions. This was a temporary arrangement and the leadership of the Task Force was soon taken over by Bradford Morse as head of the UN Office for Emergency Operations in Africa (OEOA) which was established on 18 December 1984. After that I reported to Bradford Morse and worked very closely with Maurice Strong, the Executive Coordinator of OEOA, who was to become the key person at headquarters.

Events accelerated very fast in November. I was asked to briefly visit New York to meet senior UN officials and, above all, to consult with heads of missions of the major donor countries. This was very useful in that I was able to establish contact with they key ambassadors and aid officials in New York and Washington. I also made a short visit to Geneva to meet the heads of missions there. I realised early on that there was a feeling of competition between the missions in New York and Geneva, not only with respect to the Ethiopian crisis but in general. It was a matter of prestige rather than substance and UNDRO was strongly pushing for having the focal point of donor contacts in Geneva rather than in New York. This was my initial intention, mainly because of the importance of EEC as a donor group, but my consultations in New York and the subsequent meeting of donors made me change my mind.

Before I returned to Addis Ababa I met the Secretary General and his senior aides and it was agreed that, in cooperation with the government of Ethiopia, I should, within the next two weeks, formulate a programme covering emergency relief assistance for the period December 1984 to December 1985 when the next harvest would be expected. It was also agreed that, before 20 December 1984, a meeting of donors would be convened by the Secretary General in New York to consider my report.

Time was extremely short. For the report to be in the hands of the donor representatives before the meeting it had to be prepared by 11 December. Consultations had to be held with major donors beforehand in order to obtain pledges or indications of commitments at the meeting itself.

The Relief and Rehabilitation Commission of Ethiopia (RRC), around which all emergency programmes revolved, was ready for quick action. The RRC had prepared a report setting out their own assessment of requirements for the next 12 to 13 months in terms of relief and rehabilitation, including food requirements, transport, medical supplies, sanitation, blankets and clothing, as well as agricultural inputs for the next growing season.

Taking the RRC report as a basis I consulted donor missions, UN agencies and voluntary organisations and prepared a report which represented my own independent assessment of the requirements. The number of people affected by the drought had been estimated by an FAO Crop Assessment Mission in early November 1984 to be between 6.5 and 8 million. The RRC estimate was 7,746,000 people in 11 of 14 administrative regions of Ethiopia. This figure had been arrived at using the findings of the FAO Mission as well as data collected by the RRC Early Warning System and the Central Statistical Office. The number of people affected was based on a population estimate of 42 million. This was considered conservative (except for the northern regions of Tigray and Wollo) by most people knowledgeable about Ethiopia, including demographers in the EEC. There was general agreement among donor missions, UN agencies and non-governmental organisations (NGOs) that at least 7.7 million people were in need of emergency aid. This was later revised to 7.9 million when additional field reviews had been completed.

On the basis of this estimation my report suggested that a total of 1,330,000 (metric) tonnes of food would be needed for the 12-month period concerned. This included 100,000 tonnes of supplementary food and 30,000 tonnes of edible oil. My estimate was lower than that of the RRC which stood at 1.5 million tonnes. I was not prepared to endorse this figure because I knew that the logistical capacity could not be built up quickly enough to distribute this amount of food inside the country. To ask for more than could be used would have resulted in an outcry by donors who were in any case wary of being caught providing supplies that could be spoiled or used for purposes other than relief.

The second most important assessment concerned logistics. A WFP Transport

5

Mission, which visited Ethiopia in November 1984, estimated that the monthly grain unloading capacity of the ports of Assab, Massawa and Djibouti was about 135,000 metric tonnes (MT). The Mission calculated that the unloading capacity could be increased to 150,000 MT a month with improvements in grain bulk-handling and the provision of additional equipment for the port of Assab. Equipment was later provided by donor countries and the unloading capacity of the ports was never a problem. The problem was the shortage of suitable trucks, as a result of which grain could not be transported out of the ports fast enough to avoid congestion. In my report I recommended trucks, spare parts, port-handling equipment and inland transport subsidies totalling $139.2 million. Medical supplies, materials for shelter, clothing and other survival items made up the remainder of the list of requirements. The total estimated value of the emergency relief aid for the 12-month period came close to $800 million depending on the value attached to the huge food quantity and the cost of shipment, handling and inland transport.

My report was finished on 13 December 1984 and I asked New York to set a date for the donor meeting on Ethiopia. That turned out to be more difficult than I thought. When I left New York I had a clear understanding with the Secretary General and Jean Ripert that a special meeting on Ethiopia could be held in New York. But there were second thoughts on the part of some top officials as to whether it would be appropriate to have a meeting solely on Ethiopia or whether it would be better to deal with Ethiopia in a general meeting on the 22 African drought-affected countries. There was also a strong push by UNDRO to hold the meeting in Geneva. Time was running very short because the meeting had to be held before 20 December when the General Assembly had finished but before the Christmas holidays. I was in frequent touch by telephone with New York and received evasive and contradictory answers. Sometimes I was told that the meeting would not be held and sometimes that it would but that no date had been fixed. Finally, I simply informed New York that I would be arriving on 12 December and there had better be a meeting on Ethiopia since, on the strength of the promise made by the Secretary General and Mr Ripert, I had announced this at a meeting of donors and NGOs convened by the RRC on 11 December. This settled the matter and the meeting was convened on 18 December.

My earlier experience with donor meetings on Kampuchea demonstrated the necessity for careful preparatory work before the meeting in order to avoid political controversies and to obtain pledges or indications of support at the meeting itself. During an exhausting week I met the ambassadors or representatives of all important donor countries including the USA, Canada, the EEC countries as a group, the Nordic countries, Switzerland, Australia and Japan. Of the EEC countries I met separately with the ambassadors of FRG, France and Italy.

The practice, in the case of Kampuchea, had been to hold two separate donor meetings, one with the traditional donor countries and one with the socialist countries. To the meeting on Ethiopia it was decided to invite all member countries, a decision I very much supported and which I later put into practice with respect to local donor meetings in Ethiopia. This did, of course, entail the risk of having political statements dominate the meeting, but the UN officials concerned, particularly Jean Ripert, had carried out consultations with the most important countries and it had been agreed that the meeting would be purely non-political and concerned exclusively with raising resources for the famine in Ethiopia.

The meeting itself was very well attended. Before it was opened by the Secretary General, I noticed that Mrs Jeane Kirkpatrick, US representative to the UN, was to attend. I was told earlier that the USSR Ambassador, Oleg Troyanovsky, did not plan to participate, but, as soon as the USSR delegation noticed Mrs Kirkpatrick's presence, they scurried out to the telephone in the ante-room and Ambassador Troyanovsky quickly turned up. I thought this was a good sign, particularly as it had been agreed not to engage in politics at the meeting.

After the Secretary General's introductory statement, I presented my report. It was very well received and endorsed without reservations. The estimates in the report were accepted as targets for the international community. This continued to be the case throughout the relief operation. In cooperation with the donor missions, the NGOs and the RRC, my office in Addis Ababa prepared, periodically, revised estimates which were presented at donor meetings in Addis Ababa.

I made one important procedural recommendation to the meeting. Clearly, one of my main tasks would be to help mobilise resources and a method needed to be agreed upon which would work as fast as possible. I suggested that the focal point should be in Addis Ababa where, except for Denmark and Norway, all traditional donor countries had embassies. In the case of Kampuchea this had not been possible because there were no Western embassies and only a few of the socialist countries had ambassadors in Phnom Penh. During my meetings with the missions before the conference I had discussed this proposal which was generally welcomed. At the conference itself Ambassador Stephen Lewis of Canada strongly endorsed the proposal which was supported by other speakers and accepted by the meeting. I knew that the donor country missions in Geneva would not welcome this decision but I was convinced that the missions in New York carried much more weight at home than did those in Geneva. Later I made two quick visits to Geneva to brief the ambassadors there but it seemed to me that they did not accept the central role played by their New York colleagues, although they generally welcomed my intention to concentrate resource mobilisation in Addis Ababa as the first level of action. The attitude of the diplomats in Geneva was a reflection of the keen competition that exists between the New York and the Geneva-based UN missions, a fact well-known in the UN.

2. Inside Ethiopia

There seemed to have been a widespread misconception, particularly among journalists, that my role in the emergency would be primarily coordination of the work of the UN agencies and between them and NGOs. This was based on the misunderstanding that the UN itself would provide much of the resources needed for famine relief in Ethiopia. But the UN organisations have very small allocations for emergencies; they have to mobilise resources from member states for each emergency. Another general misconception was that the UN system in emergencies has the policy of establishing a central fund to which member states are asked to contribute. This was done in the case of the Bangladesh emergency but the resource mobilisation for Kampuchea, for example, had to be organised differently. Donors were provided with estimates of relief needs and with reports on distribution inside Kampuchea and on the border between Thailand and Kampuchea. Contributions by donors in kind or in cash went to the participating agencies, UNICEF, ICRC, WFP, FAO and UNHCR. Some donors contributed cash to a small central fund administered jointly by UNICEF and ICRC but the bulk of the aid was in the form of food and agricultural inputs provided by donors through procurement and transport arrangements with WFP and FAO. Experience has shown that resource mobilisation through the setting up of a central fund controlled by the UN is impractical since most donors want to decide what channel to use in allocating their contributions, that is, the UN system, NGOs or bilaterally on a government-to-government basis.

The Kampuchea donor meetings were held in New York but the most important part of the mobilisation of resources was done by Sir Robert Jackson who was in overall charge of the Kampuchea programme as Special Representative of the Secretary General. He kept in close touch with the missions in New York and travelled extensively to various capitals to obtain support for the relief operation. A great deal of work was also done by Jim Grant and representatives of the ICRC.

The decision by the 18 December meeting to concentrate fund raising efforts in the first place in Addis Ababa meant that there had to be an appropriate mechanism for this purpose. I did not step into a vacuum in this respect in Addis Ababa because meetings had already been held among donors to review the situation and make recommendations to the home offices. These meetings were chaired by Mr Terrence Mooney, Counsellor at the Canadian Embassy, a man who played a pivotal role in the donor community at the senior working level. Mr Mooney had also organised a working group consisting of representatives of EEC, ICRC, Christian Relief and Development Agency (CRDA), the main NGO coordinating body, and the WFP.

The major gap in the existing arrangements was that there was no mechanism among donors and NGOs to systematically consider changing needs on the basis of detailed assessments made by a neutral office independent of donors, NGOs and the Ethiopian authorities, and having access to the necessary information across the board. This became one of the primary tasks of my office together with reporting on the distribution of relief.

To fill this gap I convened meetings of donors at the ambassadorial level, held monthly in the beginning of 1985 and less frequently later. With the agreement of the Western donors I invited representatives from the socialist countries to attend. I had obtained the backing for this proposal from the USSR ambassador in New York dealing with aid matters. This represented a departure from prevailing USSR policy not to participate in donor meetings, except as observers, as was the case with respect to Kampuchea. The aim was obviously to avoid any implication of responsibility for aid to developing countries whose economic problems, according to socialist thinking, are the direct result of Western exploitation. There was no objection on the part of the Western donors to participation by socialist countries, and no political problems arose. These meetings were also attended by RRC representatives and NGOs. The atmosphere was open and direct. Problems were discussed and questions answered.

These donor meetings were very well attended, a sign of the great interest the ambassadors took in the relief operation. Based upon my original 11 December report, my office prepared estimates of remaining needs in the categories of food, seeds, medical supplies, survival items and logistics. These were discussed, clarifications provided, and reports submitted on the distribution of relief. As a follow-up to these general meetings my office organised sectoral reviews on transport, health, sanitation and water supplies, supplementary feeding, seed distribution, etc. at which specifics were discussed with donors and NGOs interested in each sector. These smaller meetings proved to be very useful and resulted in sectoral programmes outlining remaining needs and targets and agreeing on which UN organisation or NGO should be the implementing agency.

Between the meetings there was constant contact between my office and the donor embassies and NGOs. The flow of information was, therefore, very satisfactory. The assessments and reports were used by donor embassies in their despatches to their home offices with clarifications and additional information being obtained from my office. The system of resource mobilisation and reporting thus consisted of two official mechanisms: meetings of all donors which I chaired, and in the beginning every two weeks, meetings of bilateral donors chaired by Mr Mooney. But there was an informal arrangement for contacts with the donors which I considered to be perhaps the most important one. Donor countries' ambassadors met in the Italian Embassy under the chairmanship of Ambassador Oliviero Rossi, who played a very active part in the emergency operation. The meetings were attended by ambassadors or chargé d'affaires of all Western donor countries plus India, Republic of Korea and, of course, Japan. I was invited to present reviews of the relief operation and raise matters that needed to be discussed in private among the main contributors to famine relief. These meetings also discussed, from time to time, questions of what attitude the donors should take towards events and problems affecting the relief operation. Discussions were very open and an atmosphere of complete trust prevailed from the very beginning. As time went on I requested meetings of this kind more frequently and found them to be extremely useful. No minutes were prepared but there was always a clear understanding of what had been agreed upon and what further action would be needed.

Meetings of donors called by the RRC were very large and included representatives of donor governments and NGOs. They were usually opened by Mr Berhanu Bayeh, Minister of Labour and Social Affairs, who was the Politbureau member in charge of the government relief committee. RRC Commissioner Dawit presented a printed report which included a brief review of the drought situation and detailed lists of aid requirements. I was asked to make a statement which usually dealt with the broader aspects of how the cooperation had developed and what particular problems had arisen. The discussions were mostly very sketchy since the RRC report was distributed only at the beginning of the meeting and no participant had had the opportunity to study it. Subsequent discussions with RRC served to clarify the contents of the reports. The RRC meetings were not attended by representatives of the socialist countries who met separately after the main meeting. The reason for this arrangement was to avoid politics.

Coordination is a much-used term which can cover many things but which can also be a sterile function unless it contains an element of initiative and dynamism. The establishment of the UN office in Addis Ababa filled the very essential need of providing a hub to the network of organisations involved in the emergency operation. It was a source of information to the donor missions for resource mobilisation and reporting and it formed the main link with the RRC and often a bridge between donor embassies and ministries concerned with the emergency. It was a place where initiatives were taken to facilitate the work of donors, NGOs and RRC. The fact that I was the only international official with access to Chairman Mengistu was of great importance. From the very beginning members of the Politbureau and other Ministers and top officials dealing with the situation accepted my practice of telephoning them in order to solve minor problems quickly. When I needed an appointment it was arranged by Suman Dhar, my personal assistant and secretary, at very short notice. This was a source of wonderment to many impatient diplomats and NGO representatives who had to await their turn.

My intention was not to involve the office in direct operational work for which it was not staffed and for which there were established UN agencies and NGOs. But as time went on my colleagues and I were drawn into dealing with operations, particularly transport, including the rental of Ethiopian trucks and the procurement of tyres and spare parts. In retrospect I think it would have been better either to keep out of direct operations or to obtain additional staff on loan from UN agencies. Early in 1986 the WFP established a truck fleet operated by a group of staff mainly from WFP headquarters. The role of the monitors, to which I will revert later, was closely related to field operations and they were often dealing with transport and port problems but their job was to monitor the relief programme and facilitate distribution rather than direct management of transport and other field operations.

To ensure coordination was thus not the principal objective of the UN office. Its task was much wider and more complex. At times it seemed that problems were insurmountable and when something went wrong the UN office was blamed, but when things went well it was not mentioned. After Kampuchea I had expected this but there were moments when I was near to desperation and cursed myself for having taken the job. It was not easy to be "the man in the middle". But the job had to be done and I was determined to do my best.

Improvisation and innovation

The UN Office for Emergency Operations in Ethiopia (EOE) on the sixth floor of the ECA building in Addis was unusual. Everything had to be improvised. Telephones were installed one at a time in the corridor outside the offices, electrical connections were hastily installed, desks and chairs borrowed from various parts of the ECA, typewriters and a photocopier were provided by UNICEF. We were first given three offices at the end of a corridor, with two ECA offices between that had nothing to do with the emergency. Eventually we managed to take over these two offices and that was all we needed. The corridor outside the offices was used to accommodate the secretaries and from time to time for informal meetings with visitors.

The EOE never had a dull moment. Every day a stream of ambassadors, aid officials and NGO representatives visited the office. Hordes of journalists descended upon it, UN staff members, officers of the Royal Air Force, Luftwaffe and the Polish Helicopter contingent as well as RRC officials stumbled over each other in the cramped space. This was all as it should be as none of the members of the emergency office cared for bureaucracy or protocol and all of us were available at any time.

I was fortunate in having been able to arrange for the secondment of Ms Suman Dhar from the UNICEF office in New Delhi. She had worked in 1980–81 as my personal assistant and secretary in Phnom Penh. In Addis Ababa she did the same job and also acted as office manager in charge of administration, transport and other related matters. She again proved to be invaluable with her sense of humour, organising ability and mixture of charm, common sense and firmness in dealing with colleagues and outside visitors. Suman arranged my daily work schedule but we had agreed that, even if no appointment had been made for an ambassador or someone else who needed to see me, I should be available immediately or at short notice. This was obviously appreciated by those concerned but it made for extremely busy days without much breathing space.

Another regular staff member was Mrs Bilge Reid, a Turkish-born American who had worked for US Save the Children for some years. She was special assistant and dealt with matters across the board such as bilateral relations, monitoring contributions and pledges, seed distribution arrangements and other duties. A lively and attractive woman in her early forties she was very popular in the donor community and took off my hands many things that had to be dealt with at the working level. She had great drive and energy.

Thomas Franklin was the third regular staff member appointed on a UNICEF post. He had worked before in Africa and was bilingual in English and French. Tom had considerable experience working with NGOs and he provided the essential link between the office and the NGO community. He tended to set himself very high standards of achievement which under the circumstances could not always be achieved. He had not worked before in the type of "pressure cooker" that the emergency office was and at times he became discouraged and a bit negative. But over the months and when he got used to the office's style of operation he did

11

excellent work and maintained good relations with the numerous NGOs working in Ethiopia.

In the middle of 1985 Finland provided, through the OEOA in New York, an information officer, Inger Wiren, who worked with the Press and prepared reports for the OEOA publication *Africa Emergency*. She also undertook *ad hoc* assignments. Inger was a competent and conscientious press officer who got along well with her colleagues and the authorities.

The World Health Organisation assigned to the EOE a full-time public health specialist. Dr Arne Sunde of Norway, the first appointee, established a sound basis for cooperation with the Ministry of Health and the Health Department of the RRC. This was a delicate task partly because of frictions between the RRC health department and the Ministry. But his long field experience and modest personality made him just right for the office. Like most of the staff Arne shared office space with several colleagues but he never raised any of the problems that might be expected from a senior official used to having his own office. Arne was followed by Ms Stephanie Simmonds, who had worked in a number of short-term assignments in developing countries, including Ethiopia, and had a thorough understanding of health problems in developing countries. She had great charm, a very straightforward approach and was above all very realistic in her appraisal of the standards one should apply in Ethiopia. She frequently found reports by NGOs' health personnel to be exaggerated or unduly alarming after she had made her own assessment on the spot. Unlike some NGO health staff her approach was to make a hard-headed study of the situation and make recommendations, rather than to run to the press and sound the alarm.

Short-term consultants for special jobs were sometimes employed by the office. One was Tom Fitzpatrick, a Jesuit who had been in charge of Catholic Relief Services in Ethiopia before it expanded into a large-scale food distribution operation. Tom, a former university administrator, excellent with figures and projections, was assigned to work at the RRC head office in Addis on distribution reports and analyses of relief requirements. Here again it was good luck that Tom fitted in with the rest of the "relief cocktail" and got along very well with the RRC.

A small group of Ethiopian secretaries and drivers had to be found quickly. This was done by UNICEF which maintained a roster of qualified candidates who had been tested for various jobs. The EOE employed three secretaries, Blene Alemselassie, Etageghnu Makonnen and Tersit Wolde Gebriel, and seven drivers, including those serving the monitors. I found the local staff very sympathetic, cheerful and loyal to the office. They were willing to work at any hour for seven days a week whenever necessary. We never had the local staff problems which frequently plagued some of the other UN agencies in Addis. The drivers had to do a variety of chores ranging from driving to acting as interpreters, following up on the status of travel permits, and sometimes acted as mediators between overzealous local officials at roadblocks and our field monitors. This was the temporary office set up to deal with the relief operation.

The emergency staff of the WFP was placed under my direction and several WFP staff members became *de facto* part of the Emergency Office. Desmond Taylor, head of the WFP office, acted as officer in charge during my field travel and infrequent trips to New York and Geneva. Desmond's calm personality and experience in food management and distribution proved very useful. Kevin Farrell, a lively, bright Irishman, spent much of his time working directly for the EOE. He had initiative, a good understanding of statistics and transport problems and a sense of humour. He worked in the RRC office for several months acting as a liaison man between the Emergency Office and the RRC.

Burke Oberle, a German-born American, was in charge of the preparation of the shipping bulletin issued by the WFP at frequent intervals. Burke was low-key, precise in his work and always on top of his assignment which involved crucial matters of keeping the donor community and the government informed of the arrival of food shipments and the stock position in ports and inland warehouses. The shipping bulletins, computerized in the middle of 1985, were one of the most important coordinating instruments.

UNICEF was headed by Dr R. Padmini from whom I had excellent cooperation. She had spent more than five years in Ethiopia and was very knowledgeable about the country. She had assigned Mrs Wendy Bjoerck, a UK citizen, as UNICEF's emergency relief officer. Wendy, who had been part of my team in Phnom Penh, travelled extensively throughout Ethiopia and was by far the best informed relief official when it came to assessing emergency needs and distribution problems. A woman of great competence, sense of responsibility and a cheerful disposition, she played an important role in the operation.

A relationship of confidence between the Emergency Office and the embassies in Addis Ababa was essential to help ensure continued support for the relief effort; field monitors' work was important in establishing and maintaining this confidence. Their task was a dynamic one, not limited to inspection and monitoring the relief distribution and the ports. Their most important function was to help the RRC and voluntary organisations to identify problems and find solutions on the spot whenever possible. They also acted as impartial observers and intervened whenever unacceptable practices were discovered, including local officials' violations of human rights. They had my full authority to act within agreed guidelines and to represent me in discussions with local party functionaries and RRC staff. Numerous problems were solved locally as a result of interventions, often in very strong terms, by UN field monitors. If a solution could not be found, they reported back to me by telephone or in person, depending on the urgency of the matter. This enabled me to take up the problem at the appropriate level in Addis. The fact, well-known to party cadres, that I had access to Chairman Mengistu and members of the Politbureau carried a great deal of weight in the field monitors' dealings with local party cadres who were much more important at the local level than the RRC officials. In dealing with the latter, my very good working relationship with Commissioner Dawit and his deputies helped the field monitors to get things done through the RRC field staff.

The establishment of a system of field personnel with monitoring, reporting and support functions was a new approach in UN emergency work. In Kampuchea this was not possible because of the attitude of the Heng Samrin Government. The Kampuchean authorities distributed food and the NGOs were allowed to work only in the field of health and education, mainly in Phnom Penh, with the exception of

ICRC which maintained a few medical teams in the provinces. Systematic monitoring was not possible under these circumstances. Instead, staff of the joint UNICEF/ICRC mission, FAO, WFP and the small group of NGOs allowed to work in Kampuchea, travelled as much as possible and reported their findings to weekly meetings that I convened. At first, access to warehouses and ports was difficult. As the chief of mission I had no problems in this respect but "guides" from the Ministry of Foreign Affairs often found excuses to delay or temporarily prevent inspection of provincial warehouses by my colleagues. It was evident that these officials wanted to avoid problems with their superiors in the Ministry when reporting on the field visits. It took numerous interventions on my part to ensure access to ports, warehouses and distribution points. This was a haphazard way of monitoring but satisfactory in Kampuchea where the relief operation was much less complex. Many problems in Kampuchea stemmed from the fact that the authorities did not understand why international officials and relief workers were assigned there. The attitude was: ship the food to our ports and we will do the rest. It took quite some time for us to convince the authorities that food and other relief supplies would not be forthcoming unless the donors were satisfied that these supplies reached the needy people.

In Ethiopia the situation was different. The authorities accepted from the outset that distribution had to be closely monitored and that independent reporting to the donors had to be ensured. But the vastness of the country, the difficult terrain, the enormous number of people to be assisted and the relentless pressure from the donor community to obtain reliable information made it necessary to establish a special system of control under UN auspices. It had to be a system upon which donors could rely but it had to work in cooperation with the authorities and the NGOs.

The UN or its specialised agencies do not have staff recruited and trained for emergency work of this nature, apart from some officials with practical experience obtained in the course of their regular careers. In Ethiopia it was necessary to make *ad hoc* arrangements through the assignment of field monitors. This experiment worked surprisingly well taking into account the improvisations that had to be resorted to under pressure of time. The monitors were on UN contracts, financed by their respective governments. UNDRO, at my request, contacted governments willing to provide this type of assistance and candidates' biographical sketches were submitted for my consideration. Time was of prime importance and there was no opportunity for me to interview the candidates. Fortunately, the men appointed to these jobs turned out to be a group of considerable efficiency and dedication. Although a mixed lot in terms of background and personality, somehow they complemented each other.

In the group were two Swiss nationals, Roman Roos and Martin Büechi, provided by the Swiss Disaster Relief Unit which always acted promptly and efficiently on requests for assistance. Both had had field experience before, Martin Büechi with the ICRC and Roman Roos with various organisations in many parts of Africa. Roman, a man in his late fifties, was a calm and highly reliable person and not easily be ruffled. He had a stabilising influence on the whole group and was a competent port and logistics specialist. Roman spent the first four months of his assignment in the principal port of Assab and when he returned to Addis I asked him to take charge of road transport. He was much appreciated by the Minister and Vice Minister of Transport to whom he had easy access. Martin Büechi was the great sceptic in the office and with his scientific background (PhD in Biochemistry) took nothing for granted. To him everything had to be proved and he always assumed the worst until he found evidence to the contrary. Because of this I asked him to compile the statistics on distribution knowing that he would certainly not err on the positive side. Young and impatient. Martin filled an important need as a true "devil's advocate".

Norway provided Asbjörn Devold who had worked earlier in Africa for the UNHCR. With a good sense of humour and common sense. he represented the middle ground in the group in terms of attitudes and the handling of delicate matters. He was very useful in dealing with tense situations in the field, particularly those concerned with returning camp dwellers to their homes in an orderly fashion.

Paavo Pitkanen, a Finnish Lieutenant-Colonel with a post-graduate degree in political science, had worked before in Ethiopia and with UNIFIL in Lebanon. Livelier than most Finns. Paavo had a way of getting along with people while acting firmly. These qualities enabled him to reconcile differences between NGOs. RRC officials and party functionaries at the local level. With his military background Paavo took strong positions and stuck to them even when risking being controversial to the authorities. Paavo, together with Martin and Asbjörn, were the three field monitors I often assigned to resolve problems involving evacuation of camps and other sensitive tasks requiring a combination of scepticism, impartiality and firmness. The famous incident at Ibenat, to which I will return later, was one in which the presence of the field monitors proved to be absolutely crucial.

Thomas Joyce, a young American who had worked for the ILO in Geneva, was highly mobile and showed a lot of initiative. That he was an American proved to be no problem and his travel permits were issued just as rapidly as those of others. Since the US was by far the largest food donor, Tom's reports were very useful and helped to reassure the USAID mission about the distribution of their food.

Sweden provided Mats Eric Douhan, a former policeman who had been with UNIFIL in Lebanon and organised training of peace-keeping soldiers in Sweden. He was the quietest of the group and took a positive view of things. Unike some of his colleagues, he was not inclined to discern subtle nuances in Ethiopian officials and his very positive character sometimes made his reports a bit too optimistic. But he was honest, direct and very active. I assigned him mainly to work in southern Ethiopia where many of the church groups, including the Lutheran World Federation, were active and where political problems did not affect the relief operation to the same degree as in the central and northern provinces.

Two of the field monitors. Paul Turnbull and John Mitchell, were from the UK. They were provided through the WFP and stationed in Asmara in Eritrea and in Dessie, the capital of Wollo administrative region, one of the worst-hit areas. Paul and John were young and inexperienced but serious. intelligent and very conscientious. Asmara and Dessie were important transit points in the storage and transport of food. Their task was therefore important and they were highly reliable. They visited Addis at regular intervals to report on their work. I found their written reports particularly informative and these were also very much appreciated by the NGOs.

A later addition to the group was Dag Hareide, a former Lutheran minister who had worked in Namibia. I had not requested a second Norwegian but one day I saw a very tall, lean man talking to Suman Dhar. Apparently he had been appointed by the UNDP to a post funded by Norway in the UNDP office in Addis. I learned that when he arrived the UNDP told him they were fully staffed and did not need his services. I welcomed him to the group of monitors and he quickly became part of the office. He had considerable experience in agriculture and I asked him to work partly as a field monitor and partly to prepare a strategy for phasing the relief activities into rehabilitation and recovery. He made a number of proposals in that respect and established good contacts with the authorities and the NGOs.

This group of volunteers was put together under great pressure of time and without any possibility of applying even minimum selection procedures. But with all their different qualities they were a remarkable group and each fitted into a certain slot in the operation as a whole. I used to joke about their being an "emergency cocktail" which consisted of good ingredients and needed to be mixed in the right way to produce the right result.

With a group like this, and given the very hectic activity, it was essential to develop an atmosphere of easy cooperation among them and between them and me. All were men of substance and dedication who had come to make their contribution to famine relief and all that needed to be done was to get the best out of them. I treated them as members of a family and encouraged them to take initiatives. They each had one or two administrative regions as their primary area of responsibility but they all undertook *ad hoc* assignments throughout the country when the need arose. Intentionally, there was no group coordinator. I dealt with them individually and collectively while encouraging a team spirit as the basis for their work. They were asked to get together informally, to agree on a work programme for the next two weeks and submit it for my approval. These programmes were adjusted when *ad hoc* assignments had to be undertaken. Reports were shared with the NGOs, the RRC and donors as appropriate. Frequently, the field monitors' findings formed the basis for my interventions with the RRC, the Minister in charge of relief, the Minister and Vice Minister of Transport and members of the Politbureau who had to be approached to help solve problems that could not be dealt with at a lower level. All in all, I found the system of field monitors to be a crucial part of the operation. They provided evidence on the distribution of food, the stock position in ports and warehouses and information on events such as coercion and other unacceptable practices by local party functionaries. I travelled a great deal myself but the monitors' reports provided much of the information I needed for an overview of the situation and to be able to intervene with the authorities whenever necessary.

The fact that, except for Suman Dhar, the field monitors and office staff were from Western countries was not looked upon favourably by most members of the Politbureau and some RRC officials. The rationale behind my choice of staff was that since practically all relief aid came from the West it was necessary to have monitors from those donor countries in order to maintain their confidence. RRC was initially not very happy with the presence of an American among the field monitors, particularly since an earlier candidate had been denied an entry visa for security reasons. I took this matter up with Minister Berhanu Bayeh who asked me not to press for a visa as the candidate was suspected of working for the CIA. After a conversation with Fred Fischer, head of the USAID mission in Addis, I dropped the matter since another candidate, Tom Joyce, soon became available.

Commissioner Dawit suggested to me that there needed to be some field monitors from socialist countries. I said I had no objection but that they needed to be appointed against UN posts financed in dollars by the sponsoring government. The USSR Ambassador, Mr V. Fomichenko, asked me if I would accept a Russian among the staff and I told him that I had no objection but that the candidate must go through the proper appointment procedures and I had to accept his candidature. Ambassador Fomichenko said, "Do you mean that we cannot send someone from Moscow?" I replied that the point was there could be no direct secondment by the government as I had established what I believed to be the sound principle that all staff should be on UN appointments. The Ambassador never returned to the matter and no staff from socialist countries were employed in the UN office.

These makeshift arrangements for the recruitment of field monitors worked well mainly because of the untiring efforts of Frank Verhagen, UNDRO's desk officer for Ethiopia, who had excellent relations with his counterparts in donor countries. But systematisation is needed. It would be important for the UN to establish a small reservoir on a standby basis of trained emergency field personnel (monitors, port and transport specialists, food managers and procurement officers) who would be available at very short notice. This would be something similar to the present arrangements for UN peace-keeping assignments but on a much smaller scale. Suitable emergency workers could easily be found among former peace-keeping personnel whose experience would be valuable for work under emergency and hardship conditions. Two of the monitors in my office were former members of UN peace-keeping forces in the Middle East.

The setting up in New York of the Office for Emergency Operations in Africa (OEOA) under the direction of Bradford Morse and Maurice Strong did not affect the Addis office very much. We had a headstart in mobilising resources and the office was already functioning. Nevertheless, the OEOA was very useful as a back-up for initiatives taken in Addis. I maintained my independence of action as agreed with the Secretary General when I assumed my assignment. The only way to act in an emergency is for headquarters to give the necessary authority and decision-making power to the head of the operation. This was done in Kampuchea, and in Ethiopia I stuck very closely to this line. It took a few weeks before Bradford Morse fully accepted this. I can well understand that he wanted to show strong action and maintain high visibility for his office. We had a few heated exchanges on the telephone but things soon settled down and Bradford Morse was always very considerate and helpful. In any event, I would not have remained in Ethiopia had I not been given the kind of freedom of action on which I had based the operation. Here again my experience in Kampuchea served me well.

Maurice Strong was the Executive Coordinator of the OEOA. He is famous in the UN as "the man who never fails". He rescued the Stockholm Environment

Conference in 1970 from a looming fiasco caused by an ineffectual consultant. His work as Executive Director of the UN Environment Programme with offices in Nairobi got that organisation off to an excellent start. As the founder of the Canadian International Development Agency and a former deputy Foreign Minister of Canada, he was very familiar with problems of developing countries. Maurice Strong visited Ethiopia three times in 1985 and we had very useful reviews of the relief situation. He made a point of saying that he had come to gather experience from the Ethiopian operation that would be useful in the other drought-stricken African countries and not to concern himself with operational matters. The success of the OEOA was to a considerable degree due to the work of Maurice Strong.

Diplomats as "relief workers"

It was fortunate that the donor community was represented in Ethiopia by diplomats who took a deep interest in the emergency. Cynics may say that they had little else to do but my own conviction was that by pure good luck a group of remarkable ambassadors and chiefs of mission were working in Ethiopia when the crisis erupted. They were all strong supporters of the UN office. This surprised me as in other countries I had found that the diplomatic corps in general was not particularly interested in UN matters whether they concerned development problems or emergency situations. In Lebanon, Pakistan and Nigeria, where I represented the UNDP, this was certainly the case with a few exceptions. In Phnom Penh there was only a handful of diplomatic missions with none from the West, whereas in Ethiopia the Western donors and the socialist countries were well represented; only Denmark and Norway had no embassies.

The diplomatic staff including the chiefs of missions spent most of their time on matters related to the emergency. They were in fact relief officials more than diplomats. The leading figure ex-officio was Ambassador Oliviero Rossi, a short man with greyish hair and strong features, whose qualities of quiet leadership, great dignity and good political sense commanded the respect of everybody around him. Ambassador Rossi was the dean among the donor country ambassadors and chaired the informal meetings to which I have referred earlier. He had a somewhat formal manner and he followed protocol even in meetings on emergency matters but always in a very courteous and agreeable manner.

Brian Barder, the British Ambassador, was the politically shrewdest diplomat and he played a very active and constructive role in anything that had to do with the famine. I met him frequently for an exchange of views and found his opinions invaluable and very sound. At meetings it was he who came up with drafts of position papers that the group of donor ambassadors were to discuss. Brian Barder had a pragmatic approach to problems and a cool head. On a more specific level, he was particularly effective in facilitating the airdrop operation to which I will revert later. I came to appreciate his humanitarian outlook which always guided his actions as an envoy representing a Conservative government in a Marxist country.

The most important donor country, the USA, was represented at the diplomatic level first by David Korn and then by James Cheek. Both were Chargés d'Affaires since diplomatic relations with Ethiopia had been downgraded to that level in 1977. David Korn was a dignified, soft-spoken man, a scholarly type who spoke little at meetings but when he did he always had some very firm opinions. His successor, Jim Cheek, was much more relaxed and showed willingness to let humanitarian considerations prevail over political expediency. He had perhaps the greatest sense of humour among the diplomats with the exception of Leslie Luck, the young Australian Chargé d'Affaires *ad interim*. Leslie Luck was followed by Ambassador John Sheppard who was in his first ambassadorial post in Addis. My first impression was that he was a bit dour and negative. I got to know him better during a four-day visit to Eritrea and Tigray and found him to be a perceptive person with sound judgement.

The Federal Republic of Germany, a very important donor of food and trucks, was represented by Ambassador Bernd Oldenkott, a genial and relaxed man of considerable dignity who took a keen interest in the emergency. He had a positive approach and was willing to stick out his neck *vis-à-vis* Bonn to push for aid which I often asked him help ensure. Good examples of this were when he persuaded Bonn to contribute another 100 long-haul trucks, a second batch from FRG, and to continue providing a Transall plane for the air drop even after it had been decided to return the FRG planes to Germany. Bernd Oldenkott and his wife were always in a good mood and there were many occasions when Bernd's calm and wise counsel were much appreciated.

The Apostolic Pro Nuncio, Archbishop Thomas White, fell into a separate category since he did not, as he frequently pointed out, represent "a donor country". A man of great charm and wit, often it was he who "cut through the fog" when discussions at meetings became too involved and seemed to lead nowhere. I was impressed by his ability to put into clear language something so many of us at these informal meetings at the Italian Embassy had been thinking but could not find words to express. Through Tom White I met the Primate of All Ireland, and Mother Theresa, occasions which I valued very much.

Among the other key members of the group of "relief diplomats" were Ambassador Nils Revelius of Sweden, Ambassador José Paoli of France, and Ambassador Marc Lemieux of Canada. Revelius spoke seldom but always made a contribution to the discussions carefully following the Swedish line of neutrality. France was not an important donor country bilaterally but it had much influence in the EEC as the head of the Commission, Jacques Delors, is French. Ambassador Paoli, a low-key personality with a very pleasant manner, was active in supporting the relief effort. But Paris was less interested in Ethiopia. When the French Minister for Overseas Development M. Christian Nucci (later involved in a financial scandal in France) visited Ethiopia in June 1985 he showed little interest in what was going on. Timothy Raison, British Minister for Overseas Development, who visited Ethiopia several times was a marked contrast to Nucci. Raison, after some initial coolness based on his political antipathy toward a Marxist regime, took a keen interest in the relief operation. He was instrumental in ensuring British participation in the air drop and was very helpful in supporting emergency aid to Ethiopia in EEC and UK itself.

Canada, an important food donor, was represented by Marc Lemieux, a former businessman in his first ambassadorial post. He was very active at donor meetings and strongly supported the relief effort, although he often complained at these meetings about too many requests for additional aid. These complaints, probably made for Canadian "home consumption", were called "Lemieux's laments". One of the most important diplomats at the working level was Terrence Mooney, the Counsellor of the Canadian Embassy dealing with relief matters.

Johann Wallner, a German national representing the EEC extended full cooperation to my office. He participated in the meetings of the diplomatic chiefs of mission but my contacts with EEC were mainly through Karl Harbo, a tall Dane with a sharp intellect and an ability for hard-headed economic analysis relevant to the famine. He was also a member of the informal advisory group mentioned earlier.

My contacts with the representatives of socialist countries were naturally more limited since they were not central to the relief effort. I made a point, from time to time, of briefing the USSR Ambassador or Chargé d'Affaires. This was important since the USSR provided 300 trucks and 700 drivers, 24 helicopters and 12 Antonov transport planes (and a small quantity of rice) My most frequent contacts with the socialist country group were with the Polish Ambassador, Andrej Konopacki, who was important in ensuring the participation of Polish helicopters in the extensive air drop. Ambassador Konopacki was a very agreeable person and, as my wife's family on her father's side came from Poland, we felt somewhat of an affinity with him.

I have sketched my impressions of the principal members of the diplomatic group during the hectic days of the peak emergency operation in 1984–85 because of their importance to the emergency operation. I have never been an admirer of the profession of diplomacy in the 20th Century when the influence of diplomats has waned with the development of rapid communications with the home offices, but I was highly impressed by the quality of the "relief diplomats" in Addis. Without their unstinting support for the relief effort, my task would have been well-nigh impossible.

At the working level, diplomats and other embassy staff dealing with the famine were just as cooperative as the ambassadors and chargés. USAID was represented by a group of five officials headed by Fred Fischer, a tall, lean man with a straightforward, honest and realistic approach to problems. He was assisted by Rick Machmer, a young man who had served before in the field including Indonesia and with the Peace Corps in Biafra. Rick had a great sense of humour and a hearty laugh. The USAID team as a whole supported the UN role very strongly and a relationship of complete trust and openness developed between us. This was important as USAID represented by far the largest donor country. Fred Fischer and Rick Machmer, although certainly not sympathetic to the Marxist regime, never let that fact influence them in their work. I greatly admired them for their dedication and their compassion for the Ethiopian people. They were true professionals who carried out their difficult task with unusual efficiency. Their reports to Peter McPherson, the USAID Administrator in Washington, were an important factor that made it possible for USAID to allocate in 1984–85 more than 450,000 tonnes of food to Ethiopia despite the pressure McPherson faced from right-wing politicians in Congress and the US administration.

At times, relations between USAID and RRC were tense. The RRC felt that too many restrictions were placed on the use of American food and other aid and too many reports and audits had to be prepared. Most of this was normal practice in the USAID and Fred Fischer could not change regulations. The position of the USAID team was not eased by the fact that they were in Ethiopia on visitors' visas renewable monthly. This was because, when US–Ethiopia relations worsened in 1977, the Ethiopian Government had placed a ceiling of 28 on the Embassy expatriate staff. The small USAID staff was over and above that quota and had, therefore, not been given diplomatic visas. This was a constant source of irritation to the USAID and many attempts had been made to change the situation. At times this matter came close to being made public and thus liable to affect the level of the US contribution to the famine relief. I therefore took up the question with Foreign Minister Goshu Wolde who said that he would be willing to reconsider it if the RRC sent him a letter affirming that the USAID mission was necessary as long as US famine aid continued. At my request, Commissioner Dawit wrote a letter to that effect but nothing happened. When I spoke to the Foreign Minister again he said the language had not been appropriate and that he needed a stronger text regarding the need for the USAID mission. A second letter was written, again the matter was delayed. The Foreign Minister was present when Bradford Morse and I met Chairman Mengistu in July 1985. When the Foreign Minister saw us to the door I took him aside and again urged him to issue the visas. He said it would be done very shortly. The visas were then issued within a few days. I was criticised by some Ethiopians for having intervened in this matter. My position was that I was in Ethiopia because of the famine and, if there was a danger of something affecting contributions from the largest donor country, I had to intervene whether or not it was considered politically acceptable.

Aid matters in the Canadian Embassy were handled by Terry Mooney who, as Counsellor, was the number two in the Embassy. I met with him very frequently either at the Advisory Group meetings mentioned earlier or at *ad hoc* meetings with a small group of major donors to discuss particular problems such as port congestion and food distribution. Terry played a key role in the whole operation. His analytical mind and ability to use statistics, plus his practical common sense, made him extremely valuable as a colleague and as a friend. I wanted him to join my office as my deputy but for various reasons this did not work out.

In most other donor embassies there was someone dealing with the famine. I found this group to be very helpful and constructive, without exception. The Italian Embassy, apart from a Counsellor who assisted Ambassador Rossi in relief matters, had a small medical team and they did very useful work, flying with the Polish helicopters to the drop zones and treating people on the spot while the air drop took place.

3. Western Private Organisations in a Marxist Country

There have been few emergencies where non-governmental organisations (NGOs) have played a greater role than in Ethiopia. Several large NGOs, including Catholic Relief Services, Lutheran World Federation and the League of Red Cross Societies had been working in Ethiopia for years. When the famine in Ethiopia became known to the outside world there was a rush among NGOs to get into the country. The government had no established policy regarding the involvement of NGOs in the relief programme. NGO staff were given visas by Ethiopian embassies often without RRC being consulted. Fund-raising campaigns were organised in many countries, particularly in the UK and USA, and on a smaller scale in Scandinavia, the Federal Republic of Germany, Switzerland, Italy and Japan. Cynics have said that for some NGOs a catastrophe such as that in Ethiopia provided welcome opportunities for raising large amounts of funds and that humanitarian considerations came second. At any rate, some Ethiopian officials, including Foreign Minister Goshu Wolde and Commissioner Dawit, complained publicly from time to time that funds raised in the name of Ethiopia's famine victims were spent partly elsewhere and that too much of the money went into administration.

The number of NGOs involved in the famine relief one way or another rose eventually to 63. These included large organisations capable of carrying out general food distributions, smaller ones that concentrated on supplementary feeding, medical care and sanitation and some which, in fact, did very little. Most of the organisations belonged to an umbrella body, the Christian Relief and Development Association (CRDA). This never became a coordinating agency of any great operational value but it provided a place for discussing common problems and deciding on action to be taken. The UN office had very close ties with the CRDA, and our NGO Officer, Tom Franklin, attended their meetings.

Coordination among the numerous NGOs working in Ethiopia was not easy. It was difficult even to obtain information on the activities of a number of organisations due to the lack of a systematic monitoring effort on the CRDA's part and because several major NGOs were not members of this organisation. In the middle of 1985 the UN office began preparing a report with the aim of showing exactly which NGO was doing what and where. The CRDA cooperated fully in this exercise. To facilitate the flow of information the UN office issued a monthly newsletter summarising the progress of food distribution, the situation in the camps, transport problems etc. But the information system was never fully developed, mainly because some of the major NGOs were extremely slow in providing information although they tried their best. Some NGOs including the ICRC, CARE, OXFAM, Save The Children, Irish 'Concern' and the Lutheran

World Federation were always on time but some of the larger ones responsible for food distribution were unable to provide precise and timely information. In order to produce the overall figures a lot of time-consuming individual consultations had to be held with these organisations. This was a slow process and the distribution figures were often unduly delayed.

The NGOs' position in Ethiopia was strong because some of the major food donors insisted on distribution by NGOs of their choice. For example, of the USA commitment of 450,000 tonnes of food, only 50,000 tonnes were given bilaterally to the RRC for distribution, the rest was shared by major US NGOs, mainly World Vision, Catholic Relief Services and CARE. Earmarkings not only to different organisations but for different regions of the country were a normal practice. This policy on the part of the donors created rigidities in the distribution system. In Kampuchea I had refused to accept this practice. The food went into a pool from which distribution was made. I was surprised the Ethiopian authorities had not objected to the system of earmarking but it was too late to change it when I arrived.

Over the months improvisations were introduced, particularly in the form of borrowings between NGOs against later shipments, and between RRC and NGOs. This introduced an element of flexibility but it was never very satisfactory from the point of view of management and reporting. A pool for all contributions with agreed responsibilities for distribution by NGOs and RRC would have been preferable. As it was, there was always a "floating" quantity of grain on loan which was difficult to trace for accounting and reporting purposes.

Over the months in 1984–85 the share of food distribution going through the NGOs continued to grow until it reached a point in November 1985 when only a little more than 30 per cent was handled by the RRC. This naturally undermined the RRC's position as the indigenous institution responsible for relief and rehabilitation of drought victims. The RRC came to grips with this problem very slowly and took belated steps to regularise the distribution system. Many NGOs had started their activities without signing an agreement with the RRC which in some cases was not, at the headquarter level, sufficiently informed of what the NGOs were doing and where. On 14 July Commissioner Dawit issued a circular letter to the NGOs to the effect that they would not be allowed to function without a written agreement with RRC and that foreign staff needed to obtain work permits. A rule was also laid down that expatriate staff should be employed only when competent workers were not available in Ethiopia. The number of headquarters staff in Addis was to be drastically reduced. The stern and somewhat high-handed style in which the letter was drafted was resented by some NGOs. Others had no objection to the principles stated in the letter but were concerned about the delays in obtaining work permits for such personnel as doctors, nurses and engineers.

I talked with Commissioner Dawit about this matter and he eventually softened his position and was quite conciliatory with the NGOs at a meeting when he explained the intent of his policy. Most of the NGOs accepted the RRC rules without much complaining and the matter soon ceased to be an issue. In fact, the number of expatriate relief workers remained at the earlier level and in October 1985 totalled 577, out of whom 446 were professionals and the remainder general service personnel. Altogether the NGOs employed at that time totalled 1,916 people.

Not all the NGOs were experienced in emergency work. Some organisations, particularly those working in small projects in health and sanitation, tended to apply Western standards and were appalled at the conditions they saw. They were not used to seeing watchmen in the camps using sticks to control large crowds. But in Ethiopia practically every young man and young boy constantly carries a stick which serves many purposes. To Western eyes Ethiopian authorities may at times seem cruel and lacking in compassion towards their compatriots, but again the methods were traditional in Ethiopia and accepted by the population. Inexperienced relief workers failed to understand a number of other things. For example, when a bag of grain was accidentally dropped from an unloading truck, children and women rushed to the place and fought for every single grain. This seemed pathetic and shocking but it was acceptable to the local people. Generally, the Ethiopian peasant population was well-disciplined and traditionally followed instructions without protests. Thousands of people could be sitting in neat rows waiting for their rations to be distributed; there was no jostling or shouting. To keep order in Kampuchea had been much more difficult and I often wondered how it could have been done on the scale of the Ethiopian operation.

Many NGOs had serious management problems. Some took on too much without having the necessary capacity to distribute what they had received from the donors. At one point in the middle of 1985 there was somewhat of a mess developing among a few of the largest NGOs responsible for huge quantities of food. Other NGOs adopted the policy of taking on only as much as they thought that they could handle and insisted on being self-sufficient in transport. This was the policy of CARE and ICRC from the beginning. The other major NGOs gradually developed their own transport and repair capacity but these arrangements came very late and long after the peak of the rescue operation had been reached. Poor leadership plagued some of the NGOs and there were too many changes in personnel, too many absences on leave and business abroad. Competition and jealousy was not uncommon. The home offices needed material for their fund-raising and pressured their field staff to show results. If I were to mention an example of excellent leadership and management, it would be Stanley Dunn, director of CARE in Ethiopia, a no-nonsense administrator who never compromised efficiency in exchange for promises of contributions. In supplementary feeding, OXFAM and Save the Children (UK) were highly efficient. The ICRC also did a good job in food distribution under difficult political and security conditions in Tigray and Eritrea.

Inexperienced NGO workers caused difficult problems. This was illustrated by the behaviour of members of Médecins Sans Frontières (MSF), a small French organisation (not to be confused with MSF, Belgium). The group was very young and consisted on average of 30 doctors, nurses and administrators who had recently finished their education and had little previous experience of Africa and none of Ethiopia. They seemed dedicated and did good work in health and, on a very insignificant scale, in supplementary feeding in relief centres at Korem, Kobo, Ketala and Sekota in Wollo province. Some of these young people were highly excitable, reacting emotionally to any events that they with their Western standards did not think appropriate. This would have been no problem had not the MSF workers constantly talked to French magazine reporters and newspapers hostile to the Mengistu regime. When the articles appeared the writers had added their own horror stories to them. The result was an extraordinary version of events that, when investigated, turned out to be highly exaggerated and unreliable in facts.

In several meetings with members of MSF, including particularly Dr Brigitte Vasset, I suggested they should first discuss these matters with RRC headquarters to try to solve problems before talking to the press. That she did, but more often than not the young doctors and nurses in the feeding centres continued their immature behaviour. The MSF was criticised by many other NGOs and some of them felt that the organisation actually wanted to be expelled. I prevented their expulsion on two occasions but there was a feeling of distrust between RRC and MSF.

I had already left Ethiopia when the MSF director told the French press that 100,000 people had died in the resettlement process. No doubt there were casualties in the very hasty and badly organised transport of people from the northern regions to the south-east of the country and conditions in many resettlement areas were bad. But MSF had no way of knowing any figures. The organisation had nothing to do with the general food distribution which represented 90 per cent of the aid. MSF staff worked in four small projects in only one of the seven provinces badly affected by the famine. None of these projects was near a transit camp for settlers which would have provided opportunities to observe the treatment of people selected for resettlement; no MSF staff visited any resettlement site. To be sure, they had seen people in poor health leaving relief camps for transport to a transit camp or to a settlement area, and had seen the often harsh way local officials dealt with these people. This was nothing new to those relief workers aware of the marks that centuries of feudalism and oppression had left on the mentality of the peasant population, but it was quite understandable that some MSF staff, young and inexperienced as they were, should have been upset at what they saw. Ethiopia is not France. What was unacceptable, however, was that MSF issued an arbitrary figure of 100,000 deaths having occurred in the resettlement programme; this was pure speculation. No one was then or is now in a position to know any casualty figures and no one will ever know how many settlers would have died in the relief camps at the height of the famine and outbreaks of disease which intermittently ravaged these camps.

A year later, the head of MSF, in an interview in November 1986 tried to justify this claim by referring to reports by the World Food Programme (WFP), to personal accounts by a Catholic priest whose organisation (Irish Concern) works in settlement sites, and to interviews with refugees. But no WFP report dealing with this subject exists (I should know since I was in charge of the WFP emergency office in Ethiopia). The priest referred to in the interview has stated that he was misquoted and that the MSF representative in Addis had seized upon some figures which came up in passing during a conversation he had had with a priest and an ambassador of a donor country in Addis. The latter has confirmed that this case of misquotation did occur. As to interviews with refugees, the MSF head, judging from an article he wrote in October 1986 for a US magazine, was referring to a survey made in refugee camps in Sudan by Cultural Survival Inc. composed of a group of US anthropologists. This survey has been convincingly debunked by the eminent Ethiopia scholar, Dr Richard Pankhurst, in an article published in a major American anthropological journal. Anyone who has worked with displaced people and refugees in developing countries knows that surveys undertaken by foreigners are frequently unreliable, because those questioned tend to provide the answers they think the interviewer expects, and which they believe may help bring aid from abroad. In any case, nothing in this very limited sample survey supported the notion that any reliable estimate could be made of the mortality rate in resettlement areas.

There were many expressions of dismay at MSF's arbitrariness. Not one of the 50-odd NGOs working in Ethiopia, most of which had a much larger role than the small MSF and worked in all the famine-affected provinces, agreed with MSF's action, and many relief workers were amazed at the lack of responsibility this indicated. It was not a question of whether or not there had been casualties in the resettlement programme. This was acknowledged by most people in the international community in Ethiopia and even in the government; Minister Berhanu Bayih had not denied this. But there should have been an attempt to establish a credible estimate using acceptable survey methods or, at the very least, MSF should have consulted other NGOs to obtain their views in this matter. But the figure was suddenly broadcast by MSF apparently without any attempt at verification. As usually happens, the press and even people in politically responsible positions, such as US Congressmen and high French officials (including the Minister for Human Rights, a former MSF president), unquestioningly quoted the MSF figure as an established fact.

The NGOs were essential in the relief operation. RRC could not have handled food distribution and other relief actions by itself. But the RRC should have exercised great selectivity in accepting NGOs. Efficiency would have increased if a smaller number of large, experienced NGOs had formed the NGO mechanism for food distribution, supplementary feeding and health and sanitation services. With this apparatus in place, the RRC and the NGOs would have known the gaps that needed to be filled by smaller NGOs with experience in specific fields. This would have provided a more manageable and more tightly coordinated NGO network. To be sure, the Ethiopian emergency burst upon the scene so suddenly that perhaps this kind of screening would have been impractical. Clearly, there were too many small NGOs involved in the relief operation creating management and political problems.

For a Marxist government to permit so many Western NGOs to function in all parts of the country was highly unusual and was viewed by some hardliners as a reflection on the government's ability to handle its own affairs. There was a genuine appreciation of the work of NGOs on the part of Chairman Mengistu. He was aware of the presence of a number of large US NGOs and in conversation with me he indicated his awareness of the support that the American people traditionally gave to voluntary organisations.

Fund-raising campaigns such as Band Aid/Live Aid and the United Support of Artists for Africa were instrumental in keeping world conscience aware of the African famine, particularly in Ethiopia and Sudan. But in terms of aid their contributions represented only a tiny fraction of the more than one billion dollars-worth of relief funded by governments for 1984–85. The practice of some fund-raising groups to do their own procurement instead of relying on experienced NGOs resulted in delays leading to a switch of policy from immediate relief to safer and increasingly popular longer-term rehabilitation projects. This was something to be supported in principle but there were times when funds needed immediately for saving lives in Ethiopia were not forthcoming. For example, some of the 100 second-hand trucks purchased in Kuwait by Band Aid/Live Aid were still not operational a year later.

I am ambivalent about the virtue of special campaigns for emergencies such as those mentioned above. To be at all sufficient, aid in cases of emergency must come mainly from government resources. The use of experienced NGOs as a channel for disbursement and distribution of aid is often desirable to ensure quick action. But improvised charity is another thing. I am not sure it is a good idea to give the impression to the general public that responsibility for emergency aid lies with individuals or private groups when it should be mainly with governments. Nevertheless, the tremendous publicity surrounding these huge fund-raising events may have contributed to pressurising governments to do more. Funds raised through these events had in fact very little impact on the aid programmes.

The tendency on the part of these fund-raising groups to get involved in project preparation and execution and to set up their own field offices raises many practical problems. The number of NGOs working in developing countries and competing for funds in donor countries is such that recipient governments face serious management difficulties, sometimes out of proportion to the benefits these projects bring. If charity drives result in additional semi-permanent structures, as now seems to be the case, their value is questionable. This is particularly true of groups getting involved in development projects by-passing established and experienced international NGOs. There are already enough problems of coordination among the NGOs, and too many amateurs looking for projects in developing countries. Fund-raising campaigns are fine but the use of funds should be left to existing organisations.

The political leadership and key officials in the emergency

I had been in Ethiopia before but only at meetings of the ECA. At that time I had no contacts with top government officials and no experience of how to approach them. By chance I was to work as head of mission in two Marxist-governed countries, Kampuchea and now Ethiopia. My political leanings are very far from Marxism but since my missions were of a purely humanitarian nature I pushed my political convictions deep into the background. In Kampuchea I decided it was necessary to make my position clear from the beginning, because the Heng Samrin regime was new and inexperienced except for some senior officials in the Ministry of Foreign Affairs who had worked for Norodom Sihanouk. When I first met President Heng Samrin I told him that I was not a supporter of Marxism but that I had come to try to help the Kampuchean people, and if my political leanings were not acceptable I would return on the next Red Cross plane to Bangkok. Heng

Samrin, who spoke only Khmer, did not seem startled by my statement and replied through an interpreter that he understood the purpose of my mission and that my political views did not matter. Throughout my assignment in Kampuchea there was never any problem in this regard.

This kind of approach was not feasible in Ethiopia where the political leadership is highly-educated and sophisticated. The Head of State, Chairman Mengistu Haile Mariam, has a habit dictated by his very busy schedule of not giving the exact time of appointments and thus keeping visitors waiting until he was free to receive them. On 12 November 1984 I was sitting in the lobby of the Ethiopia Hotel in Addis Ababa waiting for a UNICEF colleague. The lobby was full of people and the din of conversation was loud. Suddenly a young man entered, looked around and asked something from several people. He seemed very nervous since he obviously got no answers, and finally he shouted "Is Mr Jansson here?" He was an official of the Chairman's staff and told me with great relief that the Chairman was waiting for me at his office.

Chairman Mengistu received me in his main office, one of the former minor mansions of Emperor Haile Selassie. I had to wait for about five minutes before the Chief of Protocol ushered me into a large room filled with television cameramen and journalists. Chairman Mengistu stood in front of a huge table some distance from the door with a portrait of Lenin high on the wall behind the table. I had seen pictures of the Chairman in the press but I was surprised to see how short he was and how dark his complexion compared to many of the Ethiopians. With television cameras whirring and flashlights popping, he stepped forward with a friendly smile and greeted me in English. We then sat down in a part of the large room reserved for meeting visitors. He began with the normal words of courtesy and asked about my family and whether my wife had arrived with me. Then he explained to me, in quite some detail, the situation in Ethiopia caused by the prolonged drought and the earlier regime's neglect of the needs of the peasants. His statement centred on the historical position of Ethiopia among hostile countries and the struggle to preserve its independence and Christian faith among the Muslim multitudes. Turning to the famine he warmly welcomed the establishment of the UN Emergency Office in Addis and my own assignment. He stated with a smile that he had been informed of my assignment in Kampuchea and added, very graciously, that he hoped the UN role in Ethiopia would be as successful as it was in Kampuchea.

Chairman Mengistu stressed that he would like to see me at regular intervals to be briefed on the famine situation and that he was willing to see me any time I needed his support to fulfil the task to which I had been assigned. During the year I spent in Ethiopia I was to see him many times, mostly at his request but sometimes at mine. He spoke slowly and deliberately in a very low voice and I remember particularly that he looked me steadily in the eyes not only when he made a statement but also when the interpreter put it into English. I knew he had a good command of English and I therefore replied to him in that language. He sometimes helped the interpreter and obviously did not need interpretation from English into Amharic. He was clearly well-informed and was briefed by a minister or RRC senior official before our meetings.

I spent a day with Chairman Mengistu on 8 May 1985, visiting the port of Assab.

I had met with him two days earlier about the Ibenat incident and when we had finished he said, "Well Mr Jansson, will you come with me to Assab the day after tomorrow?", adding, with a typically faint smile, that since I had complained so much about the insufficient offtake in the port we could go down together and see what could be done about it. We travelled in Mengistu's personal plane, a Twin Otter. At the airport a number of Politbureau members were present, some of whom took part in the trip. Chairman Mengistu arrived in a Land-Rover, escorted only by two soldiers who acted as his bodyguards. On the plane he sat with his back to the cockpit in a type of easy chair before a folding desk. I was placed opposite him and next to Feseha Desta, the number three in the Politbureau and Chairman of the transport committee dealing with famine relief. The other members of the party including Berhanu Bayeh, Minister of Labour and Social Affairs and Chairman of the Politbureau's famine relief committee, and RRC Chief Commissioner Dawit Wolde Ghiorgis were placed according to protocol.

During the almost two-hour flight Chairman Mengistu did not say very much except to point out some of the landmarks below. Feseha Desta acted as interpreter. At the airstrip in Assab we were met by a large party of local officials and then proceeded to make an inspection tour of the port facilities, guided by the Minister of Transport Youssuf Ahmed. The port was full of military and civilian trucks loading relief grain. Obviously this was a bit of a show put up because of the Chairman's visit and to indicate that my request for the use of military trucks was being implemented. We stopped for some time to survey the damage caused by a freak rainstorm two days earlier which, it later turned out, had destroyed about 10,000 tonnes of wheat. After a tour of the port Minister Youssuf gave a briefing in the port clubhouse. He spoke in Amharic and Chairman Mengistu made sure that I had someone by me to interpret. Minister Youssuf went into some detail about the port operation and outlined the need for further unloading equipment and storage space. He stated that the daily offtake by truck from Assab would be doubled to around 4,500 tonnes. At that point Chairman Mengistu turned to me and said, "Did you notice this important commitment?" The briefing was followed by lunch which was also attended by the North Korean Ambassador who took part in the visit because of an ongoing project to build a new fishing harbour in Assab with North Korean aid. During lunch Chairman Mengistu conversed almost exclusively with Feseha Desta and me and I noticed that throughout the trip he seldom talked with other members of the Politbureau. This somewhat surprised me but it could perhaps be explained by my presence and that of the Ambassador of North Korea. It did indicate to me a tendency on the Chairman's part to keep his distance from his entourage but it may well be due to his reserved manners. The visit to Assab helped me in later contacts with the transport authorities since I could always refer to the fact that a commitment had been made in the Chairman's presence to raise the offtake from the port.

My overall impression of Chairman Mengistu was one of intelligence, quiet dignity, reserve and great courtesy.

That I had access to Chairman Mengistu was of great importance to my work. Ambassadors of donor countries dealt with the Minister of Foreign Affairs, Goshu Wolde, who was not a member of the Politbureau and not important politically. At my meetings with the Chairman I raised matters of general importance to the relief effort such as port congestion, food distribution in sensitive areas, the use of military transport for food distribution, freedom of action for NGOs and the policy of resettlement. The Chairman usually reacted positively to my proposals. Only once was I firmly turned down. That was when I suggested that UN or ICRC food convoys be permitted to move into the interior of Eritrea and Tigray, a matter to which I will revert later. Otherwise he generally supported my initiatives (except those regarding resettlement) including my action to prevent the forcible evacuation of the large Ibenat camp which had attracted worldwide attention. Sometimes he did not reply directly to proposals I made but I adopted the attitude that if he did not object he agreed at least in general terms. In my dealings with the authorities in Addis and at the regional and local levels I referred to the Chairman's views whenever necessary in order to get action. This never failed to help.

There has been much speculation about Chairman Mengistu's actual position as head of state. Rumours had it that he was being pressured by the hardliners to adopt a more radical Marxist economic and social policy and that the moderate elements in the Politbureau resisted that. My experience convinced me that Mengistu was clearly in charge and that there was no one who could challenge him. He discreetly tried to steer a middle course in internal politics and in Ethiopia's relations with the outside world. He was interested in improving relations with the United States and, on one occasion in 1985, asked Commissioner Dawit, the head of the Relief and Rehabilitation Commission who was then visiting Washington, to sound out State Department officials about this. By all accounts Chairman Mengistu, while pursuing strongly his policy of friendship with the Soviet Union, maintained a certain distance from his main ally. This has to be seen against the background of the fierce patriotism and deep nationalist feelings of the Ethiopians nurtured by centuries of struggle against outside aggression. I am convinced that Ethiopia could never become a satellite of the Soviet Union. It simply is not in the nature of the people and their leaders. This is a far cry from Kampuchea where the Soviet Embassy was in charge acting mainly through the Vietnamese advisers present everywhere.

Rhetoric apart, Chairman Mengistu seemed to harbour no antagonism towards the US. At a meeting with him in June 1985, when I asked him to ensure that the American NGOs be given all facilities needed to carry out their humanitarian work, he seemed surprised that this was considered a problem. He told me that he had spent some time in the US and understood the people of that country. He assured me that everything would be done to facilitate their humanitarian work.

My cordial relationship with Chairman Mengistu and his keen interest in famine relief were instrumental in obtaining decisions on crucial problems in the relief effort. Senior Ethiopian officials told me that there was resistance in the Politbureau to the establishment of a special UN office for emergency operations in Ethiopia. Some of the Politbureau members thought that this would be a reflection on the ability of the Marxist regime to handle its internal problems. The fact that the office was established at the level of Assistant Secretary General added to the reluctance of some officials to accept the arrangement. But Chairman Mengistu showed absolutely no sign of having any reservations in this regard. My assumption was that he felt that since the blame for the recurring famines was constantly attributed to the policies of Emperor Haile Selassie, the present regime could not be blamed for the consequences. But when I got to know many of the senior officials in the government and the general attitude of the people, I am more inclined to attribute Chairman Mengistu's position to a deep concern for the fate of his own people. He was aware of the fact (proved earlier in Kampuchea) that sufficient food and other relief aid would not be forthcoming from his socialist friends. Their assistance came in other forms. Humanitarian aid in large quantities was desperately needed and Chairman Mengistu knew that it had to come from the West.

Another moderating factor was the influence of the Ethiopian Church dating back to the 4th Century. Since the present regime came to power there seems to have been an upsurge in church attendance. The Patriarch of the Church of Ethiopia is treated with great respect. At the May Day celebrations it was Chairman Mengistu who went over to greet the Patriarch and not the other way around. The latter remained seated and anyone who wished to greet him had to walk over to where he sat. When Minister Berhanu Bayeh gave a farewell reception for my wife and me at the end of 1985, the Patriarch was present as a guest. He stood by a French window in the reception room of the Ghion Hotel and never moved around in the group. Here again he was in a special position of respect reflecting the influence of the Church in Ethiopian society.

Apart from Feseha Desta, the most important Politbureau member concerned with emergency relief was Berhanu Bayeh, a former army officer like most of the others. He ranked number five in Ethiopia and as Chairman of the Politbureau's Relief and Rehabilitation Committee had a central position in famine relief. A handsome, small-boned, short man in his early fifties, Berhanu Bayeh belonged to the moderate group in the party leadership. He was Commissioner Dawit's direct superior but left all operational matters in Dawit's hands. Berhanu Bayeh was always accessible when I asked to see him and we frequently dealt with problems by telephone. I found him quite open to suggestions and criticisms and often very helpful in solving particular problems. One example was when an Australian grain vessel was kept waiting off the port of Assab while some Russian ships were unloading equipment for the armed forces. The Australian Chargé d'Affaires, Leslie Luck, was in a real dilemma because the press had discovered the situation and Canberra was pressing him for action. I asked Berhanu Bayeh to arrange for docking space for the grain ship since we had agreed that relief cargo should be given priority in the ports. Berhanu Bayeh telephoned the Minister of Transport, Youssuf Ahmed, who happened to be in the port of Assab. After a conversation in English with Minister Youssuf the Australian ship was docked and the grain unloaded.

Feseha Desta was a friendly man with a good sense of humour. I dealt with him only when I could not get the necessary action from Minister Youssuf or Vice Minister Asseged Wolde Amanuel. Feseha Desta was usually very positive and took quick action. He was always accessible by telephone and was most prompt in returning telephone calls.

Of the other top officials important to the relief operation, I was particularly impressed by Transport Minister Youssuf Ahmed. He was a member of the Central Committee but not of the Politbureau and a transport economist by profession. Always in a good mood and ready to be helpful I found working with him very easy. I must have been "a pain in the neck" to him and I used to joke with him that when he was ill in bed it was because I gave him nausea and he had to disappear for some time. The Vice Minister of Transport, Asseged Wolde Amanuel, was a difficult person in many ways and subject to a lot of caustic remarks by NGO representatives and diplomats. Initially, I found him somewhat arrogant but when I knew him better I came to like him. He was frank and always willing to discuss problems. When he made a commitment he always carried it out.

The Minister of Agriculture, Tekola Dejene, was one of the first officials I met when we discussed the seed distribution problem. Easily approachable, open and friendly he was one of the most sympathetic among the ministers. Our cooperation was invariably smooth.

Chief Commissioner Dawit Wolde Ghiorgis of the RRC was my real counterpart. He was a former army major with a master's degree in International Law from Columbia University. He returned to Ethiopia from the United States after the 1974 overthrow of Emperor Selassie. His most important earlier assignment had been as Chief Administrator of Eritrea for two years. Commissioner Dawit, a handsome man with much drive and initiative, highly regarded by most people involved in the relief operation, was a true extrovert who could laugh at jokes even at the expense of the RRC. He could be very stubborn when it came to sensitive political problems but in relief matters he took quick decisions and stuck by them. His job was in many respects impossible. He was a member of the Central Committee but not of the Politbureau and had to deal mainly with Western donors and NGOs. Inevitably, Politbureau hardliners looked upon him as pro-West, and because of his prominent position he figured a great deal in the world press and the local news media. This created jealousies on the part of top officials who often undercut him. His sometimes abrupt manner irritated some diplomats and NGO staff, but everyone respected him for his tremendous drive and dedication.

Commissioner Dawit was in a position where he was under pressure from all sides and he had to be extremely careful in balancing his openness towards the Western donors and NGOs with political considerations and his delicate relations with hardliners in the Politbureau who doubted his loyalty to the regime. After visiting Washington in 1985, where, at Chairman Mengistu's request, he had tried to sound out US officials on improving relations, he was grilled for hours by the Central Committee and accused of betraying the Ethiopian revolution.

At the field level, when the Ethiopian Workers Party, established in 1974, became stronger, regional and local party secretaries always had to be kept in the picture and frequently made decisions on relief matters, although that should have been the task of the RRC regional and local representatives. The power structure at the provincial and local level was rigidly clear. The Regional party secretary was supreme and even the regional army commander, usually a major general, was under his control. Then came the chief administrator and only after him the RRC regional representative. During my frequent trips throughout Ethiopia with

Commissioner Dawit and his senior staff I found that Dawit was a personal friend of many of the party secretaries. That made it easier for him to get their cooperation and to reduce interference from the party cadres in the relief operation.

Since the beginning of the full-scale operation in December 1984 Commissioner Dawit was immersed in his work day and night. He was ably assisted by Deputy Commissioner Berhane Deressa and his two other deputies Taye Gurmu and Haptemariam Ayenachew. Some of his department heads at the next level were hardworking young men, particularly Ahmed Ali, head of Aid Coordination. He was truly overworked since it fell upon him to keep statistics and prepare reports to donor meetings and the government. I had great respect for Ahmed Ali. Each time I saw him he looked thinner and frailer. My wife and I thought he should get married and I said I would try to help him find the right girl. I didn't succeed and we joked that he always managed to escape because he had been alerted by the RRC's Early Warning System.

4.   The Logistics Nightmare

Road transport

Food and other relief supplies were shipped to the two Ethiopian Red Sea ports of Assab and Massawa, and to the port of Djibouti linked by rail to Ethiopia. A WFP mission had estimated in November 1984 that the unloading capacity of Assab port, through which most food and other relief supplies were shipped, was 135,000 MT. When additional equipment, such as dumper lorries, bagging machines and port tractors and trailers had been provided and more workers employed, the port could, in spring 1985, unload 180–200,000 MT a month. Massawa port's capacity was 15–24,000 tonnes a month and Djibouti could unload about 15–20,000 tonnes for Ethiopia.

My office, and later the WFP, had a port officer in Assab to help the port authorities and monitor relief shipments for which three berths had been reserved. Roman Roos spent the first five months of his assignment in Assab and introduced many improvements to speed up unloading and truck offtake. All three ports functioned quite efficiently as far as unloading was concerned. The congestion at Assab throughout the relief operation and the fact that ships had to wait for up to nine days before docking, with demurrage being the responsibility of Ethiopia, was due not to unloading problems but to a shortage of trucks, resulting in transport out of the port area being unable to match the rate of unloading. Another factor was the difficulty of scheduling relief shipments in a way that would make the most efficient use of port capacity possible. WFP issued regular bulletins listing forthcoming arrivals and projecting the unloading and storage situation in the ports. Donors tried to plan their shipping schedules accordingly but the availability of vessels and the intricate commercial shipping arrangements and freight rates often meant that ships arrived at the wrong time. The offtake problem was compounded by the import of fertilisers and commercial grain which had to be unloaded at a time when there was the greatest need for food. Storage became increasingly difficult as grain piled up in the port and could be stored only partly under cover. Stacking practices were not up to par and available storage capacity was not satisfactorily utilised. To protect grain bags from the sun and possible freak rains my office and WFP obtained large tarpaulins with assistance from UNDRO. The quickest response came from the Disaster Unit of the ODA in London which was very efficient in matters of this type not requiring large budget allocations.

The offtake out of Assab was also affected by very cumbersome handling procedures; about 42 pieces of paper had to be prepared and signed before the trucks could leave the port area. Some of these procedures were later simplified after many efforts by my office but that came only in the second half of 1985. Roman Roos tried to persuade the port authorities to use more direct delivery from ships to trucks to avoid the kind of double-handling that was the rule in the port, but this recommendation was never implemented. Perhaps it would have reduced the much-needed revenue the government collected in handling relief goods, particularly food. The offtake was helped by Roman Roos' initiative in getting the port authorities to add a third work shift. But insufficient offtake from Assab continued to plague the relief programme because of a shortage of trucks, and port and transport management problems. My office monitored port activities very closely and daily telexes were received from our port officer showing the unloading and offtake rates. My interventions with the Ministry of Transport and its operating agencies were often based on these telexes which provided up-to-date information for immediate action.

I expected many problems in relief transport because of Ethiopia's formidable geography, but they turned out to be infinitely more difficult than I had foreseen. In Kampuchea there were enough difficulties because of maintenance problems and the poor condition of the roads, except for one of the main arteries running from Phnom Penh to the port of Kompong Som. But the trucks carrying food travelled mostly over plains and there were rivers by which the light river-craft with outboard motors and the large motorised barges provided for the relief operation could transport a lot of food.

Transport in Kampuchea was child's play in comparison with Ethiopia, where elevations range from 100 metres below sea level to plateaux rising to nearly 4,000 metres. Abrupt escarpments and deep gorges cut the landscape into a mosaic of high plateaux and steep mountainsides where tiny hamlets and isolated small homes were situated.

Ethiopia, twice the size of France, has one of the poorest road networks in the world. There is a total of little over 30,000 km of primary, secondary and feeder roads of which less than half are all-weather asphalt or gravel roads. The mountainous interior had practically no roads and large parts are accessible only by foot or donkey transport. The generally poor condition of the roads, and the difficult terrain in the highlands made for heavy wear and tear of vehicles. Only one operating railroad runs from Djibouti to Addis, a distance of 781 km of which 681 km is inside Ethiopia.

These conditions were bad enough in normal circumstances but now transport was affected by the activities of rebel groups, particularly in Eritrea and Tigray, and to a lesser extent in the provinces of Wollo and Gondar. These areas, except for the towns, were frequently under rebel control or consisted of "grey areas" controlled by neither side. Road transport through many of these parts mostly needed armed escort. This involved cumbersome arrangements taking up to one month of preparations and the convoys proceeded at snail's pace. Road transport was also frequently interrupted, on the main road from the port of Assab leading to Kombolcha, a major storage and transit place for transport north, west and south, and Hararghe in the south-eastern region next to Somalia.

Despite efforts to provide sufficient maintenance services, including a large RRC garage in Addis with a West German technical team, the heavy 4-wheel-drive trucks and trailers carrying up to 22 tonnes frequently broke down. The average number of vehicles put out of action each month was 50. Four sets of tyres specially manufactured for conditions such as those in Ethiopia were needed annually for each vehicle and even that was not enough for routes in the most difficult areas.

The Ministry of Transport and the RRC were responsible for government-operated vehicles. The National Transport Corporation (NATRACOR), the operating agency running government-owned vehicles and controlling private vehicles under contract arrangements was under the Ministry. At the local level was the "Ketena" through which private truck owners did their business. About 5,400 trucks were under NATRACOR's control. Of these, in a letter to me dated 25 June 1985, the Minister of Transport stated 4,039 were allocated to carry relief cargo. Taking into account the long turn-around time, this meant deploying 135 NATRACOR trucks a day for relief transport representing, according to the Minister, 90 per cent of the total number of operational civilian trucks in Ethiopia. Increasing numbers of trucks had to be written off as beyond repair, and maintenance took a lot of time; there was a constant struggle to keep trucks on the road.

In February 1986, RRC had 329 long-haul and 703 short-haul trucks. In early 1985, the larger NGOs began to establish their own truck fleets totalling 557 vehicles at the end of 1985. This took time and created distribution problems for organisations such as World Vision and Catholic Relief Services. To ease the situation the latter made an expensive but necessary US-financed contract with a Kenyan trucking company involving 55 trucks.

To help finance transport I established a UN Transport Fund to which donor countries quickly contributed a total of $2.9 million. These funds were used mainly to procure tyres and spare parts and to subsidise NGO food transport. In November 1985 the UN and the WFP established a transport unit with 100 trucks provided by USAID and Band Aid/Live Aid.

The total number of trucks committed by donors for the relief operation eventually rose to over 1,100 at the beginning of 1986. This was a very satisfactory outcome of efforts to overcome the transport bottleneck and another manifestation

35

of donor generosity.

Management of this kind of hastily assembled truck fleet created a lot of headaches. One problem arose from the number of makes and types of vehicles brought into the country; at one point there were some 47 makes and over 100 models. An indication of the technical problems involved was the fact that in May 1985, 70 tractor-trucks donated to RRC were parked in the port of Assab awaiting semi-trailers, while some semi-trailers without tractors were offloaded for NGOs. Attempts to combine tractors, trailers and semi-trailers proved to be impossible because the couplings did not match. One donor shipped a large quantity of tyres but not of the type that could be used in Ethiopia. Some NGO trucks were unsuitable for conditions in Ethiopia because of such factors as unsatisfactory clearance height and unsuitable trailer couplings. Manufacturers had not intended these models for operation outside Europe and they proved practically unserviceable in Ethiopia. Standardisation would have been important from the beginning but pressure of time in the emergency, transport authorities' lack of coordination and failure to control NGO imports, made this impossible. In Kampuchea, with 1,074 trucks received in 1980–81 under the emergency programme, my policy was to accept only a few types of vehicles suitable for conditions there and to always insist on sufficient initial spare parts. But the famine relief operation in Ethiopia had to be started very quickly and in an emergency improvisations are often unavoidable.

To balance the unloading capacity of Assab with the transport out of the port it would have been necessary to deploy 150 long-haul 22–30 tonne trucks per day. This number was reached only infrequently despite my constant pressure on the Minister and Vice Minister of Transport and my interventions with Feseha Desta. In May 1985 the congestion in the port of Assab reached 101,000 MT, with cargo consigned to the RRC and NGOs. An unexpected brief rain on 5 May lasting one hour and nine minutes spoiled over 10,000 tonnes of grain, mainly from Canada. There had not been rain in Assab at that time of the year for decades. According to a review by a grain storage technologist from the Tropical Food and Research Institute in London, much of the food could have been saved if quick action had been taken immediately after the rain. This was not done because of inexperienced port authorities and food management personnel. The whole quantity was eventually discarded. This was reported in the world press under sensational headlines such as "food rotting in Assab while famine victims starve". In fact it represented a mere one per cent of the food shipped to Ethiopia by that time. This was a record achievement in this type of huge relief effort. It caused no starvation since food stocks were adequate for distribution.

The issue of increasing the offtake out of Assab became one of the most serious causes of friction between donors and the government. In all this I was squeezed from both sides, the donors insisting on strong measures to increase the use of government trucks and the government maintaining that they had made available all the trucks that could be spared, taking into account that agricultural and industrial needs for the rest of Ethiopia had to be met as well. The press came into this and the debate reached a point where loose estimates and figures were thrown about. US Vice President George Bush stated erroneously in one interview that only five per cent of the Ethiopian trucks were used for relief. In my opinion the government did all it could to provide transport for the relief operation; Roman Roos was of the same opinion. The fact that highest priority was given to fight the rebels in the North was often criticised by conservative visiting politicians. But drawing parallels with what their own governments would do to preserve their countries' integrity usually helped to wind up the discussion.

I spent much of my time, together with Roman Roos and Burke Oberle of the WFP, on questions of transport trying, on the one hand, to squeeze more commitments out of the donors and, on the other, to continue to increase pressure on the authorities to assign more trucks, including military vehicles, to the relief programme. The culmination of this came when I met Chairman Mengistu on 5 May 1985 in connection with the Ibenat incident, described later. I took the opportunity to urge him to ensure that the maximum number of trucks, including military vehicles, the economy of Ethiopia could permit be used for relief transport during the next several months. The UN would continue to press donors for additional transport aid including inland transport subsidies; but this would not come in time to solve the problem decisively. Chairman Mengistu assured me that immediate action would be taken to increase the government's transport capacity. To raise the daily offtake out of Assab he assured me that military vehicles would be made available on the Assab–Kombolcha, Assab–Addis and Nazareth routes. The latter had a storage capacity of 100,000 tonnes. It was agreed that, to avoid any suspicion of diversion of food, military trucks would not be used for secondary transport to distribution points. The Chairman added that he had sent the Minister of Transport to Assab to review the situation and invited me to join him on a visit there three days later. The results of that visit have already been mentioned.

Some donor embassies continued to doubt that the authorities made sufficient efforts to clear the port of Assab and they were sceptical of the figures they gave. One concern of the donors was that trucks were diverted from relief to resettlement, a programme not supported by major donors. I asked Roman Roos to investigate this and he concluded that the effects of the resettlement programme on relief transport was marginal. The 300 USSR trucks and 700 drivers were mainly used for transporting food to resettlement areas from the Ministry of Agriculture's stores. I knew the capacity of these trucks from my experience in Kampuchea. They were very inefficient, capable of transporting only three to five tonnes depending on the terrain and had refuelling problems because they ran on petrol and older trucks consumed one to three litres per kilometres. It would have made little difference had all USSR trucks been deployed for general food distribution.

At a private meeting in the Italian Embassy Western donor countries' ambassadors decided to ask for a meeting with Chairman Mengistu to express concern about the resettlement programme's effects on the relief effort and about a number of other points related to the resettlement programme. A paper for use in presenting the issues, but not for transmission to Chairman Mengistu, was drafted at several meetings. The approach to the Chairman was to be informal and presented as a local initiative by the ambassadors not speaking for their governments. I participated in discussions of the draft but told the ambassadors that I could not be part of the delegation since it would represent only one political grouping of the UN member states. The idea fizzled out because some ambassadors needed to have instructions from their home offices. This made the matter look more formal than intended. The proposal was also leaked to the EEC Commission in Brussels and therefore became too politically involved and impractical. Some ambassadors later had a meeting with the Foreign Minister.

On 15 June 1985 Maurice Strong and I had a meeting with Chairman Mengistu. In preparation I had drafted a four-page *aide memoire* reviewing problems affecting the relief operation, particularly the port situation and problems of offtake and distribution. The draft had been discussed at a meeting with ambassadors of the major donor countries held at the Italian Embassy on 13 June.

Chairman Mengistu listened very carefully to the presentation of four-pages and then responded, point by point, to the eight suggestions it contained. Maurice Strong and I were impressed that he did not miss one single point, although he had not seen the text in advance. The upshot was that the Chairman confirmed that these suggestions had his backing. This was something that I had particularly wanted, and I used that fact frequently in pressing the authorities for action.

One point we raised at this meeting was the question of increasing offtake from the ports. My office had estimated that the amount of emergency food in the delivery pipeline at that time exceeded the projected distribution capacity during the next seven months by about 270,000 tonnes. We concluded that donors should be advised that no further contracts for the shipment of food should be signed until a concomitant increase in distribution capacity was provided by the Ethiopian government and by donors. We pointed out that this should not be interpreted as suggesting that there was sufficient food aid in the pipeline to meet Ethiopia's need but rather that, in view of the damages that could occur, it would be irresponsible to accept more food aid than the foreseeable distribution capacity would permit. It was important to establish an approximate equilibrium between food aid deliveries and distribution capacity. I had discussed this earlier at a meeting of the major grain donors, the USA, Canada, EEC and Australia. The press got wind of this and, with the exception of BBC's Michael Wooldridge, they all interpreted it as meaning that a decision had now been made to stop further grain shipments immediately. The government, particularly Feseha Desta and Berhanu Bayeh, were very unhappy when they saw the news story and many of the NGOs were highly critical. I sent out a clarification to all concerned and the matter was closed. This event showed the extreme sensitivity with which the government reacted to any measures that might possibly have a negative effect on food aid commitments. The NGOs, whose distribution depended on food they received from the major donors, were also jittery about such matters. But it was necessary to be firm with the authorities and to make sure that they were clear about the consequences of the logistics problem and its effects on the food pipeline.

One problem affecting the Assab offtake was the rather inefficient management of the trucks resulting, among other things, in extended turn-around times. I approached Minister Youssuf about this problem and he was as always well informed and cooperative. At his initiative, a plan was prepared, with the help of US consultants, to improve management efficiency and reduce the trucks' waiting time at Assab from an average of 18 hours to 10 hours from the beginning of August

1985. This was not achieved. but relay stations were established on the Assab route where drivers were rotated so that the trucks could continue uninterrupted; this helped. but the turn-around time remained very unsatisfactory.

Port charges in Assab. among the highest in Africa. were another point of friction between donors and the government. WFP had long tried to get them reduced but to no avail. After long negotiations with the Vice Minister of Transport, I finally succeeded. in October 1985. in having the port charges considerably reduced for all relief cargo whether shipped by governments or NGOs. The Minister and the Vice Minister agreed to this against the advice of the Maritime and Transit Services Corporation (MTSC) and the Marine Transport Authority (MTA). Some people. including World Bank officials. were not sure that reducing port charges was wise because of the government's great revenue need. but constant complaints from donors and NGOs made the reduction necessary.

The end result of various steps taken to increase the transport capacity was that the daily offtake from the port of Assab reached 2,500 to 3,000 tonnes a day with fluctuations up to 4,000 tonnes — twice as much as when the relief operation began.

Air transport

Airlifting was an important means of getting food to the famine victims in Ethiopia's northern regions where the security situation was such that road transport needed armed escort, infrequently available, and ordinary traffic was often suspended. Airlifting to camps and distribution centres in Tigray and Northern Wollo, hard hit by the famine, became a necessity. Several countries were willing to provide transport planes with crews for this purpose. An airlift operation was initiated in November 1984 right at the beginning of the peak year of the relief effort. By the end of 1984, 27 transport planes and 24 heavy helicopters had been provided by seven donors: UK, USSR, FRG, USA, GDR, Italy and Libya. At the beginning of 1985 three more helicopters came from Poland and — for a short period — one transport plane from France. The ICRC contracted four transport planes with crews from the Belgian and the Swedish air forces and from Air Botswana. The latter also supplied one transport plane to the Lutheran World Federation. Several NGOs working in Ethiopia had their own light aircraft.

The planes provided by donor countries were originally expected to stay in Ethiopia for only two to three months, but most of them remained throughout 1985. That year there were 76 aircraft in Ethiopia doing relief transport. In February 1986, when the need had decreased, the number dropped to 45.

In 1985, these aircraft transported nearly 15 per cent of the food distributed in Ethiopia, enough for over 800,000 people. The planes flew mainly from Assab and Asmara to air strips in Tigray and Wollo, and on a smaller scale to Hararghe and Gondar. Apart from participating in relief transport, aircraft from the Soviet Union, the German Democratic Republic and Libya also carried settlers from central and northern regions to the south-west. No planes from Western donor countries were involved in resettlement.

The air transport operation was coordinated by the RRC Air Service, except for the USSR aircraft (24 MI-8 helicopters and 12 Antonov AN-12 transport planes) whose deployment was coordinated by the Ministry of Transport.

As I have indicated, the problems of transporting food to inaccessible locations in the Ethiopian highlands were formidable. For example, it took ten hours to reach Sekota from Korem in the northern Wollo region, a distance of 96 km. The turn-around time on these roads was excessive and the wear and tear of trucks extremely heavy. During the 1985 rainy season, trucks which had reached their destination frequently had to remain there for days while roads were repaired. Refuelling and truck maintenance was also a great problem.

On the rugged high plateaux there were no airstrips suitable for airlifting. Under these circumstances dropping food seemed to me to be a possibility. I approached the RRC regarding this matter in January 1985 but there was very little enthusiasm for the idea. Dropping food had been tried ten years earlier when the famous Swedish flier, Count Carl Gustav von Rosen, experimented with it using Saab aircraft. The technique was primitive and wastage very heavy. Deputy Commissioner Berhane Deressa thought it would not be worthwhile to start an airdrop operation. For a while I let the matter rest.

Some time later the FAO Director General Edouard Saouma visited Ethiopia and among his entourage was a Swedish–Italian staff member, Staffan De Mistura. He was very keen to get out from FAO headquarters for a while and asked me if he could spend his unused leave helping the relief effort. Mr Saouma agreed and Staffan turned up one day to report for work. I did not know exactly what to do with him and thought at first perhaps he would not be particularly suitable for this kind of rough field work. A nobleman, elegantly dressed and of the hand-kissing type, he seemed, initially, to belong in a more conventional office. This assessment turned out to be completely wrong.

The idea of again suggesting the airdrop came when I looked through Staffan's *curriculum vitae* and saw that he had taken a course in airdropping in Sweden and been involved in actual operations in an African country. I asked him to come up with a proposal taking into account that British and West German transport planes were flying food and that Russian and Polish helicopters might be available. Staffan set to work with enthusiasm and untiring drive. Very soon a plan had been prepared involving one Royal Air Force Hercules, which could quickly be modified for airdropping, and one Luftwaffe Transall aircraft as well as two Polish helicopters. The Russians had first shown interest in participating but one of their helicopters had a bad accident and Moscow had adopted a policy of not flying civilians in their helicopters.

On the basis of the new proposal, RRC agreed to the airdrop and gradually became a strong supporter of the operation which utilised a new airdropping technique developed in the United States. The grain was rebagged into double or triple sacks containing 25 kg each and placed on wooden pallets which were dropped from a height of about 6 to 10 metres above the ground. No parachutes were used. The RAF planes, making four flights a day, carried 16–17 tonnes, and the Transall planes, which flew three daily flights, eight tonnes on each drop. The technique was called "heavy free drop" and the drop zones had to be carefully selected to find a level surface and enough manoeuvring space between the hilltops to make the highly precise drops. The drop zones also needed to be sufficiently close to groups of villages so that the grain could be carried to distribution points and to the homes of the famine victims.

The operation was called "Tesfa" ("hope" in Amharic) and the first airdrop was carried out on 13 February 1985 near Rabel, a village situated on a 4,000-metre high plateau in the region of northern Shewa about 200 km north of Addis. My wife and I took part in one of the first airdrops aboard a RAF Hercules. The procedure was very exacting. The pallets, 16 in the RAF plane and eight in the Luftwaffe plane, were pre-positioned on a set of rails fitted with small steel rollers, ready to be pushed out. The plane first made a dry run over the drop zone to be sure everything was in order. Then followed a loop around the plateau and an approach to the drop zone where, at a signal from the pilot, the pallets were pushed out, one at each approach. The crew handling the pallets were secured by attachment to a rail running along the sides of the plane. When the drops had been completed hundreds of people, supervised by RRC officials, rushed down a slope, picked up the bags and carried them to a collection point nearby. Every single grain on the ground as a result of damaged bags was collected. Two Polish helicopters, carrying a British ground party of two or three men and members of an Italian medical team, were the first to fly out each day to select and prepare the drop zone. Polish helicopters were also used occasionally to carry grain from the drop zones further into the interior inaccessible by other means of transport.

The population in these isolated areas showed great appreciation. They were simple peasants, many of whom had never left the plateau on which they lived. Their wonderment over what was done to help them seemed limitless.

One day my wife who had flown with me to a drop zone to observe the operation on the ground was approached by a woman carrying a baby. My wife was not sure how to react. She thought the child may be sick and the mother wanted her to take it to a clinic in the village we were to visit next. Suddenly the woman bent down and kissed her feet. This, we were told, was a way to show her gratitude.

Opinions about the airdrop operation varied. Some people felt it was too costly and the quantities that could be transported too small to make much difference. My position was that, since this was the only way to reach many people in inaccessible areas on the most isolated high plateaux and their lives depended on airdropping food, it had to be done. Furthermore, donor countries were willing to finance this operation which also provided good training. The costs were shared by the military and civilian budgets. Most of the funds used for the airdrop would thus not have been available for other famine relief. In the case of the RAF, the expenditure for the airlift and the airdrop was $1.5 million a month with the lion's share provided by the Ministry of Defence. The Luftwaffe participation cost about $1.2 million per month. The quantity of food airdropped was sufficient to keep alive about 200,000 people and to provide medical aid to over 12,000. In my opinion the exercise was fully justified and worthwhile from a humanitarian point of view. That the air forces of two NATO countries cooperated extremely well with helicopters from a Warsaw Pact country added to the value of the operation.

The airdrop was coordinated by a committee consisting of two RRC officers, the Commanders of the Royal Air Force and Luftwaffe contingents, the Commander of the Polish helicopter group and a representative of my office. The rebagging of

41

grain at the airport was financed mainly by UNDRO through my office and put under the supervision of the RAF which also endorsed payments by the UN to the local contractor. The pallets and bags were flown in from the UK and FRG on planes rotated on a regular basis for maintenance. Cooperation among British, FRG and Polish contingents was excellent. They included RAF Wing Commander Derek Kingsman, who was instrumental in getting the airdrop started, and the Polish Colonels Kazimierz Pogorzielski and Kazimierz Chojnacki. On the Ethiopian side Colonels Eshete Wagaye and Tsegaye Wolde played a pivotal role in the operation. The UN office was represented by Paavo Pitkanen whose enthusiam for the airdrop was almost boundless.

It was fascinating to follow the activities of the group of pilots and air-crews from seven countries taking part in the air transport operation. The RAF performance was considered first-rate both in the airlift and airdrop. They were more experienced than the FRG crew in airdrop techniques and had assigned more trained crew than the Luftwaffe. It was therefore natural that the RAF assumed responsibility for the rebagging and for ground arrangements in drop zones. One criticism of the RAF was that the attitude of commanding officers varied quite a lot. Some of them took an interest in all aspects of the operation, including arrangements in the airdrop zone, rebagging, and the accommodation of the crew; others were more interested in flying and seemed less active in supervising the crews. But these were small problems and on the whole the reputation of the RAF was excellent. The group had strong and active support from Ambassador Brian Barder who took a very keen interest in the operation.

The Luftwaffe performance was poorer during the beginning of the airdrop due to lack of experience. Another factor was that the Transall plane used an automatic dropping mechanism which did not function properly and not as well as the RAF's manual technique. During the initial days of the operation the Luftwaffe made some disappointing drops resulting in considerable breakage of bags but their performance improved consistently and they soon reached the same level of expertise as the RAF. The West German Ambassador, Bernd Oldenkott, strongly supported the Luftwaffe team. When, at the beginning of September, the two Transall planes were withdrawn to West Germany with the intention of discontinuing participation in the airdrop, I asked Ambassador Oldenkott to try to get the decision reversed in Bonn. Based on an analysis my office made on the need for further FRG participation and a request from RRC, the planes returned on 23 October and stayed until the end of 1985. Cooperation between the British and the West German contingents was always excellent and it was interesting to note that the Luftwaffe personnel followed without hesitation the more experienced RAF's lead in such matters as the selection of drop zones, arrangements on the ground and rebagging techniques.

In their own field the Polish helicopter squadron fully matched the performance of the RAF and the Luftwaffe. They were highly trained and disciplined and always behaved like gentlemen. The contingent lived in tents at the old airport in Addis and was self-sufficient in respect of all services including maintenance. The Polish pilots were true professionals and had top rating in their own country. I flew a number of times in Polish helicopters and always marvelled at the precision of their work and the unflagging courtesy the crew showed to the passengers. The Poles were popular in our office and there was a joke that every time members of the Polish squadron came into the office all the girls had their hands ready to be kissed. The Polish Ambassador, Andrej Konopacki, took a great interest in the airdrop. His support was invaluable.

The USAID contracted two private C-130 Hercules planes which took part in the airlift for a year beginning in November 1984. Since the payments were based on the number of hours flown, USAID supervised the performance very closely. From the point of view of cost efficiency, American planes were highly rated. There was a small incident when the contractor suddenly decided without reference to USAID to change his base from Asmara to Addis, which raised the operating costs unnecessarily. When the USAID threatened not to renew the contract, the position was reversed.

The ICRC airlift was well planned and efficient, using planes on contract from the Swedish and Belgian air forces with financing from EEC and ICRC resources. The ICRC also had a commercial contract with Air Botswana. The airdrop from Asmara to Maychew in Tigray region started badly because of the Belgian crew's lack of experience but improved later after assistance from the RAF. The Lutheran World Federation had a contract with Air Botswana flying a Hercules C-130 from Assab and Asmara to Mekelle and Axum in Tigray.

There is little to say about Italy's participation, which lasted for only three months, or France's which lasted no more than two months and transported only 360 tonnes of food.

The USSR planes and helicopters began their operation in November 1984. The capacity of the Antonov AN-12 aircraft was slightly over half that of the UK's Hercules C-130 and a little more than the Luftwaffe's C-160 Transalls. The USSR transport planes took part in the airlift from Asmara and Assab to airstrips in northern Wollo and Hararghe but were deployed mainly in the resettlement programme. Their contribution to the transport of food amounted to about 40,000 tonnes by the end of December 1985 as compared to 122,000 tonnes transported by planes from Western donor countries during the same period. Deployment of the Soviet contingent was inefficient. This was due to many factors and the Russians often blamed the Ministry of Transport for the fact that so many of their planes were often sitting idle at airstrips and at the airport in Addis. The contention was that cargo was not ready for loading, that workers did not turn up for the loading itself and that fuel was sometimes not available. On the other hand, the Russian crews showed less dedication than such other contingents as the British, West German and the Polish and could not compete with commercial planes in cost-effectiveness and performance in general. Since much of their work involved the transport of people, the Russians may have had the most difficult task, partly because of delays in gathering settlers at agreed times for transport, and poor communications between Addis and the air strips from which the planes took off. In addition, Russian helicopters had four serious accidents in 1985 due to what was referred to as "pilot error" or "inexperienced pilots". In one accident, at Gondar, three Russians died when the helicopter hit a tree and fell to the ground. In Maychew in Tigray, a Russian helicopter collided with three others on the ground.

luckily without casualties, and another ran into a hill just north of Addis. The Russians sometimes had a bit of fun when they landed their helicopters close enough at the airstrips to stir up a lot of dust around Western planes being loaded. The British crews were annoyed when Russian aircraft transporting settlers were being cleaned with fire hoses near the RAF area at Addis airport and the dirty water ran near the British tents. But apart from such trivial incidents there was no friction between the Russian contingent and those of the Western donors.

At the beginning of April 1985 I attempted to obtain 100 additional helicopters from the USSR to transport food to inaccessible areas too far from Addis to be feasible for the ongoing airdrop operation. My idea was to organise food transport by helicopters based on air strips in selected parts of the country which would operate for a limited period until the transport system got into full swing with more trucks. I talked with Commissioner Dawit about the initiative and, with his concurrence, visited the USSR Chargé on 1 April 1985 to discuss this possibility. I had beforehand made sure that he had heard of the idea through the very effective Addis "grapevine". The Chargé did not seem surprised at my suggestion and did not rule out the possibility of the provision of a considerable number of additional helicopters. He said he would willingly take the matter up with Moscow if a formal government request was made. But he pointed out one major problem, which was the under-utilisation of the 24 Russian helicopters already in the country. He estimated that only about 50 per cent of their capacity was being utilised and that this had to be corrected before additional helicopters could be provided. I reported these problems to the RRC Air Service and at a meeting shortly afterwards the matter was discussed with the General-in-Charge of the USSR air transport contingent. On 9 April I wrote to Commissioner Dawit to the effect that if the government made a formal request to the USSR Embassy for additional helicopters it would probably be favourably considered, provided sufficient justification was given and that the deployment of the present helicopters could be decisively improved. Commissioner Dawit did not pursue this matter and I decided that he must have had good reasons for not doing so. I therefore dropped the matter.

The GDR first used one Ilyushin aircraft and later two Antonov-26 planes. They worked out of the airport in Dire Dawa in the Hararghe region. Like the USSR, the East Germans were involved in the resettlement programme and had a small role in the transport of relief supplies. Generally, their performance was highly regarded.

Libya's participation through three Antonov-26 planes was somewhat of a joke. The pilots often turned up in the morning, took a look at the weather and decided it was not a good day to fly. They returned to their hotel and that was it for that day. The small capacity (4 MT) of the planes added to the impression that the presence of the Libyan planes in Ethiopia was mainly symbolic. They transported little more than 3,200 tonnes of food in a year.

The airlift and airdrop operation entailed highly complex management and maintenance problems. It first developed in a haphazard way and management was difficult. The cost-effectiveness of the programme was not high (about $600 per tonne or six times more than by truck) but this factor must always remain in the background when it is a question of saving lives in emergencies. In retrospect I do not see how the food distribution could have succeeded without the air operation.

5. Reaching the People

Food aid commitments increased steadily from December 1984 and I never doubted that the target of 1.2 million tonnes would be reached. My optimism, criticised by some NGOs, was not based on guesswork but on close consultations with the major food donors. I knew what commitments were forthcoming long before they were publicly announced and frequently received confidential indications of new commitments likely to be made during the next few months. This kind of monitoring was possible because of the relationship of confidence that had developed between the UN office and the donors. When asked by journalists and visiting politicians about the food situation I used a standard phrase: "We are right on target".

Naturally there was a timelag of some months between a commitment and the arrival of shipments in Ethiopian ports. This meant that the food available for distribution was low for December 1984 and the first months of 1985, but by June a total of 801,000 tonnes had arrived. Pledges for the period December 1984 to December 1985 totalled 1,273,260 tonnes, of which 975,000 tonnes had arrived by October 1985.

The largest food donor was the United States which provided over a third of the total. EEC as an organisation and EEC members making bilateral commitments, other European countries outside the EEC, and Canada and Australia made up the bulk of the remainder. The World Food Programme contributed 82,000 tonnes from its own resources in 1985. Calculated in terms of money, the US food and non-food aid for the period 1 December 1984 to 31 December 1985 amounted to $391 million, EEC totalled $82.6; FRG $72.2 million including $55 million in non-food aid, mainly trucks; Italy $56.3 million of which $49.3 million represented trucks and other equipment; Canada $52 million, UK $44.8 million and Australia $24.3 million. Of the smaller Western countries, Sweden, Finland, Norway and Denmark contributed a total of $27.5 million. The UN system provided food and non-food items valued at $72.1 million. Of this total, $33 million came from UNICEF, $20 million from WFP and the remainder from UNHCR, FAO, UNDRO and WHO.

Figures obtained from the Socialist countries showed a total of $321 million, of which USSR contributed $260 million mainly for the resettlement programme, and the remainder came from Bulgaria, Rumania, Poland, GDR and Czechoslovakia.

The donor community's response was slow in the beginning. This created a great deal of criticism and controversy, but when the aid flow started the donor community showed great generosity. By the end of 1985 the value of food and non-food contributions had risen to $1,253 million of which food aid represented $685 million. It has to be noted here that it is difficult to make a comparison between the money values attached by donors to their contributions. Some figures, like those for the USSR, represented actual disbursement, others included commitments with corresponding disbursements coming later. There may also have been some double-counting between bilateral and UN contributions since

WFP handled shipments for some food donors. Furthermore, there were differences among donors in methods of calculating money values. For example, how does one account for the salaries and upkeep of 700 Russian drivers? Were standard Western salary rates applied or the lower wages prevailing in the USSR? My experience from Kampuchea led me to believe that, for statistical purposes, Socialist countries applied Western rates. In the UN office we tried to adjust the statistics but found that the only way was to use figures provided by donors themselves, despite the pitfalls they entailed and despite the incompatibility of these figures. What really counted was the tonnage of food, the number of trucks and the quantities of other relief supplies provided. At any rate, regardless of accounting problems, the contributions made to the relief operation in Ethiopia during 13 months were a new record in emergency aid.

The overwhelmingly positive response by donors to our appeals meant that distribution, not availability of food, was the real challenge. Ethiopia's unbelievably difficult geography, the size of the country, the poor road and railroad network, the shortage of transport and severe maintenance and management problems all contributed to these difficulties. The large number of organisations taking part in the distribution complicated planning, management and reporting; and rebel activity in northern Ethiopia hampered distribution.

Because of the absence of passable roads in most of the interior distributions had to take place along the main roads. People had to walk long distances, sometimes several days, to fetch their monthly rations. This was considered by some Western relief workers as a cruel system but it was the only one possible. I discussed this matter with several Ethiopian and expatriate sociologists and agriculturists who knew conditions in Ethiopia intimately. It was clearly impractical to try to reach far into the interior away from the roads. At one point I considered mobilising thousands of donkeys for food transport but concluded this was also impractical. The system adopted proved to be right. Ethiopian peasants have traditionally moved long distances in search of food during droughts and other emergencies and for them it was not difficult to understand that they had to do this again. Distribution had to be regularly carried out on a predetermined day and this had to be communicated to the peasant associations which, in most areas, were responsible for assessing the need for relief aid. As long as this could be maintained, those registered turned up at the distribution points, of which, at the peak of the operation, there were 257.

The RRC, established ten years earlier when famine struck Ethiopia, was the centre of the relief programme. It had a staff of some 12,000 including the head office in Addis, regional offices and local staff. RRC is unique in Africa and I believe has no equivalent in the developing world. As an organisation it was unusually efficient but, nevertheless, one of its problems was that it was highly centralised and had a strictly hierarchical structure. Decisions on aid distribution and logistics, even at the regional level, were made in Addis. Anything of importance eventually landed on Commissioner Dawit's desk. Very little freedom of action was left to the RRC regional representatives most of whom were competent and dedicated to their task. This was in part due to the fact that they were subject to the control of the regional party secretaries. The RRC head office in

Addis was staffed by officials gathered from various government departments, most of whom were competent and serious about their work. The structure of the RRC did, however, slow down the decision-making process, creating delays that could have been avoided. I discovered soon that some decisions made by Commissioner Dawit, Deputy Commissioner Berhane Deressa and the other deputy commissioners were not carried out by the staff at the operational level. It was necessary to follow through on decisions I had reached with top-level officials in RRC by telephoning personally the department heads and division chiefs on matters that had to be implemented. The presence of a liaison officer from my office working at RRC headquarters was very helpful in this respect.

All things considered, RRC's performance was surprisingly good. As Deputy Commissioner Berhane Deressa often pointed out to the press, Ethiopia is a developing country and Western standards of efficiency could not be applied. I cannot imagine how the emergency could have been handled without the RRC.

Apart from this general distribution, an emergency programme for Ethiopians who had returned from neighbouring countries was being carried out by the UNHCR in the Hararghe region in south-east Ethiopia. The work was being done through contract arrangements with World University Service of Canada (WUSC) and provided relief and rehabilitation assistance to 317,000 returnees. The UNHCR had issued a special appeal for this programme but it was agreed with the RRC that the returnees would be included in the overall food distribution if that was necessary because of lack of UNHCR resources.

At the beginning of the emergency, the NGO's share of the food distribution was small but grew steadily, due to earmarkings by major donors, and reached an average of 65 per cent for the last months of 1985 and 67 per cent for the period December 1984 to June 1986. The NGOs handling large quantities of grain made one initial mistake which plagued them throughout the operation. In accepting responsibility for distributing US, EEC and Canadian grain they should have insisted on being provided with the transport capacity needed for distribution. I put this to the major NGOs but their commitments had already been made and they had to approach the donors separately for trucks. Several donors provided inland transport subsidies but that did not help very much since there simply were not enough trucks available in Ethiopia. The failure of some NGOs to obtain sufficient transport assistance meant that distribution was slow until the donors had been persuaded to provide trucks, and this took considerable time. NGOs such as ICRC and CARE were from the beginning self-sufficient in transport and thus enabled to carry out their task efficiently.

Food distribution in Eritrea, Tigray and Northern Wollo posed particular problems because of rebel activity. The ICRC, and the Catholic Secretariat, an umbrella organisation for several Catholic charities, distributed over 65 per cent of the food, with ICRC assuming responsibility for the most sensitive areas. During the second half of 1985, World Vision and Catholic Relief Services also began food distribution in the north. RRC itself gradually became less important in these regions due to its shrinking share of food donations and to security problems.

In planning the distribution of relief food, one had to remember that Ethiopia had had a good harvest in November 1984 to January 1985 in two surplus provinces.

Some food was thus available on the market but at high prices. Also, the peasants had set aside small quantities from earlier harvests, a traditional practice in Ethiopia to get through recurrent food shortages. Food distribution, therefore, did not necessarily have to reach full speed during the first two months of emergency operation. The amount of food distributed had to be increased from February 1985 when the population had consumed whatever food they may have been able to set aside. A critical period would come in March–April before the "small harvest" (5 to 10 per cent of the total) available in some areas in August to early November, before the next main crop was expected. The real crunch would come in September–October. In planning distribution, another factor was the rains expected in June to August when many secondary roads would become impassable; the same was true of many of the air strips. This planning framework and general timing of food distribution turned out to be correct and gave the operation a good basis for pressing donors to provide the necessary food and transport when the need was the greatest. I presented this scenario in my report to the meeting of donors in New York on 18 December 1984.

The intensive phase of food distribution got off to a satisfactory start with 35,000 tonnes reaching beneficiaries in December 1984 despite shortage of transport. In September 1985, at the most critical time, the level of 82,000 tonnes was reached and in October the distribution was about 76,000 tonnes. With the new harvest beginning to have its effect the distribution decreased in November–December to an average of 64,000 tonnes a month.

The original distribution target had been 100,000 tonnes a month but that proved impossible to achieve. On 6 June 1985 a meeting I had with the major food donors, the USA, EEC, Canada and Australia, a target of 70,000 tonnes was set and this was achieved and exceeded. The number of beneficiaries increased from 3.2 million in the period December 1984 to March 1985 to nearly seven million a few months later. The RRC could not deliver full standard rations on a regular basis because of its shrinking share of food donations, and security problems, but the main NGOs such as ICRC, CRS, World Vision and CARE did manage to distribute full rations most of the time. It should be noted that Ethiopian peasants traditionally share their food resources with relatives and neighbours during periods of famine. That the number of people registered for food distribution did not reach the estimated level of 7.9 million in need of food aid did not mean that they starved to death. The cohesion of the Ethiopian extended family system prevented that.

Supplementary and intensive feeding for infants, young children and lactating mothers was an important part of the relief programme. In 1985 special feeding programmes, carried out in the relief centres, reached at times over 300,000 beneficiaries. These programmes could be successful only if the basic food rations could be distributed. This created difficulties from time to time as a result of irregular deliveries of food to the relief camps. Some NGOs responsible for these feeding programmes sometimes became very agitated about the shortage of basic rations, and special measures had to be taken through borrowing food and deploying trucks from other regions. Save The Children (UK) and OXFAM, which worked mainly in the Wollo region, were very much "on the ball" and together we managed to ensure a minimum delivery of food to Wollo and thus maintain the special feeding programmes.

Among the worst hit regions were Tigray, Northern Wollo and to a lesser degree, Eritrea and Gondar, all areas where rebel activity hampered distribution and where the RRC had limited possibilities to act because of security problems. The main rebel movements, the Tigrean Peoples Liberation Front (TPLF) and the Eritrean Peoples Liberation Front (EPLF), had established their own relief associations which distributed food transported from Sudan, a slow and risky method. They had powerful lobbies in the UK and the USA including War on Want headed by an articulate Labour Party politician who figured frequently in the press. This organisation advocated a safe-passage agreement with the Ethiopian government to ensure food transport directly from the port of Massawa. War on Want, very hostile to the Ethiopian regime, had no way of negotiating directly with the Ethiopian authorities and, instead, attempted to arrange for an approach to the Ethiopian government through a commission headed by Willy Brandt. Other members included Pierre Trudeau, the former Canadian Prime Minister, Olof Palme, former Swedish Prime Minister and Leopold Senghor, former President of Senegal. This initiative was doomed to failure. First, War on Want openly took the rebels' side which made the whole idea suspect from the beginning. But the main obstacle was that according to the plan suggested by War on Want the Commission was to deal openly both with the TPLF and the Ethiopian government. This implied recognition of the rebel movement was impossible for Ethiopia to accept. As expected, the safe-passage proposal was firmly rejected out of hand by the Ethiopian government. This naïve initiative indicated that the personalities involved lacked sufficient understanding of the political situation in Ethiopia. War on Want lost much of its credibility with Western governments despite all the noise it made in the press.

One of the first major subjects I raised with Chairman Mengistu was exactly the matter of extending food distribution into rebel-controlled areas. At a meeting on 1 February 1985, also attended by Minister Berhanu Bayeh and Acting Relief Commissioner Berhane Deressa, I made two proposals. One was to organise regular food convoys under UN auspices using local distribution personnel. The plan was to transport food from Asmara to agreed locations in Eritrea, and from Mekelle, the main town in Tigray, to distribution points in that region. I did not mention safe-passage, but I did indicate very carefully that for safety reasons I needed somehow to let the rebel groups know that unarmed food convoys would be moving to selected locations. This would be done strictly unofficially through a circuitous route; I would not deal with the rebel organisations. My plan was to lead the convoys personally during the first week. UN field monitors would then continue to accompany the convoys as long as necessary. My experience in Kampuchea led me to believe that the rebels would not attack UN convoys bringing food to the population. As a fallback proposal I had asked the ICRC to suggest a distribution plan that they could carry out. The ICRC attached three conditions to their proposal: that the roads in the areas concerned would be continuously de-mined; that the convoys would be unarmed; and that no Ethiopian authorities would be present.

In discussion with Chairman Mengistu I emphasised that a great deal of attention was being focused on food distribution in Tigray and Eritrea and that the UN was under pressure to find ways to ensure that famine relief reached all Ethiopians in need. In his response the Chairman first gave a lengthy review of the background to the insurgency in Eritrea and Tigray, which he said was part of a longstanding effort of some Arab countries to dismember Ethiopia. Regarding the distribution of relief supplies in these regions he stated emphatically that there could be no arrangement, tacit or open, with what he termed "the bandits". He repeated the official position that the government can reach all people in need of relief in any part of Ethiopia. When I asked how this could be done, he replied that he would arrange for a greater number of food convoys under military escort to step up food distribution. He also pointed out that UN and ICRC convoys would be attacked by "the bandits" and he could not permit that to happen. I said I was not concerned about that possibility and that emergency relief always entailed a certain risk which I was willing to accept. After a few additional exchanges I concluded that it would be futile to press my proposals further. The position of the government was unshakeable. The only way to increase food distribution in Eritrea and Tigray would be by shipping larger quantities of food over the border from Sudan. The Ethiopian government had tolerated this, although unofficially it branded this operation as an infringement of Ethiopian sovereignty.

In March 1985 during the UN Geneva conference on the African drought emergency which was attended by an American delegation led by Vice President Bush, food distribution in Tigray and Eritrea was discussed very discreetly between the Americans and the Ethiopian delegation headed by Foreign Minister Goshu Wolde and including Commissioner Dawit. The Americans were pushing for what they called "the northern initiative" aiming at increased distribution of American-donated food in Tigray and Eritrea. I had a marginal role in these bilateral negotiations but was kept informed by both sides. Knowing the firm position of the Ethiopian government, I was surprised that Commissioner Dawit engaged in negotiations with the American delegation on such a sensitive issue. I felt that the Ethiopians simply "went through the motions" of not wanting to give the Americans the impression of unwillingness to go along with reasonable proposals but avoiding any concessions having political implications. I asked Commissioner Dawit whether he had cleared the matter with his superiors in Addis and he replied that he had full authority to negotiate with the Americans. This reinforced my expectation that whatever was agreed upon could not be a new departure of any significance. At any rate, at the request of the US delegation and with the concurrence of Commissioner Dawit I telephoned my office in Addis and asked Bilge Reid to select, in cooperation with the ICRC, an additional four or five locations in Tigray and Eritrea through which more food could reach people living in rebel-controlled areas. This was done and the proposal from Addis was accepted by both sides. Arrangements for actual distribution were later made with two NGOs. The "northern initiative" turned out to be "more of the same" rather than a geographical extension of food distribution in Tigray and Eritrea at new locations away from towns and into the interior.

The UN's concern to ensure maximum food distribution in Tigray and Eritrea continued throughout the emergency. One way of doing this was to ask our monitor stationed in Asmara and those working out of the office in Addis to make frequent visits to observe and facilitate food distributions. I also took the initiative to arrange for visits to Tigray and Eritrea by ambassadors and aid officials from major donor countries. One such visit took place in August 1985 and included Joseph O'Neill, Minister Counsellor of the US Embassy, Leon de Riedmatten, Chief Delegate of the ICRC, our Swiss field monitor Martin Büechi, who was familiar with distribution in the Northern regions, and Commissioner Dawit together with RRC department heads. We toured the two regions during four days and discussed food distribution problems with the NGOs working at camps and distribution points, and with RRC local officials. Upon returning to Addis the group had two meetings, one on Tigray and one on Eritrea, to review our conclusions and ensure that the figures, compiled by Martin Büechi on the basis of data collected from NGOs and RRC, had everyone's agreement. Our conclusion was that considerable improvement had been introduced into the relief camps in Tigray, including the largest one situated in Mekelle. The nutritional situation of the camp population was much better than two months ago and hygienic conditions were satisfactory, including availability of clean water. Displaced people no longer collected around major shelters due to improved distribution of take-home food rations. As to distribution figures, we concluded that a total of 1,120,000 people out of an estimated 1.5 million needing relief food were reached in Tigray, about 65 per cent being distributed by NGOs, mainly ICRC, the Catholic Secretariat and other NGOs, and the remainder by RRC. The ICRC distributed full rations (15 kg per person per month) but the Catholic Secretariat could distribute only partial rations (11.1 kg). The RRC rations varied from 5–10 kg due to shortage of supplies. In Eritrea, where the situation had from the outset been better than in Tigray, no relief camps had been established. Slightly over 600,000 out of an estimated 827,000 people needing relief aid were being reached by NGOs (mainly ICRC) and RRC.

I reported these findings to OEOA in New York, emphasising that they represented not only my estimates but the joint views of the group as a whole, representing the most important donor country and the NGOs doing most of the food distribution in Eritrea and Tigray. The OEOA issued a press release quoting these figures and this resulted in an outcry from the TPLF. I received a letter from the Executive Board of the Relief Society of Tigray (REST) located in Khartoum enclosing a lengthy memorandum full of invective and political propaganda. Earlier I had received a more moderate letter from the Coordinator of the REST office in Washington DC. The distribution figures as such were not questioned, but TPLF's estimates of the number of people in need and those put forward by the RRC and accepted by the donors differed because of the use of a different figure of the population in Tigray. REST was using a figure of five million whereas the estimate of 1.5 million people in need of relief food was based on a population figure of less than three million. The Population Division of the UN Economic Commission for Africa confirmed to me in a note in October 1985 that the population of Tigray was indeed under three million. There had been a national census in 1984 and the preliminary estimate for Tigray was 2.4 million of a total population of 42 million. This was based on a pre-revolution sample survey in 1967, updated in 1982 using an estimated growth rate for each province. This estimate was carried forward in 1984 for Tigray, applying a generally accepted national population growth rate of 2.9 per cent. Reports by the Central Statistical Office before the revolution showed that Tigray's growth rate was lower than that of the country as a whole. A small change in the boundaries of Tigray, made by Emperor Haile Selassie, had very little effect on the population figure. I had no reason to doubt the correctness of the ECA figures produced by a highly competent group of African demographers and statisticians.

The REST Coordinator in Washington DC was upset that I had termed the cross-border operation from Sudan "marginal". She wrote that 3,000 tonnes a month were being transported to Tigray that way. This quantity represented less than 20 per cent of the food distributed in Tigray, and diversion to rebel forces further diminished its value. In spring 1985, a dispute between TPLF and EPLF forced the former's trucks to use a much longer and slower route, which badly affected their food distribution. There is no doubt that the food distribution organised by RRC and NGOs was decisive in helping the Tigrean people. The ICRC Chief Delegate, Leon de Riedmatten, confirmed to me that, at many of their distribution points, up to 90 per cent of the recipients came from rebel-controlled areas of the interior. Allegations that the Ethiopian authorities were deliberately starving these people were untrue. To be sure, there were incidents when local party officials interfered with food distribution, which they believed helped the rebels, but such actions were few and isolated and had little effect. Every time such incidents were reported to me I intervened with RRC and, when necessary, with Minister Berhanu Bayeh. Even the extreme right-wing members of the US Congress could not sustain their contention of "deliberate starving" or genocide when hearings were held in October 1985 on a proposal to impose economic sanctions on Ethiopia.

In August 1985 it was brought to my attention that food supplies had run out in the town of Sekota in Northern Wollo where immediate emergency supplies were needed to feed about 25,000 people. The food was normally transported from the relief camp at Korem, 96 kilometres east of Sekota but the road had been badly damaged by rains and road transport had to be interrupted. Sekota was a heavily fortified town in an area largely controlled by the rebels. I raised the possibility of an airdrop with Ambassador Barder and the RAF Commander. The security problem was such that a decision needed to be made in London by the MoD and the ODA of the Ministry of Foreign Affairs. As agreed with Ambassador Barder I sent him a letter requesting that the RAF be allowed to carry out an airdrop of up to 500 tonnes of food pending the repair of the road to Sekota. I pointed out that among the people in Sekota were many returnees from the Ibenat camp and that, according to information received from NGOs working in the town, the nutritional situation was very poor and the death rate high. According to RRC reports 351 people had died between 1 July and 10 August.

In order to get London's approval steps had to be taken to ensure that no action would be taken by the rebels which would endanger the RAF crew or the aircraft. Obviously the TPLF had to be informed of the airdrop and their assurance of non-interference obtained. I could not be in direct contact with the TPLF but I asked my counterpart in Sudan, Winston Prattley, to act as a communication channel. I sent him the following message, using the coded British Embassy circuit:

Air drop in Sekota in Northern Wollo essential to feed around 25.000 people who cannot be otherwise reached since road transport cut by rains. RAF willing to initiate airdrop for limited period from Addis on understanding that TPLF conveys to local units in area that flights which are purely humanitarian should not be put at risk and that no action of any kind be taken to endanger crew or aircraft. Aircraft will be marked with white cross. My office will provide monitoring and assistance at Sekota to ensure that distribution will be only to those in need and that no food will go to the Ethiopian military. Need TPLF assurance of above understanding as soon as possible. Local TPLF units will also be informed of airdrop through voluntary organisations working in the Sekota area. Please use the same channel for reply as that used for this message and do not inform TPLF that this channel used. This message must under no circumstances become known to the Ethiopian authorities.

The TPLF replied through Prattley that they would cooperate subject to several conditions including airdrops at other locations selected by TPLF. TPLF was clearly trying to use this humanitarian operation to gain political advantage and an implied recognition by the UN and the British government. I therefore suggested to Ambassador Barder that the airdrop should go ahead without any further contacts with TPLF. This was not acceptable to London for security reasons and it was agreed that the TPLF should simply be informed that the airdrop would take place. Again using British Embassy circuits I sent the following message to Prattley:

The British Government has agreed that the Royal Air Force should airdrop 350 tonnes of grain to Sekota as emergency stop-gap remedy pending longer-term road transport arrangements. Operation is due to start on 28 September. I have agreed with British Ambassador, Addis Ababa, that it would be prudent to inform TPLF of our intention. Immediately before the operation is due to begin, i.e. on 27 September, but not before, I should be grateful if you would tell the local TPLF representative primo that it is impossible to accept their demands, secundo that attachment of political conditions for promise not to interfere with a humanitarian operation is unacceptable, and tertio that a limited airdrop operation will start soon and that the United Nations and British Government expect the TPLF to instruct their local commanders to do everything possible to ensure the safety of the Royal Air Force aircraft and crews involved. The United Nations office here and the British Government are taking extensive measures to ensure that all food dropped reaches those in need for whom it is intended.

The airdrop was successfully carried out without any incident and Paavo Pitkanen, whom I had assigned to monitor the operation, reported to me that the distribution had started immediately and that the large Ethiopian army contingent in Sekota did not in any way attempt to divert food. This was confirmed later by the NGOs working in Sekota.

The Sekota airdrop was exceptional in that neither the RRC nor anyone else in the government knew of my contacts with TPLF in Sudan. In this I took a considerable risk in terms of my relations with the Ethiopian leadership including particularly Chairman Mengistu who had strongly emphasised to me that even informal arrangements were excluded. But humanitarian considerations outweighed everything else. In the event, the attitude of TPLF was a great disappointment to me and showed once again how politics affected the aid effort in Ethiopia. TPLF soldiers' later attacks on relief workers, several of whom were killed, cast doubt on the feasibility of safe passage arrangements in internal armed conflicts. Colonel John Garang, the leaders of the rebels in Southern Sudan, did not agree to safe passage for relief transport despite the efforts of the UN to obtain at least his tacit concurrence. I acted as a channel of communication between Winston Prattley and Colonel Garang, who was based in Addis. That at the end of 1986 the Sudanese government expelled Prattley shows the delicacy of international officials' positions.

6.   Aid Distribution: Control and Verification

The distribution of food and other aid to millions of people is no simple task. In a country as vast as Ethiopia the problems were immense not only in terms of logistics but with respect to the methods of actual distribution to the population and control of distribution. Briefly, this was the way it was done. Food distribution was divided, with the RRC and NGOs each having their target population and area to serve. At the start the population was informed through the peasant associations, the basic economic and administrative units in rural Ethiopia, that those in need of food aid should report at a given time and place for registration. Initial screenings were made by the peasant associations. During the actual registration by RRC and NGOs, which could take days, each family head was given a ration card devised by the distributing organisation. These cards, marked and coded in different ways to avoid cheating, had to be presented at each distribution. The usual practice was to distribute rations once a month on a given date. Between distributions recipients returned to their homes, normally over a long distance and by foot. Although the authorities had no objections, to monitor recipient families or groups of individuals back to their huts which, in the highlands, were mostly scattered over immense, roadless areas, would have been utterly impossible both from a logistical and manpower point of view and has never been attempted in any large-scale relief operation. Quite possibly in some areas under anti-government guerrilla control some food was taken from famine victims. But the quantities could not have been large because there was no feedback from the otherwise vocal peasant leaders, and the presence of guerrillas in most provinces, except Tigray and Eritrea, was scattered and thinly spread in the interior.

Confiscation of food by Ethiopian soldiers was never reported by any food distributing organisation. Had it happened it would have been easy to detect since the Ethiopian army was stationed in population centres and not spread out in the interior where the bulk of the aid recipients lived. Former RRC Commissioner Dawit told me on 18 January 1987, after his defection to the United States, that soldiers did not engage in robbing people of their food rations. On the contrary, Dawit emphasised, they often helped famine victims with part of their own food. He also emphatically affirmed that there were no incidents of the Army having confiscated food from relief stocks. There could be no more authoritative refutation of this allegation, made mainly for political reasons by MSF and some individuals in France.

The aim of the aid effort was to save lives and, as was evident by the regular return of registered recipients to distribution points, food distribution kept the people alive. Quibbling about possible small food losses is irrelevant and borders on the absurd. The matter was never raised by food donors and the distributing NGOs, and was mentioned only by a few spiteful individuals who consider themselves to have been badly treated by the Ethiopian authorities.

In and around the relief centres, where at the peak of the famine about 800,000 people were fed, the distribution system was similar. Each family prepared its own meals except those in supplementary or intensive feeding programmes, for whom food was prepared in kitchens set up for that purpose.

The system worked well after some initial difficulties. The main problem was to ensure a steady supply for general distribution and for the special feeding programmes. This was dependent on the transport capacity and the management of the truck fleet by RRC and NATRACOR, as well as those NGOs with their own means of transport. From time to time shortages of supplies occurred in various parts of the relief system. This was mainly due to earmarkings by donors to different NGOs and regions, which meant that at times there was more than enough food in some places and not enough in others. Borrowings between NGOs and between RRC and NGOs had to be resorted to making record-keeping more complicated. Another problem was that some NGOs running special feeding programmes suffered from the fact that they were not participating in general food distributions and had to rely on other agencies for a supply of basic rations indispensable in order to maintain their special feeding programmes. This problem plagued the Wollo region in particular because it was supplied mainly by RRC which, due to earmarkings by donors for other regions, suffered intermittent shortages.

In every large-scale operation it is of prime importance to be able to report to donors how their food and other relief supplies were being distributed and what control mechanism had been established to guard against diversion. In Kampuchea this had been difficult because of the Heng Samrin government's distrust of foreign relief workers, and the poorly functioning administrative machinery established after the fall of Pol Pot.

In Ethiopia, however, the bulk of the food (67 per cent during the period December 1984 to June 1986) was distributed by Western NGOs which were accountable to the food donors, and with their own control mechanisms: there was no problem in verifying their distributions. Some NGOs, such as ICRC and CARE, were always up-to-date but, initially, some other organisations were slow to provide figures. But there was never any question of food being used for unauthorised purposes. RRC had a reporting and auditing system, beginning from the local level, of distribution points and through their regional offices to headquarters in Addis. This system was slow and it was time-consuming for my office to check figures against those obtained by our monitors during visits to regional offices, warehouses, relief centres and distribution points. The quantities of food distributed each month could be verified but it was at times difficult to know quickly what the rations had been during each periodic distribution. The UN staff, including Martin Büechi, Tom Fitzpatrick and Tom Franklin, together with WFP colleagues, with the RRC Aid Coordination Department, reviewed the RRC figures monthly in order to verify the distribution figures in terms of tonnage and number of recipients. A computerised system using data supplied by the NGOs and the RRC would have made it more efficient. CARE initiated a project of this type but it did not become operational during 1985.

Press stories about diversion of food to Soviet ships in the port of Assab or to the Ethiopian army and the blackmarket were based on rumours which always circulated in abundance, particularly in Addis. Our Swedish port officer who monitored all aid shipments in Assab port laughed at the allegation of transshipments to Russian or any other ships. As to allegations of diversion to the army, one of our British monitors once found an entry in an RRC regional warehouse's books indicating the transfer of 4,000 tonnes of wheat to an army depot. I raised the matter with Commissioner Dawit who, after investigation, reported that this was a loan and would be recovered. I had no way of personally verifying the return but no incidents of this kind were discovered again despite increased attention to this possibility by our monitors and the NGOs doing most of the food distribution. Stories about highjackings of trucks by the Ethiopian Army were totally untrue. One highjacking was carried out by a minor guerrilla group on the road from Nazareth to Gondar, and there were incidents of armed robbery by guerrilla soldiers in some relief camps in Tigray and northern Wollo. But these were insignificant in terms of food supplies lost.

Some relief food found its way to the market in Eritrea. The EEC chief economist in Addis Karl Harbo, a Dane, investigated this and concluded that some food-aid recipients had sold part of their rations at the market to buy other necessities. Aid bags were reused for a variety of purposes and some inexperienced observers took this to mean diversion of food aid. The fact that the small peasant militia helping to provide protection against guerrilla attacks received food rations could not be considered wrong since they would have received food aid whether or not they served in the local militia. What was objectionable was that their rations were often higher than those for the rest of the recipients. When I raised this matter with the authorities it was explained that peasants were reluctant to do the job and an incentive was needed; the food ration was their wage.

There were repeated reviews of food distribution by teams despatched by major food donors. One review was carried out in spring 1985 by inspectors from the General Accounting Office, the investigating arm of the US Congress. They informed me that they had concluded that diversion of food was marginal. The same conclusion was reached by missions from EEC, Canada and several smaller donor countries. These monitoring and auditing missions applied rigorou standards required by their governments or decision-making bodies. As regards food donated directly to RRC (about a third of the total food aid), donors usually arranged for an NGO to monitor the distribution. For example, USAID used CARE as their monitoring agent for the distribution of 50,000 tonnes of food provided to the RRC.

The possible diversion of relief aid was discussed repeatedly with donor missions in Addis. At my last meeting with the ambassadors in the Italian Embassy in late October 1985, it was concluded that the diversion was less than five per cent, an exceptional achievement in any relief operation of this magnitude. As a rule-of-thumb, relief workers agree that, if diversion is limited to 20–30 per cent in African countries, it is acceptable. Most observers, even those strongly opposed to the Ethiopian regime, thought there was little general corruption in the country, a fact which does not apply to many other countries receiving aid. The opinion of the donor community was summed up by Fred Fischer, the USAID director in Ethiopia, when he stated in an interview with the *Washington Post* (1 December 1985) that "There has been very, very little corruption. The food has gone where it was supposed to go".

Upon my arrival in Ethiopia I was surprised that very little had been done to look into the need for distributing seed in the drought-affected areas. In Kampuchea that was the first thing I took up as a matter of high priority. In Addis I met with the Minister of Agriculture, Tekola Dejene, and he estimated that up to 40,000 tonnes of seed would be needed for distribution. After discussions with the Ethiopian Seed Corporation I discovered that seed from abroad was mostly unsuitable for use in Ethiopia. The main local crop, teff, was grown only in Ethiopia and seed could be procured only internally. Farmers in the country did not use hybrid seeds and the conclusion was that the only maize seed could be bought abroad. Funds had been made available by donors and, in cooperation with FAO, my office tried to find other African countries willing to sell maize seed. Malawi indicated a willingness to sell 2,500 tonnes but before an order could be placed even that amount was embargoed for domestic purposes. Seed had, therefore, to be procured in Ethiopia and as much as possible processed and packed by the Ethiopian Seed Corporation. A number of NGOs were interested in helping finance the procurement and help in distribution. One constraint was the Seed Corporation's insufficient capacity to process improved seeds; another was, again, shortage of transport. My office became the coordinating point for a seed distribution scheme that proved to be very difficult to handle; too many government organisations and 23 NGOs were involved. Eventually 26,000 tonnes was made available to the drought-affected areas, with 18,300 distributed by NGOs. The overall target of 40,000 tonnes could not be reached in the time available but the Minister of Agriculture assured me that Ethiopian peasants would rather starve than eat the seed they had set aside and that the balance would be procured from farmers in regions where there had been a crop. When I expressed my doubts about his optimism he smiled and said, "You do not know the Ethiopian peasants but you can be sure that my prediction will come true". The Minister turned out to be right and the seed distribution programme must be counted as a limited success despite its many crises. Some quantities of seed came only in the nick of time before the planting season but all of it arrived in time.

During recurring food shortages and outright famines the peasant population of Ethiopia had for centuries moved long distances in search of food. This happened again in 1984–85 on a very large scale. The peasants did not leave their homes until they had used up all their food reserves and had sold their belongings to buy food. This migration resulted in a number of large conglomerations of people around towns waiting for help from the authorities. One camp after another sprang up and hundreds of thousands of people gathered outside to receive food rations. In March–April 1985 the population in and around the camps rose to about 800,000. In the camps themselves, some of which had existed for more than two years, the RRC and NGOs gradually established basic services such as kitchens, medical services, water supplies and sanitation. Supplementary and intensive feeding programmes were started in most camps. Nevertheless, until about the middle of 1985, conditions remained very bad and the death rate, especially among children, was high. New arrivals from the interior were in extremely poor physical condition and help came often too late. Funerals occurred daily and cemeteries expanded quickly around the camps.

One of the largest concentration of famine victims was around Mekelle, the main town of Tigray province. My first visit to Mekelle was in January 1985 and it was a real shock. The camps were severely overcrowded, with very poor facilities. People not admitted to the camps for medical treatment or supplementary feeding had practically no shelter against the cold and the strong winds sweeping the high plateau. Even for a Finn the cold was uncomfortable. I remember standing one morning at dawn on a hill overlooking the road leading to Mekelle. I saw a never-ending stream of people walking slowly up the slope towards the camp. The latter was already full and the new arrivals moved on. I wondered where they were heading. Following the stream of people for a while I realised that they simply stopped at some point hoping to get food.

The next day, in the company of RRC officials, I visited one of these sites. The new arrivals had dug a hole in the ground or piled up stones as protection against the wind. They had no belongings, their clothing was in rags. They had no blankets or anything to cover themselves. This was a shocking sight of human misery. How these people survived until help arrived was a mystery. But perhaps I did not quite understand the staying power of the Ethiopian peasant families, very likely the most enduring in the world.

The same thing happened around other camps mainly located in the northern provinces, except Eritrea. These large groups of people created many problems, including outbreaks of diseases such as cholera, acute diarrhoea, respiratory diseases, typhus and measles. One outbreak of measles in a camp in Wollo killed hundreds of children in a week before it was brought under control. Here it should be said that the Ethiopian health authorities acted with speed and efficiency as soon as they were alerted to problems in the camps.

Sanitation was deplorable; following is an excerpt from a report prepared by Stephanie Simmonds, Senior WHO Health Adviser in my office:

The latrines in the compound are an affront to human dignity. To expect people to urinate and/or defecate in view of anyone who walks by is both unacceptable and unnecessary. It is also a pity that time, money and other resources have gone into building latrines without a simple addition of ventilation pipes which would have reduced the smell.

Stephanie was a level-headed and experienced public health specialist not given to exaggeration or hasty judgements. Her description was a truly British understatement. I could add a few comments of my own but that may not be necessary. Suffice it to say that the sanitary conditions and lack of shelter were in many of these makeshift camps shocking. As time went on many improvements were made and by autumn 1985 conditions in the camps had become acceptable.

A basic principle in relief action is that the establishment of more or less permanent relief centres and camps should be avoided whenever possible because of the problems involved. No such camps were set up in Kampuchea, but in Ethiopia this was unavoidable because the relief operation started on a large scale only in December 1984 after the international community had been stirred into action. By that time huge numbers of people had gathered in many locations. In spring 1985 the government adopted a policy of returning as many as possible from the camps to their homes. This was generally considered a sound step because it reduced the health and other problems usually associated with large numbers of people collecting in a confined area with primitive services and because it was important to help peasants return to their homes and grow food. There was no disagreement among donors and NGOs on the principle of a returnee programme of this type. But everyone agreed that it should be done in an orderly fashion at the right time of the year. Parallel to the gradual evacuation of camps, a sufficient number of additional distribution points within the returnees' reach should be established and an initial food ration, seeds, basic agricultural hand tools and survival items such as blankets should be provided.

I repeatedly discussed this matter with Commissioner Dawit and occasionally with Minister Berhanu Bayeh. We had reached an understanding that no camp evacuations would be undertaken without appropriate preparations, careful screening of returnees able and willing to leave the camps, and the provision of agreed quantities of supplies. It was agreed that organising the return of the camp population should be undertaken jointly by the RRC and the NGOs working in the camp, under constant scrutiny by UN monitors. In each case a target would be set for the number of people to be returned. Only able-bodied people willing to leave the camp would be accepted and those remaining would continue to be fed. Medical services and feeding programmes would continue.

It was, therefore, with considerable surprise that I received a telephone call early one morning in late April 1985 from Rick Machmer of USAID informing me that he had been told by an American NGO that the camp at Ibenat in the north-western province of Gondar was suddenly being emptied and that some ugly incidents had occurred. His information was that people had been forced to leave the camp and sent on their way without any medical screening or supplies. The army was reportedly involved, the RRC representative had been bypassed and the regional party secretary had taken charge of the operation. I asked our monitors to verify the information. We discovered that over the weekend of 28–29 April 1985 some 36,000 people were suddenly evacuated. The world press cited much higher figures, which my monitors did not accept. But the number of people expelled was of less importance than the unacceptable methods used and the precedent that had been set for camp evacuations.

I called Commissioner Dawit the same morning and he was clearly unaware of what was happening in Ibenat. I asked him to intervene but most of the people had already left Ibenat and no one knew their fate. I flew there the next day together with Deputy Commissioner Berhane Deressa and other officials of the RRC. Michael Wooldridge of the BBC and William Shawcross of the *Observer* were invited to come along. At the small airstrip near Ibenat we were met by the party secretary, known as "the butcher of Gamo Gofa" for his role in the "red terror" after the overthrow of Haile Selassie, the chief administrator and the RRC regional representative.

The party secretary was a short man with a fanatical look in his eyes. He obviously did not welcome our visit. When we stepped off the Twin Otter one of the Ethiopian officials whispered to me, "Look at the eyes of that bastard". The party secretary sidled away from the group and took very little part in our discussions. He maintained that the population had returned home, that no force had been used and that there was no need to be concerned about their fate. He showed no sign of understanding the severity of his actions and the repercussions it had already had on world opinion. The visit convinced me that the Gondar party secretary had initiated the evacuation, without authorisation by the central authorities in Addis. This was later confirmed to me by Chairman Mengistu.

The incident was reported first in the *Washington Post* and then picked up by the press worldwide. It became a real *cause célèbre*. We in the UN office were very much concerned about what had happened to the camp population. The party secretary's unsatisfactory explanations reinforced my anxiety about the people forced out of Ibenat. We knew that somewhat over half of them came from districts in Wollo region and the rest from Gondar. It was important to discover where they had gone and what could be done to assist them. Two of our field monitors and I took off in a Polish helicopter trying to locate the people expelled from Ibenat. We landed during the first day in several locations in Wollo and talked to members of peasant associations and village leaders. The answer was that none or very few people had recently returned from Ibenat. We returned the next day to Addis as the search had to be discontinued because of bad weather. We were surprised that we could not locate any of the returnees. I asked the party secretary in Wollo, a friendly man, to telephone his counterpart in Gondar, the man responsible for this mess, in order to find out whether he had any information on the matter. The latter replied that the people had left the area and were now the responsibility of local authorities. The whole thing seemed a mystery but suddenly it dawned on me that the camp population must have remained somewhere in the vicinity of Ibenat rather than continuing unaided to walk to their homes, which would have taken several days. This turned out to be the case, the people had walked for a few hours into the hill around the camp where they received no help.

I returned the next day to Ibenat to try to find some further information. The party secretary was nowhere to be seen but the RRC regional representative was very helpful. He showed me the records of the camp population and two of our field monitors made further checks on the figures. I had previously agreed with Dawit that if any of the camp population returned to Ibenat they should be taken back and given assistance.

My numerous discussions with donor ambassadors and NGOs reinforced my belief that something drastic had to be done to assist the population still hiding in the hills around Ibenat, and to stop such incidents recurring. I asked for an urgent appointment with Chairman Mengistu and saw him on 6 May 1985, together with Commissioner Dawit. He had been briefed on the subject and listened intently when I outlined my findings. At one point I said that the action taken at Ibenat was "stupid". He looked clearly startled by this and I added that I was sorry to use such language but this was a matter of great importance. He said he did not mind and asked me to continue. Chairman Mengistu confirmed that the action at Ibenat had been taken by local officials and that neither he nor members of his government had authorised it. He stressed that he neither agreed with nor approved of it and that such actions would not be allowed to recur; appropriate measures would be taken against the local officials responsible. He denied army involvement in the burning of empty straw huts and stressed that information in the world press that the camp itself had been burned was not true. My visits to Ibenat after the incident showed this to be correct, although the allegation was repeated in many news stories.

At the end of our meeting I said to Chairman Mengistu that, since the international uproar continued, it was essential for him to issue a statement confirming the position he had taken. He exchanged a few words in Amharic with Commission Dawit, something quite unusual since he never consulted officials during our meetings, and then said that if I really insisted he would consider issuing a statement. He added that on the basis of our meeting he would prefer that I do it, which I did, in a statement to the news media the same day and it was widely published in the international press. During a field trip to resettlement areas a few days later, Chairman Mengistu made a stop at Gondar and reprimanded the party secretary, who was then absent from his post for several months. Mengistu certainly took the Ibenat incident seriously. When next I saw him, a few weeks later, he said only half jokingly, "Everyone is talking about Ibenat. I had never heard of it before".

The results of my meeting with Chairman Mengistu created a sensation in diplomatic and government circles in Addis. Just three days earlier the Ministry of Foreign Affairs had issued a vitriolic press release denying that anything wrong had happened at Ibenat. The Ministry stated that the people had left Ibenat of their own free will and been given sufficient food, seeds and farm implements. The press release was directly particularly against the United States and stated *inter alia* that,

In the light of the above facts, the so-called incident at Ibenat is therefore a clear demonstration that officials of the US Administration will not spare the slightest pretext no matter how detached it might be from reality, in their effort to besmirch, and, if possible, to sabotage the striving of the Ethiopian Government to contain the effects of the debilitating drought affecting the country.

Mengistu's position thus contradicted this position of the Ministry of Foreign Affairs. Diplomats in Addis knew of no precedent for such an intervention by Chairman Mengistu. The Ethiopian ambassadors in donor countries were bewildered by the turn of events and when I was in the RRC Acting Commissioner's office the next day many of them called in for clarification. They naturally had to follow the line taken by Chairman Mengistu, and the Foreign Ministry's press release was quietly forgotten. For days before and after my meeting with Chairman Mengistu my assistant, Suman Dhar, was kept busy taking telephone calls from all over the world including Scandinavia, USA, Australia, UK, FRG, France and Italy, mostly from very excited individuals and representatives of voluntary organisations. Governments had been informed by their diplomatic missions in Addis Ababa.

Ibenat became a milestone in the policy of dealing with the camps. The strong position taken by the UN was appreciated by the donor community and the NGOs. Ambassador Barder telephoned me the morning my statement appeared in the press and said: "Many congratulations for the coup you pulled off." At a hearing in the US House of Representatives on 16 October 1985, Mr Chester Crocker, Assistant Secretary of State for African Affairs stated:

> The role of the UN coordinator on the spot in Ethiopia has been a very important one from the standpoint of us and other donors, precisely because of his intervention on a number of specific areas of abuse and problems of delays and what have you. He has been able to say and do things that would be hard for any individual outside donor to do.

Asked by Mr Crocker to comment further, Mr Theodore Morris, deputy director of the Task Force on African Famine, stated:

> Certainly the role that the United Nations played in Ibenat we considered critical. A lot has been said about Ibenat today. We were in the vanguard, but we couldn't carry that banner alone. Our political relations with that Government were not sufficient that we could carry the message alone. The United Nations joined us, took the leadership, put a stop to Ibenat in the first situation. When it threatened to repeat itself, it was the UN deputy, a Finnish man under the Coordinator, who went up and said "thus far and no further" and stopped it again. I think we have been very pleased with their willingness to stand for the human rights principles that we stand for as a nation.

The people who left Ibenat returned there over the next week and were cared for as agreed with Commissioner Dawit. An orderly programme of arranging for able-bodied people to return voluntarily to their homes was organised by the RRC using the services of two NGOs, World Vision and Irish Concern, the latter represented by a calm and level-headed Irish nurse. Those who left were provided with a food ration for one month, a quantity of seed, some agricultural hand tools and blankets. The previous incident had created tension between these NGOs and the RRC local administration and the first two days of the operation were difficult. I decided to have one of our monitors constantly on the spot supervising the operation and helping to resolve problems. These monitors, Paavo Pitkanen, a Finn, Asbjörn Devold, a Norwegian, and Tom Joyce, an American, took turns and reported to me any problems that needed my attention in Addis. This turned out to be very helpful and the programme proceeded quite successfully. After completion, the heads of both Irish Concern and World Vision confirmed to me independently that they were fully satisfied with the way things had been handled. The supplementary feeding programme for children and the medical services continued to function at Ibenat and it was agreed with Commissioner Dawit that any new people in need who turned up would be admitted for assistance.

After this experience UN field monitors were always present when programmes for returning camp populations to their homes were organised. The Emergency Office took great care to prevent any further "Ibenats" from happening. During July and early August 1985, programmes on a larger scale were arranged at the Mekelle relief centre from which about 50,000 people were returned to their homes. This was done along the same lines as the Ibenat programme. During a visit I made in July 1985, with Commissioner Dawit, the Counsellor of the US Embassy, and the Chief Delegate of the ICRC as well as RRC department heads, arrangements for the Mekelle programme were discussed and procedures agreed upon in detail. I wrote to Commissioner Dawit confirming my understanding of these arrangements. The number of people to be returned would depend on the availability of food, seeds and farm implements, the exercise would be voluntary and an RRC task force and the four NGOs working in Mekelle would do the work. Those unwilling or unable to return home would be permitted to stay in the relief centre. Here again I assigned two of our monitors, Martin Büechi and Paavo Pitkanen to help with the operation and to supervise it from beginning to end. Food distribution points nearer the homes of the people returning were established. This was the last large-scale relief camp returnee programme in 1985 and came just in time before the planting season ended.

There was a serious incident during the Mekelle operation. Some 70–100 men who had been registered by the ICRC and RRC for receiving rations and supplies in order to return home were suddenly rounded up by the peasant militia and placed in a resettlement transit camp near the Mekelle airport. Our monitors tried in vain to have them released and returned to the relief centre. The efforts of the ICRC also failed. I took up the matter with Commissioner Dawit who agreed that it would be very damaging if this matter was not resolved and that it would have a very adverse effect on future programmes of repatriation from the relief centres. Dawit telephoned the party secretary of Tigray, his former classmate at the Military Academy in Addis. The latter immediately called Martin Büechi and informed him that the men were to be sent back to the relief centre. ICRC verified that this had been done.

The return of populations from relief centres continued to attract the interest of the press and the donor community. False rumours arose from time to time. One of the most annoying was that the camp at Korem in Wollo, a major relief centre, would be emptied and the population sent to Sekota about 96 km to the west. This was without foundation but it was picked up by the press and even by voluntary agencies with relief workers in Korem. The head of Save the Children (UK) sent me a telex, with copies to a number of organisations in Europe, protesting strongly against the alleged evacuation and blaming me. I could not resist the temptation to telephone the person in London responsible for this telex and give him a piece of my mind for spreading rumours and not contacting me to get the facts. I am afraid I lost my temper on that occasion but not without good reason.

The result of the camp reduction programme was that the relief camp population fell from about 800,000 people in and around the relief camps in March–April 1985 to about 15,000 at the end of 1985. By May 1986 the number had been reduced to a few hundred remaining in the camps for medical care. This was a considerable achievement and a tribute to the efficient work by the RRC, NGOs and our field monitors.

7. Resettlement

Although my UN mandate excluded dealing with resettlement, a matter which was the concern of the Resident Coordinator of the UN Development Programme (UNDP), I followed the programme from the point of view of its effects on the relief operation and on human rights, a matter that must be of concern to every UN official.

The resettlement of people from drought-prone and ecologically degraded areas in the northern regions to more fertile areas in the south-west of the country is considered by agricultural specialists as a necessary aspect of Ethiopia's economic and social development. This problem was the subject of a massive study undertaken in 1983–84 by the FAO and the Ethiopian Ministry of Agriculture. Entitled "The Ethiopian Highlands Reclamation Study", it produced some 30 research papers and employed about 50 specialists, mostly expatriates. The study showed that of the 5.9 million hectares of farmland in the highlands, about 2.7 million are highly eroded, 1.4 million seriously eroded and 0.2 million are already lost to agriculture which, under cultivation, loses about 100 tonnes of soil per hectare every year. At this speed, by the year 2010, soil degradation would destroy the farmlands of some 10 million of the highland population. Continued soil erosion would reduce grain production by about 120,000 tonnes a year between 1983 and 1990. Serious erosion mostly affects the highlands in Wollo, Tigray, Northern Shoa (Shewa), Eritrea, Eastern Gondar and parts of Hararghe and Bale regions.

These are stark facts and there can be little doubt that resettlement, as part of a comprehensive agriculture and reafforestation programme, is needed. The World Bank recommended such action as early as 1971 on the basis of surveys undertaken by Western specialists. Spontaneous migration from the highlands had taken place over the centuries but rapid population growth and primitive methods of cultivation continued to aggravate the situation to the point that food production could not even sustain the peasant population.

The resettlement scheme began in February 1976, although some small projects had been undertaken earlier. During the period 1976–79, roughly 48,000 families were resettled in some 80 locations. In 1984 the resettled population totalled about 200,000.

The programme reached a new stage in November 1984 when the government decided to move nearly 600,000 people, mainly from the provinces of Wollo, Shoa and Tigray, to areas in Wollega, Illubabor, Gojjam and Kefa in the south-west of the country. According to instructions issued by RRC, the selection of settlers was to be based on the willingness of heads of families to be resettled and to take their families with them, to engage in agriculture, and on satisfactory physical condition (age and health). Screening committees, comprising leaders of peasant associations, local administrators and RRC representatives were established at sub-district level to select settlers. Registration records were kept centrally in Addis with copies in the RRC regional offices and the offices at the settlement sites. Transit centres were established in a few locations from where transport to the settlement sites, by Soviet planes, buses or trucks, was organised.

This seemed a reasonable system on paper but in practice it worked badly. The time-frame given to the authorities for settling hundreds of thousands of people within a year was quite unrealistic. Targets or quotas for the selection of settlers were given to the screening committees with a tight time-table obliging them to act under pressure.

Insufficient preparations were made at the settlement sites and in most areas basic services were non-existent or very poor. Huts had been erected and land cleared around them, some roads had been built and water was available but that was about all in many areas.

By January 1986 a total of 592,994 people had been resettled. Of these, 63 per cent came from Wollo, 18.1 per cent from Shoa, 15.2 per cent from Tigray and the remainder from Gondar and Gojjam provinces. The fact that only 15 per cent were from Tigray and none from Eritrea, the two provinces where civil war continues, showed that frequent allegations in the media at the beginning of the scheme that the settlement programme's aim was to depopulate these provinces for political and military reasons cannot be sustained.

I visited several settlement sites and what I saw convinced me that most of the projects would fail unless large-scale international aid was provided. The authorities were under the illusion that the settlers would be self-sufficient in food, and the new communities would become viable, within one year. This was completely unrealistic but this assumption was at the base of the resettlement policy. Another important factor was the government's very limited resources for investment in the programme. Experience of similar schemes in other countries shows that it normally takes roughly $5,000 per family and a period of some five years for a new settlement to reach the stage of economic and social viability. This is, of course, a very rough yardstick and the situation varies from country to country and from site to site, but it gives an idea of what is required in terms of investment and time. These facts were known to the Ethiopian authorities concerned. In one of the older settlements (Assosa) the cost per family had been $3,500–$4,600 over a five-year period (1979–84). To settle nearly 600,000 people would be enormously expensive and far beyond Ethiopia's means if properly done. When I had my first meeting with Chairman Mengistu I expressed serious reservations about the resettlement programme. I pointed out that on the basis of experience obtained in other countries (I had dealt with resettlement in Burma and the Philippines) the Ethiopian programme would not succeed the way it was planned and implemented. I particularly emphasised that, unless the programme was genuinely voluntary and families were kept intact, the settlers would inevitably return to their places of origin. I suggested to the Chairman that the selection and movement of people should be suspended or slowed down pending the preparation of a more realistic plan and the mobilisation of resources to carry it out. I put to him the idea of inviting the FAO to send a small group of experienced resettlement specialists to help the authorities. Chairman Mengistu took note of what I said but the programme continued as before. At my last meeting with him in late October 1985 Chairman Mengistu confirmed that the resettlement programme would go on and that within a year another 600,000 would be resettled. It was clear to me that he was totally convinced about the necessity to implement the resettlement programme and that no amount of argument would help to dissuade the government from doing so.

During the first phase of the resettlement programme in the winter and spring of 1985 most observers agreed that the programme was voluntary and that people who had lost everything were willing to migrate to other parts of Ethiopia. In fact, migration was nothing new to the highland poulation which over the centuries has moved to other regions in search of food. In the second half of 1985 it became difficult to find people willing to be resettled partly because of the beginning of good rains and the much improved food distribution. The local authorities had problems filling their planned targets of settlers. It was during this stage that force and coercion were being used, although this was against the announced policy of the government in Addis. Several NGOs told me of incidents they had witnessed and some of our monitors had been able to verify. In March 1985 I decided to list the incidents reported to me and to take them up with Minister Berhanu Bayeh. I presented him with a list of six incidents where coercion or other unacceptable methods had been reported. These included withholding relief grain from people who did not sign up for resettlement, and the use of force or coercion to make people sign up or to prevent them escaping from transit camps once they had been registered. These incidents had taken place in six locations in the northern provinces.

Minister Bayeh questioned the veracity of these reports which he thought were based on misunderstandings on the part of relief workers who were not sufficiently familiar with conditions in Ethiopia. He promised to investigate each incident and I persuaded him to invite a small number of journalists to interview him on the subject. He did so in March 1985, during my absence in Geneva to attend the OEOA conference on the African drought. According to press reports, Minister Berhanu Bayeh denied the incidents had taken place but pressed by persistent questions from the journalists he admitted there might have been incidents in which coercion had taken place.

In July I again took up incidents related to the resettlement programme with

Berhanu Bayeh. One was reported to have happened at Wukro in Tigray where an NGO had opened a new distribution point. The RRC had cooperated in organising the registration of about 1,000 new beneficiaries for the first distribution. When people began to arrive some were taken to resettlement transit camps. According to the NGO concerned the new distribution point had been used as "bait" for involuntary resettlement. Earlier, near Axum in Tigray, two of our monitors had observed an enclosure with about 100 men under armed guard awaiting transport for resettlement. In reply to my questions Minister Berhanu Bayeh observed that, again, the NGO and our monitors must have misunderstood since people for settlement were no longer needed from Tigray and Wollo. It was agreed that Commissioner Dawit would carry out an investigation into this incident. I never received a satisfactory explanation.

Even after I had finally left Ethiopia, my office reported to me in London (where I had stopped to meet Timothy Raison, Minister for Overseas Development) that NGOs at Korem had estimated about 12,000 of the camp population at the relief centre had fled into the surrounding hills for fear of being registered for resettlement. Our monitors had been informed that they would not be allowed to fly to Korem to look into the matter, and the office was beseiged by telephone calls from the press. I tried to telephone Minister Berhanu Bayeh but he was not at home. Instead I asked Mrs Bayeh to relay my concern to him and to ask him to arrange for our monitors to visit Korem. That was done and the situation was resolved when the people returned from the hills and were readmitted to the relief centre. But this was one more indication that the resettlement programme was running into increasing difficulties.

The US Embassy was very sensitive to anything that happened in the resettlement programme, to which the US was adamantly opposed. Their lead was followed by UK, FRG and several other EEC countries. Canada was more ambivalent and in autumn 1985 decided to authorise the distribution of Canadian food in settlement projects. The country that took the most positive attitude was Italy which, late in 1985, decided to make a large allocation for the development of infrastructure, agriculture and social services in resettlement projects.

The major NGOs were slow to get involved in work in resettlement areas, partly because they did not want to go against the policy of the USA from which many of them got their resources. The first NGO to start a project in a resettlement site was a small Austrian organisation *Menschen für Menschen*, funded and run by Karlheinz Böhm, a former well-known actor. I visited this site in early October 1985 and found that the project had got off to a good start. But assistance on a much larger scale was needed and I tried to encourage other NGOs to participate.

In 1986 Irish 'Concern' and Band Aid/Live Aid (UK) initiated projects in settlement areas to help provide roads, water supplies and other services, as well as agricultural development. By that time major food donors, with the exception of the US, had withdrawn objections to food distribution to the resettled population. Some of those trying to find fault with the relief operation considered this distribution to be diversion of food aid, an absurd claim since the food was being distributed with the approval of the donors. Allegations that trucks donated for relief transport were being used for resettlement purposes were also groundless as I have indicated in Chapter 4. There may have been occasional abuses by local officials but the fact is that the resettlement areas were being served by 300 Soviet trucks and 700 drivers and by Soviet Antonov transport planes.

My position concerning the resettlement programme was from the beginning that, while the UN was certainly not advocating in any way the movement of people (I had warned Chairman Mengistu about the likelihood of complete failure because of poor planning and lack of required resources as well as objectionable aspects of the selection of settlers), it was necessary on humanitarian grounds to provide food and other assistance to the settlers. It was obvious to me that unless massive foreign aid from governments and NGOs was forthcoming the programme would result in widespread human suffering.

Early in 1986 the programme was suspended, not because of a change in policy and certainly not due to pressure from the West, but because of lack of resources for agricultural inputs and a shortage of transport which had to be used for the coffee export and the transport of food crops. In April 1986, it was announced that the programme would resume.

8. Fact and Fiction: Media Reporting of the Crisis

From my experience as a part-time reporter during my student days in Helsinki, and from my dealings with the press in previous UN assignments, I knew that it was essential to cooperate with the media representatives. To avoid them would simply have created a suspicion that there was something to hide. But I was not prepared for the onslaught that followed.

Western reporters temporarily stationed in Addis Ababa and based in Nairobi understood the operation better than those who came for short visits. Among them were several excellent journalists and radio reporters with whom I had first-class cooperation. Hardly a day went by without journalists and radio and television reporters waiting for me in the office. The WFP had assigned an experienced press man, Dennis Craig, to help me deal with the press. He developed a good working relationship with the media representatives and was very helpful to me.

I had little dealings with the press representatives of Socialist countries. I met the Soviet TASS news agency reporter attached to the USSR Embassy, but he never asked any questions. My only serious encounter was with the representative of the East German news agency. I gave him a briefing intended for background purposes but his dispatch quoted me out of context and in a highly controversial way. His story, published by the official Ethiopian news agency (ENA), created some surprise among Western donors in Addis. I was greatly upset, but my relationship of confidence and trust with the donor countries was strong enough to ride out this "storm in a teacup".

On reflection I believe that the reporting on Ethiopia in the Western press was greatly coloured by hostility towards its Marxist regime. But gradually, when facts became known and journalists revisited the country in the second half of 1985, when the relief operation was in full swing and conditions in the camps and elsewhere had greatly improved, their reports began to reflect the true situation.

The most difficult problems arose when journalists from major newspapers came on short visits. Some of them had little experience of Africa, had not been in Ethiopia before, and were unwilling to use facts available in my office and from NGOs and donor missions. In many cases, the stories they filed were based on limited or inaccurate information and statistics and, at times, hearsay and gossip, and consequently served only to exacerbate an already difficult and delicate situation.

But there were many exceptions to the "visiting firemen". For example, Michael Wooldridge of the BBC always produced balanced and factually accurate reports in the admirable tradition of the BBC. He was not looking for sensational incidents or controversies, and if he found any always checked his facts before filing his report. John Edlin of the Associated Press was another highly professional and accurate reporter. He did not fuss over details such as exactly how many people had been at Ibenat when the first evacuation took place, but was more interested in the substance and his stories were written in a fittingly sober style. Barry Schlachter, also of the Associated Press, stationed in Nairobi, was another highly responsible journalist with many of the qualities of Mike Wooldridge and John Edlin.

Clifford May of the *New York Times*, always active and alert, began, after a few months, to write not only about the problems but about the achievements of the relief effort. I spent some time with him, going through distribution figures and other facts about the relief operation and our relationship became increasingly one of mutual trust.

Blaine Harden of the *Washington Post* "scooped" the forced evacuation of Ibenat camp which created a storm of protest worldwide. One of his reports I found deeply upsetting, but after we had discussed it he understood my reaction. After returning to his regular post in Nairobi, he wrote some excellent articles.

Jonathan Steele of the *Guardian* who visited Ethiopia a few times was a quiet-mannered, highly experienced journalist who could be relied upon to ascertain that his facts were in order. When he came to Ethiopia in September 1985, I was fed-up with the press, but when he turned up at the airport, hoping to visit Ibenat, I asked the Commissioner to invite him to join the ambassadors and relief workers who formed the party. In the presence of my information officer, Inger Wiren, I asked Jonathan Steel to rigorously apply his professional standards of honest and unbiased reporting. This he did on our four-day trip and, to some extent, his article helped restore my faith in independent journalism.

Unfortunately, however, there were also disappointments. Some journalists, basing their reports on inadequate information, or disregarding reliable information, not only misinformed the public, but risked injuring the good faith of donors.

Jacques de Berrin, a reporter from *Le Monde* stationed in Nairobi, came to Ethiopia in April 1985. He never came to see me but obtained his information mainly from the ICRC. This body, however, did not have an overview of the relief operation as a whole as it was responsible for only about 15 per cent of the food distribution and worked in four of the eleven provinces affected by the famine. De Berrin filed a story with *Le Monde* in which, among other things, he stated that only two to three million people — as against the generally agreed 7.9 million — in Ethiopia were in need of food aid, and that the authorities were diverting 30,000 tonnes a month. I asked the ICRC Chief Delegate how De Berrin had come by this information and was told that he had apparently misunderstood that the figures referred only to the provinces of Tigray, Eritrea and northern Wollo and not to the population as a whole. Regarding the allegations of diversion of food, if, like most reporters, de Barrin had contacted me for information, I could have told him that distribution as a whole at the time of his visit amounted to 40,000–45,000 tonnes a month, mostly distributed by Western NGOs. He had thus, indirectly, accused these organisations of misusing relief food; this was pointed out by the French ambassador, José Paoli, in a letter to a French magazine.

Unfortunately, as invariably happened in such cases, the *Le Monde* article figures were taken up by other journalists, including William Shawcross of the *Observer*, one of whose articles was headed "A Conspiracy of Silence". Inevitably this phrase was repeated by other journalists and the misinformation it implied was thus afforded a degree of credibility in the English-language press. William Shawcross' article disappointed me because I had spent considerable time with him, providing the information he was looking for.

I also gave quite a lot of time briefing Paul Vallely, a reporter of *The Times* in London. Whilst he was in Addis his articles reflected the facts of the situation, although clearly coloured by his dislike of the regime. But his particular concern was whether or not there was cholera in some relief camps. I discussed this with the Minister of Health who said that there was no cholera but a severe type of diarrhoea. I told Vallely this but he filed an article in which he said *inter alia* that the Minister had declined to show me results of laboratory tests for cholera — which I had not asked for, and would have been unable to interpret even if I had seen them. On a plane to London in February 1985 Vallely showed me the text he had telexed to *The Times* in which he had written of the Minister's refusal to show me the laboratory tests. By telephoning the appropriate desk editor I was able to have this passage deleted from all except the northern edition of the paper.

After Vallely returned to his post in London, he wrote an article from Khartoum stating that the large relief camp in Korem was being emptied and the people sent to the town of Sekota, 98 km east. This was not so. On 19 August 1985 I wrote the following letter to Vallely:

Dear Mr. Vallely,
Your article entitled 'Starving Wollo: an empty excuse' has just come to my attention. It is full of misinformation and misunderstandings which cannot go uncorrected. You say that the warehouses at Nazareth are 'once more full of food which the Dergue is refusing to distribute'. The fact is that most of the food

in Nazareth and other central warehouses belongs to voluntary organisations and not to the RRC. The voluntary organisations have full control of their grain which has been earmarked to them by major donors, particularly the US, for distribution in specified regions.

To say that the government is 'unable or unwilling to feed almost nine million of its subjects' (the correct figure of those in need is 7.9 million) is wrong. At present 65–70 per cent of the food distribution is done by voluntary organisations because of the insufficient quantities of grain sent to the RRC by the donors. Thus, even if the Government were 'unwilling or unable' to distribute the food consigned to it, the majority of those in need would still be fed by international voluntary organisations working on the basis of cooperative agreements with RRC. RRC's problem in not having enough grain to distribute is shown by the fact that for the period May–December food aid imports totalling 427,000 tonnes were consigned to voluntary organisations and only 181,000 to the RRC. The monthly average to be received by the RRC during this period is 23,482 MT while the RRC monthly requirement is between 35–50,000 MT. Shortages of food for certain regions at given periods of time cannot be blamed mainly on the RRC since a major part of the food is being distributed by international voluntary organisations which have control over the grain consigned to them by donors. There is a complete consensus here among representatives of donor countries and voluntary organisations that the RRC is doing its utmost to distribute whatever grain has been consigned to it. There is certainly no unwillingness to distribute food but there are problems of management and transport of which you should be aware.

You refer to a programme 'to close down most of the big refugee camps'. This is a policy that all the private organisations have fully accepted and are trying to help the RRC to carry out. It makes no sense to keep people in large camps with all the attendant problems when it is possible to help them return to their places of origin with seed, agricultural implements and blankets and with the establishment of new food distribution points near their homes.

To say that there is a systematic attempt in Ethiopia to deprive Wollo of food when it is the region most severely affected, is complete nonsense which can be shown by the reports of our monitors and the voluntary organisations working in the affected provinces. It is true that Wollo had not received a fair share of the food distribution [but] not as a result of government policy but due to the fact that RRC has not had enough grain to distribute because of the heavy earmarkings by major donors to voluntary organisations mostly working in regions other than Wollo. This is the reason why we have approached the EEC for additional shipments to be consigned to RRC and distributed in Wollo. The first such shipment of 14,000 MT has by now been practically unloaded in Assab. Since very little of the 'huge stocks' can be used by RRC, there is no justification in blaming the Commission for inability to provide enough food for Wollo.

Your report on Ibenat is utterly wrong. I enclose a copy of a telex I sent to UN Headquarters summarizing the way the programme was carried out. I must stress very strongly that Father Finucaine who is in charge of Irish Concern and Mr. Searle who is head of World Vision have once again confirmed to me that they were fully satisfied with the returnee programme at Ibenat. These were the two organisations responsible for the returnee programme at Ibenat and they are the ones who know the facts. During the entire Ibenat operation my office had monitors (one Norwegian, one Finn and one American) on the spot following every step of it and assisting in the work. I take it as a direct insult to the integrity of these dedicated men to imply that they had permitted anything unacceptable to happen. There was at the beginning of the operation some tension between the RRC local representative and the voluntary organisations involved but this was worked out with the assistance of our monitors and the programme then proceeded as originally agreed between them and the RRC. But a journalist who wants to dwell on isolated incidents to make a good story will always find some 'anonymous relief workers' who are willing to relate imaginary incidents. You would have done well in checking your information with the heads of Irish Concern and World Vision in Addis since these two organisations together with the ICRC carried out the returnee programme in Ibenat. Your reference to RRC officials arbitrarily picking out men, women and children for return home is again wrong. The fact is that there was a screening committee which agreed on who should be registered for return home and who should be permitted to stay at the feeding centre and the clinic.

As regards Korem you are again completely wrong. The rumour about transferring the Korem population to Sekota was just a rumour and no returnee programme has started in Korem. The only tentative plan is to return about 7,000 Tigreans from Korem to Maychew but my agreement with the RRC and the voluntary organisations involved is that this will be done only to the extent that food, seeds, agricultural implements and blankets can be distributed at Maychew where the Tigrean camp population originally came from. Here again you could have verified your facts by a telephone call to Save the Children Fund in London or Oxfam in Oxford which are the two principal organisations that would be participating in the programme if it were to take place. It is astonishing that you are basing your story on Korem on a rumour that was scotched a month ago, a fact which I have communicated to the agencies concerned. My last point is that the consensus here among the voluntary organisations is that the RRC is cooperating very well with the multitude of private organisations assisting in the relief programme. When Mr. Bradford Morse, Director of the UN Office for Emergency Operations in Africa and I saw Chairman Mengistu here on 20 July he went out of his way to thank the voluntary organisations for their work and to assure us that he has given instructions to the effect that their work should be facilitated by the government in every way possible.

My first impulse was to write a letter to the editor to correct the misinformation contained in your article. But I know that the readership of the letters to the editor is limited. However, I am sending a copy of this letter to the editor and to the U.K. Ambassador in Addis. You owe me an article which will correct this misinformation in an appropriate way. After all I was completely open with you when you were in Addis and it is only normal to expect you to show fairness to me as well. Does it not bother your conscience that articles such as yours grossly distorting facts and making up nonexistent incidents will influence the attitudes of donors towards the emergency relief effort in Ethiopia? The indirect result of these kinds of articles is to increase the suffering of the people through an insufficient supply of relief aid. And does it not give you some pangs of discomfort that you have never written an article mentioning the achievements of the RRC and the many voluntary organisations and relief workers, thanks to whom a population equivalent to that of Denmark is being assisted despite the enormous difficulties caused by the size of the country (two times that of France), the unbelievably difficult terrain, few roads and only one railroad and security problems in several parts of the country. The operation here has in fact been very successful and I will once prove this by facts which will finally triumph over fancy.

I sent a copy of this letter to Ambassador Brian Barder and to the Editor of *The Times*.

Possibly my letter was an over-reaction to the often biased coverage the relief operation received in the Western press antagonistic to the Mengistu regime. But it reflected my feelings of frustration with the media at that time. My letter found its way to voluntary organisations and to some politicians in Britain; a former leader of the Labour Party tried to get *The Times* to publish the letter. Vallely's article came up again, to my annoyance, when in February 1985 I appeared before the Select Committee on Foreign Affairs of the House of Commons. Later, Vallely adopted a more balanced approach to the Ethiopian crisis.

A number of television programmes on the Ethiopian famine were made for showings in Europe, USA and Africa. Those programmes I have seen were mainly Scandinavian, including Norwegian, Swedish and Finnish. They were mostly comprehensive and reasonably objective although some of them had a number of factual errors. One TV programme was produced by Bill Moyers, Vice-President of the CBS. Moyers is a well-known writer and journalist and, as his programme was to be shown at prime time on the East Coast of the US, it was bound to have a very wide audience. Moyers had insisted that his friend Maurice Strong accompany him. The team spent five days in Ethiopia and I went with them for a day to one of the resettlement areas, Assossa, near the Sudanese border. It was my understanding that the programme would look at problems as well as achievements and since the US was the largest donor country I expected the programme to have an important impact on public opinion there. At the end of our trip to Assosa Bill Moyers interviewed me at the Addis airport for more than half an hour, against the background of an RRC light aircraft. I tried to outline the difficulties experienced by RRC and NGOs in food distribution and cited facts showing what had been done to help the famine victims. Bill Moyers sent me a copy of the tape and, when I saw the programme, I was greatly disappointed. It was thoroughly political, emphasising that the American people were supporting what he said was the regime of a Marxist dictator. He also repeated the favourite line of many journalists that "food was rotting in the ports while people were starving". As I have shown earlier, this was not true at all. All in all the programme was almost entirely negative and had nothing good to say about the donors (other than the USA) or about RRC, NGOs or the UN system.

The role of the media, particularly the press, in keeping the public informed of the situation in emergencies is of great importance to help ensure a flow of aid from governments and the public at large. Irresponsible reporting, however, can be very damaging, and journalists solely engaged in looking for sensational stories can do irreparable harm to emergency operations. One can only hope that at least some of the most influential newspapers and magazines will endeavour to select only those reporters sensitive to humanitarian relief efforts as observers of emergency operations.

Epilogue

For months after I had left Ethiopia I had what my wife termed "withdrawal symptoms". My thoughts were in Ethiopia and I found myself wondering about such matters as port offtake, distribution levels, truck maintenance and above all the condition of the people in the areas affected by the famine.

My experience in Ethiopia was in many ways exceptional. I left my quiet home in the hinterland of southern France to be dropped into a cauldron of pressures, politics and practical problems that at times seemed insurmountable. The donor governments and NGOs looked to the UN for leadership in this vast operation. The UN could be either the *primus motor* or the scapegoat.

The results of the international relief operation prove beyond doubt that it was a success. It is regrettable that many people died in 1984 and during the first months of 1985 until distribution of food and other aid started reaching people on a large scale. There is no way to be sure about how many deaths occurred and here again loose estimates and guesses abound. On the basis of the collective judgement of donor missions, relief officials and representatives of NGOs working in various parts of Ethiopia, including the large relief camps, my very tentative and reluctantly arrived at view is that during 1984 and 1985 probably up to 500,000 people died as a result of the famine. This very rough idea is based on information gathered from Ethiopian and international agencies working in relief centres, special feeding programmes and at distribution points. The most reliable figures came from the relief centres where records were kept and from NGOs (including the Ethiopian Red Cross) in touch with the peasant associations and local RRC and party functionaries. Information was also received from Ethiopian priests who were able to circulate freely in areas controlled by resistance groups. But it has to be emphasised that this is nothing more than an indication of the human tragedy that occurred in Ethiopia.

On the positive side it has to be recorded that the relief operation kept alive more than seven million Ethiopians and enabled some 800,000 people displaced by the famine to return home and begin to grow food. The distribution of seeds and tools, although it did not reach the established target, was an important factor in preventing another exodus towards relief centres. In terms of these quantifiable results the famine relief and rehabilitation programme was astonishingly successful against what, at the beginning, seemed impossible odds. Fred Fischer, head of USAID in Ethiopia, considered the relief operation to have been "one of the world's great success stories" (*Washington Post*, 1 December 1985). As one who was there I pay tribute to the donors, RRC and the NGOs who together with the UN achieved results nobody could have foreseen when news of the famine hit the media.

The food shortage, chronic in Ethiopia for a long time, continued beyond 1985. In 1986 there was a need partially to assist about five million people who had not yet recovered from the drought. This was to be expected after years of severe food shortages and disruptions in food production. But it was a good sign that peasant grain production in 1986 was 29 per cent higher than in 1984. In several regions of Ethiopia inadequate rainfall, shortages of seed and oxen, hailstorms and pest damage limited overall peasant production to about 20 per cent below normal as compared to average annual production for the period 1979 to 1983. Three provinces had above normal production. But distribution of foods was not a problem in 1986 as the mechanism existed for this work and there were sufficient food aid supplies and transport capacity to get the food to the people.

Food aid will not solve Ethiopia's continuing shortages. Rehabilitation of agriculture and improved services to increase food production through greater use of better seeds, fertilisers and agricultural extension work will be absolutely essential. There is plenty of water in Ethiopia for irrigated agriculture but these resources need to be exploited. Existing pricing and marketing policies provide no incentives to farmers to expand production and market their surpluses. These policies were being reviewed in 1985 and 1986 with the participation of the World Bank and it is hoped that a more efficient agricultural system will be developed.

The UN has been criticised for not acting more promptly and vigorously in 1983–84 when information about the food shortage became known. There is some justification for this criticism. But in the famine relief operation itself, the Ethiopian authorities, the donor countries and NGOs relied heavily on the UN office for leadership and initiative in the mobilisation and distribution of resources. Any important problem that could not be solved otherwise, such as port congestion, transport bottlenecks, uneven distribution of food among the administrative regions, human rights violations by local party officials, unauthorised relief camp evacuations, travel restrictions and so on were referred to the UN office. And the UN staff had to be constantly on the move to monitor aid distribution, help prevent problems in the field and anticipate difficulties before they became real problems. Inevitably, the UN office was placed right in the middle of conflicting pressures and politics that swirled around the huge relief operation.

In this very complex situation, full of political pitfalls and almost unbelievable organisational problems, there was never a quiet moment. It was truly an incredibly hectic task for which everyone had to be available around the clock. There were critics of the UN role. Some people thought that I was not firm enough with the Ethiopian government and did not speak loudly enough in public when something untoward happened. To those who expressed that view I recommend reading the letter I received from US Vice President George Bush quoted below. Others, including some top Ethiopian officials and Eastern-bloc diplomats, felt that I was too much on the side of the donors and the NGOs. In any event, I leave it to others to evaluate the performance of the small UN Emergency Office in Ethiopia and to choose the criteria on which to make their assessments. There have been a number of reviews and evaluations of this performance by donor agencies, individual researchers and NGOs. Some of the material will be published in the course of 1987.

The most significant assessment came from US Vice President Bush in a letter to me dated 26 November 1985, in which he commends the UN *inter alia* for its strong leadership role in the operation and for its "direct humanitarian interventions in cases of forced resettlement and the precipitate closure of the emergency feeding camp at Ibenat which served to protect against violations of human rights."

Coming from the Vice President of the country most strongly opposed to the Mengistu regime, and usually critical of the UN, this must be of interest to those "knights on white horses" always ready to run to the media — often with unverified information — but who accomplished little. My approach was different. It was based on two premises: 1) in order to be firm with the authorities I had to convince them that the UN was acting in each individual case in the best interest of the relief operation and not owing to pressure from any quarter; and 2), I had to be absolutely sure of the facts and act in a way that would not unnecessarily embarrass the government and thereby harden its attitude. Events proved this to be the right approach. It would have served no useful purpose to dramatise incidents greatly or to provoke the government into reacting publicly to alleged abuses of human rights by local party officials. I am convinced that firmness must be based on trust and confidence and that "quiet diplomacy" was the best way of getting results in the politically charged atmosphere in Ethiopia. My approach had the undivided support of the donor community.

When, upon the completion of my assignment, my wife and I left Ethiopia, Commissioner Dawit was travelling on the same plane on his way to the UN General Assembly session. At the airport he did not enter the guest lounge which was full of well-wishers but went directly to the plane. Earlier Dawit had told me several times that he would quit his job at about the time I was to leave Ethiopia but not that he would defect. During the flight we had hours of frank discussions about the relief operation, of which he was justifiably proud as head of RRC. The fact that two-thirds of the food had been distributed by NGOs did not worry him because his interest lay in helping the famine victims by any legitimate means available; and he had great respect for the integrity of the major NGOs doing the distribution. Dawit considered the whole operation as having been very clean with only marginal diversion of aid supplies for unauthorised purposes.

When he told me he would defect to the West he explained that he was at his wit's end because of relentless pressure from Politbureau hardliners. Dawit was considered much too pro-West and was blamed for having given Western organisations too great a role in the relief programme and thereby facilitating Western penetration of Ethiopia. He was critical of the resettlement programme but, when I spoke with him again a year after his defection to the US, he dismissed the MSF death-rate figure as pure speculation. In his opinion, based on inside information only he possessed, the MSF claim was "highly exaggerated".

Whatever Dawit's future as a political refugee he remains the hero of the relief operation. Without him it would have been impossible to achieve the aim of saving millions of people from death by starvation.

In autumn 1986 Médecins sans Frontières (MSF) resumed its attacks on the resettlement programme. It was joined by some of the French "new philosophers", one of whom made the bizarre statement in a magazine article in October 1986 that the very success of the relief operation and the absence of corruption in it enabled the Ethiopian government to carry out the resettlement programme. This is true only to the extent that if the relief effort had failed there would have been no people left in the highlands to be resettled.

MSF's renewed publicity campaign, coinciding with the organisation's tenth anniversary, was not limited to the resettlement scheme but spilled over into insinuations and loose statements casting doubt on the performance of other NGOs. Even the absurd allegation that "food was rotting in Assab port while people were starving" was repeated; I have dealt with this falsehood in chapter 4. MSF's behaviour prompted strong reactions from NGOs which had carried the main burden of relief aid in Ethiopia. In comparison with their work, MSF had made an infinitesimal contribution. In September 1986 the American Council for Voluntary International Action issued a statement on behalf of Africare, Mercy Corps, Church World Service, Save the Children and World Vision, taking strong exception to statements made by MSF, calling them "an affrontery to truth". In November 1986 all NGOs working in Ethiopia, including two French ones, refuted MSF's attacks stating *inter alia* "all [involved in the aid effort] have every right to be proud of what is widely recognized as the greatest humanitarian effort in recent memory". The main donor agency, USAID, issued a statement along the same lines, as did Maurice Strong in his capacity as Special Advisor to the UN Secretary General. The result of all this was that MSF is totally isolated from the rest of the large NGO community, and its credibility is seriously undermined. Given this fact, the longer-term effect of MSF's action will have only a nuisance value. But it demonstrated how easily irresponsible individuals can create a nuisance through the media which do not take the trouble to check facts.

An appropriate way to end this part of the book is to quote from a report of the US Senate Judiciary Sub-Committee on Immigration published in the summer of 1986:

> Seven million men, women and children have been saved from starvation. Today, thanks to the sustained efforts of the international community — and to the incredible work and sacrifice of the international and voluntary agencies — a remarkable success story of international relief has been accomplished in Ethiopia.

SECTION 2

Before and After

by
Angela Penrose

Acknowledgements

This book grew out of research carried out by Michael Harris, without which it could not have been written. I am indebted to him for the information he sought out in Ethiopia, Europe and the USA and to the many people involved in the emergency operations during the recent famine who provided that information.

I would like to acknowledge a great debt to Fred Halliday and Maxine Molyneux for their book *The Ethiopian Revolution* and to Peter Gill for his book *A Year in the Death of Africa*; both books were invaluable in building up the background to the situation in Ethiopia before and during the famine. Robert Chambers' works on seasonality have also provided essential material. I am grateful to Richard Pankhurst for permission to quote from his recent book *The History of Famine and Epidemics in Ethiopia prior to the Twentieth Century* — I did not think I could improve on his summary of famine so I have included it in full. Dick Grove of Downing College, Cambridge was kind enough to give advice on the section on climate. I am particularly grateful to Edith Penrose for her practical support and editorial assistance.

I would like to thank all those still actively involved in attempting to prevent further famine who took time to talk over the issues whilst I was in Addis Ababa. But my special thanks go to the staff and student colleagues of the University Famine Relief and Rehabilitation Organisation with whom I worked during the famine of the 1970s, who taught me so much about Ethiopia and its people and much else besides.

Angela Penrose,
Cambridge, 1987

Introduction

Study of the history of drought and famine in Ethiopia shows that the calamities of our time, with which the world has in the last year or so become familiar, are but the last of a long series of such disasters.

Famines were due to both natural and socio-economic factors which were often interconnected. The former comprised drought, locusts, caterpillars, and in the case of the great famine of 1889–1892, rinderpest; the latter included deforestation, soil erosion and exhaustion, fragmentation of land holdings, the subsistence economy with its primitive agricultural tools and inadequate grain storage, obsolete and inegalitarian systems of land tenure, arbitrary taxation and other dues, civil wars and external invasions, as well as, according to some observers, the observance of an excessive number of holidays. Though there were many years with good harvests, famine was a frequent, at times almost

*endemic occurrence in many parts of the country, and was almost invariably
followed by the outbreak of epidemic diseases.*

*Famine in Ethiopia in former days, as in other countries at a similar level of
economic development, was perhaps inevitable, in that it could not be overcome,
given the socio-economic conditions of the time.*

*The situation today is, however, vastly different, for the technological and
other achievements of the twentieth century can — and must — be harnessed for
the good of man.*

This view, with which Richard Pankhurst introduces his *The History of Famine and
Epidemics in Ethiopia Prior to the Twentieth Century* (published by the Relief &
Rehabilitation Commission, Addis Ababa, 1985) and with which few who have
experience of famine in Ethiopia would disagree, speaks of 'the calamities of our
time' in the plural. As all are aware, the disastrous famine of the early 1970s, from
which it was universally agreed so much must be learned, was followed in the 1980s
by an even more catastrophic famine. How could a second 'calamity' have occurred
within such a short space of time? Why were the lessons not learned?

Although a number of African countries were affected in the period 1980–85 by
inadequate rainfall and harvests this book is concerned primarily with Ethiopia.
Generalisations about poverty, rural development, agricultural policies, climate
and so on, can be useful in this context but there is no doubt that Ethiopia is a
special case where additional constraints on development, needing some
discussion, exist. This study sets out to provide a background to the recent famine in
Ethiopia, a survey of the responses to it, a resumé of the current situation as
emergency action shifts into rehabilitation and development and an outline of those
types of action necessary to avert another disaster. It does not go into every issue in
depth, but I hope that all aspects of the natural and man-made disasters, and the
handling of them, have been touched upon.

The famine in Ethiopia can only be properly understood in the context of the
country's unusual history. Part One, therefore, considers the historical background,
the reign of the Emperor Haile Selassie and the establishment of the Provisional
Military Administrative Council after the revolution of 1974. The revolution took
place against the background of widespread famine and national and international
outrage at the spectacle of mass starvation. That famine is considered in some detail
for it affected the same social groups, in the same areas, for many of the same
reasons. The economic, political and social policies of the Ethiopian government in
the decade between the major famines are considered.

It is to be hoped that anyone finding this historical section too long will remain
patient as it seems clear that the impatience, frustration and prejudice
demonstrated by foreign governments, international agencies and non-governmental
organisations (NGOs) towards the Ethiopian government and its departments
during the recent crisis have, however understandable, contributed to the
misconceptions, delays and dismissals of requests for aid which aggravated the
effects of that crisis.

In Part Two the build up to the most recent famine and the reasons for the
inadequate response on the part of international agencies and voluntary

organisations are examined. A brief description of the improved response since October 1984 and current developments is given.

Part Three describes some of the healthy attempts to reappraise approaches to development that are being made in the climate of positive criticism that prevails after the famine. Some areas in which action can be taken to prevent the reoccurrence of such devastating famines are reviewed and the question is posed: have the lessons been learned? Only experience in the future will show whether they have. In the meantime the Ethiopian people grapple with the complex problems which beset their country. Whatever policies are implemented, however, there are two factors which, at least in the short and medium term, are beyond the reach of government programmes, however rigorously implemented: the climate and the rate of population growth.

The last part of the book discusses these issues in an attempt to underline the fact that the people of rural Ethiopia should be able to expect more than periodic handouts and blanket condemnation of their government.

The Ethiopian government has received a great deal of criticism since the crisis became internationally known, much of it justified, some of it misinformed. Those who are seeking to prevent further serious famine in the country are not, by either their actions or their concern, condoning the Ethiopian government's expenditure on arms or its repression of nationalities within the country. They recognise, however, that if their involvement is to be effective in helping to avert famine a realistic approach to what is feasible within Ethiopia today must be made.

For a number of interconnected reasons even a series of rain failures do not automatically result in famine. In late 1984 Kenya suffered a major harvest failure in some areas whereas Ethiopia was undergoing its fifth. In that year Kenya received well over half a million tonnes of food aid in addition to its extra commercial imports. With a population one half of Ethiopia's, Kenya thus received a total emergency aid inflow three times greater than Ethiopia did, with no comparable international clamour. The reasons may be obvious, but if the 'humanitarian' edict is to mean anything, ways of improving Ethiopia's status as one of the least favoured in terms of international assistance per capita must be found.

Part 1:
Historical Background

1. Historical Introduction

In many ways Ethiopia is unique. Being the single African country to escape prolonged colonial domination, it was able to preserve its distinct precolonial social structures and culture throughout the period of European colonialism. It thus became a symbol of political independence and cultural continuity within Africa and exerted an almost mythical fascination over Europeans. Its survival as an independent state, and the personal prestige of its last monarch, were the main reasons it was chosen as the headquarters of the Organisation of African Unity (OAU) in 1963.

Ethiopia's first significant contact with Europeans was in the early 16th Century when the Portuguese, at the peak of their powers of exploration, discovered the Christian King of Ethiopia in their search for the Prester John. Only the intervention of a small Portuguese force preserved the Christian state from complete destruction by the Islamic forces of the Somali leader Ahmad Gran. The Portuguese Jesuits' arrogance and insensitivity towards the rituals and traditions of the Ethiopian Orthodox Church a short while later led to their expulsion from the country and the return of Ethiopia to her former isolation. The disappointing contact with outside influences reinforced a tendency towards xenophobia and helped maintain the country's remoteness.

Most of Ethiopia was not embroiled in the 19th Century division of Africa by European states. The Italians annexed the port of Assab in 1869 and from there gained control over a wider coastal area along the Red Sea, which in 1890 they called Eritrea. They were unable to impose a protectorate over Ethiopia as a whole, losing 8,000 of their own troops and 4,000 native soldiers at the battle of Adowa in 1896. The creation of a new central government in the 1880s that was capable of defeating European armies and preventing internal disunity, which European states could have taken advantage of, maintained Ethiopian independence, but that Ethiopia was a Christian Kingdom, claiming centuries of religious organisation which resisted both Islamic incursions and paganism, played a further role in holding off European intrusion. It is a mistake, however, to look upon the Ethiopian system of Empire and its conquests under the Emperor Menelik in the late 19th Century as analogous to the modern European colonial empires.

Many Ethiopian scholars, as well as Ethiopians of non-Amhara descent, resent the tendency of Europeans to continue to identify modern Ethiopia with the ancient Abyssinian kingdom of the north. Recently a number of studies of the interaction between the expanding Imperial state and the peoples of the southern areas of Ethiopia have thrown light on the formation of the modern Ethiopian state and the evolution of different social and economic structures in the southern provinces.

Italy tried to redress the defeat of Adowa by reinvading Ethiopia in 1935 but received no international support and was ejected in a joint Anglo–Ethiopian campaign in 1941. Ethiopia's strategic location on the Red Sea enhanced her importance in the post-war period, as the dependence of the West on Middle East oil supplies increased and control of the Indian Ocean became of greater concern to the Great Powers. British and later US aid helped Emperor Haile Selassie maintain his regime and re-establish control over the country. Although the British administered Eritrea until 1952 and part of the Ogaden until 1955, these areas were returned to Ethiopian control despite the protests of a significant section of the population in both regions, and despite, in Eritrea's case, UN guarantees that this would not be allowed to happen. Ethiopia remained, therefore, an apparently independent but rather isolated kingdom until the revolution of 1974.

With the re-establishment of Haile Selassie, the ethnic and cultural dominance of the Amhara people were also maintained. Culturally, ethnically and linguistically related to the Tigreans, this dominant group was formed by the mingling of Semitic invaders from the Arabian peninsula with the aboriginal Hamitic Agau people. After conversion to Coptic Christianity in the 4th Century the Christian monarchs maintained power, although only in the late 19th Century did it finally rest with the Amharas based in the province of Shoa. More than one-third of the population, however, is of Oromo (or Galla) origin, a different ethnic group still speaking its own language, who moved steadily into large areas of southern Ethiopia from the 16th Century onwards. There are many other groups, principally the Sidama, the Somalis and the Danakil-Afar.

In the 1920s Haile Selassie had expanded health and education services; in 1931 he announced Ethiopia's first constitution and in the post-war period, encouraged and assisted by Great Britain and the United States, he took these reforms further and began the construction of a new government machine and army. But such changes as were made did not extend to the creation of a modern economy or provide an alternative social base to the existing order. Even the revised constitution of 1955 did not dilute the autocratic nature of the state. The level of political concentration at the centre increased during his reign at the expense of the provincial nobles. He never tried to break the control of the aristocracy but he undermined it and removed some of its functions. In return he had to allow its members to take critically important posts in the government and the bureaucracy, and to accept and promote capital ventures in which both he and they took and held primary shares. This need to offset the power of the nobility often outweighed the mounting need for reform in all areas. Haile Selassie, despite his charismatic image, possessed neither the institutional strength nor personal vision to introduce political, economic and social reform on any effective scale. He allowed his rural reform measures, modest enough in themselves, to be blocked by the interests of provincial opposition.

The most striking aspect of the last 300 years of Ethiopian society is its stable nature and continuity. The practical strength of the system lay not in the mystique of the House of Solomon nor the religious sanctions of the church, important though they were. It lay in the control of the economic base of the Empire — land. Commerce never succeeded in supplanting land as the source of wealth, prestige, or influence in the society. The medieval land structure remained essentially unchanged until the land reforms of the Provisional Military Administrative Council (PMAC). Details of obligations on the land have changed at times and new nobility emerged, especially in the southern provinces, as the power of the Emperors fluctuated *vis-à-vis* the nobility, but not until the 1960s was any attempt made to alter the hierarchical, virtually feudal, structure arising out of the control of the land.

Haile Selassie's total control lessened in the 1960s and 1970s and he appeared unaware of the extent of the crisis which was building up. Many of the problems which later confronted the revolutionary government were the result of his policies, particularly the institutionalisation of Amhara domination at the expense of the ethnic groups, especially the Oromos, and the arbitrary handling of the Eritrean and Somali question. The resources of his regime were inadequate for the task of modernisation facing it but nevertheless the traditional landowners' control of local taxation was left more or less untouched. Little effort was made to enforce taxation on those who could pay and the severe inequality of the tax burden persisted despite the growth of manufacturing industry and some commercialisation of farming in the 1960s.

Whilst it had been obvious for many years that the Ethiopian polity could not continue without major changes, none predicted the extent of the upheaval that was to occur. The indulgence shown to Haile Selassie by Western governments, other African states and those classes whose interests were linked to his own, obscured the dangerous realities of the failures and omissions of his rule. Towards the end of his reign a much-used defence against criticism was that only a gradual rate of reform would secure the modernisation of a traditional society without serious disruption. Not only was this clearly disproved by events but a comparison of his own actions before and after the Second World War clearly shows that the pace of change was far faster from 1930–35 than at any later time. Even in 1974, however, his reputation remained enormous and his admirers were world-wide. He remained a spokesman and figurehead of African and, to some extent, non-aligned states despite the fact that Ethiopia remained one of the least developed countries in the world.

This paradox was brought home to many Ethiopians, including military officers, who travelled overseas to study in the 1960s and early 1970s, or who were dispatched on OAU missions and UN military missions. Their foreign experience to some degree contradicted their belief in their own superiority. The proclamation of the 1960 military rebels who attempted an unsuccessful coup whilst Haile Selassie was abroad began 'It is clear that the fantastic progress achieved by newly independent African states has placed Ethiopia in an embarrassing situation. The new government will have as its aim to restore Ethiopia to its appropriate place in the world.' Whilst nothing as explicit as this was said in 1974, well-educated Ethiopians no doubt face a difficulty in reconciling the knowledge that by any internationally accepted indicators they are among the handful of nations at the bottom of any table with their traditional perception of themselves as an independent, civilised nation, culturally superior to the rest of Africa. This compounds the problem many petitioners face in their relationships with aid donors.

2. The Eve of Famine and Revolution: Economic Conditions

Ethiopia is a country of 395,000 square miles, about twice the size of France with a population estimated at 26 million in the mid-1970s and 31 million in 1981. A 1984 government census, however, caused all former estimates to be drastically reappraised. The estimated population in 1987 is over 45 million. Climatic and geographic conditions vary enormously. The centre of the country is formed by a vast block of mountains and plateaux. In this exceptionally difficult terrain cut by deep gorges and unnavigable rivers live 80 per cent of the population engaged in agriculture. The diversity of altitude gives a diversity of climate within a small area; the Ethiopians themselves divide the highlands into three main zones according to altitude and the resultant climate with its influence on vegetation and crops: *dega* is the temperate zone of 7,000 feet and above; *woyna dega* is the intermediate zone of 5,000 to 7,000 feet and *quola* is the low-lying, hot area. To the south-east and south this central region falls away steeply to the arid lowlands of the Danakil and the Ogaden bordering the Red Sea and Somalia, whilst to the west it slopes more gently to the plains of southern Sudan.

Communications are notoriously difficult. Traditionally there is no movement in the main rainy season from the middle or end of June until September. The Ethiopian Orthodox Church festival of *Maskal* is, like many religious festivals, seasonal in that it heralds the opening up of communications and the resumption of work. Ethiopian Airlines, the inauguration of which in 1946 was a revolutionary landmark in internal transportation, ceases its services to Lalibela on 30 June until the end of the rains, whenever they occur in September or October. There is no indigenous wheeled transport. As late as 1974 there were estimated to be 14,000 miles of road of which only 1,250 were asphalted and about one third all-weather. Forty per cent of the population lived more than a two-days walk from the nearest educational or government centre and 90 per cent more than a day's walk from a road. Rivers, instead of being avenues of communication and trade are, like the great escarpments, a type of barrier.

Whereas it may be true that no region or country has pure or absolute subsistence production, about four-fifths of the population were subsistence farmers and only about 25 per cent of agricultural produce was marketed. Peasants were persistently at or below subsistence level because their meagre production was constantly flowing out in the form of taxes, rents, debt payments, and forms of bribery and extortion. In these circumstances of marginal living there is little capacity to save, and peasants therefore have no potential for raising the productivity of their lands through some form of investment. There was little alternative to remaining dependent on traditional methods of production.

Most peasants remained outside a market economy partaking in few cash transactions and incapable of commercialising their farms. A landless, agricultural labouring class was beginning to emerge, especially in the southern provinces, working on larger mechanised modern farms which were often foreign owned.

There has been considerable debate as to whether the system of land-holding and social stratification could be properly termed feudal. Certainly many divergencies between the feudal systems of Japan or mediaeval Europe and the socio-economic system of Ethiopia can be discerned. Possibly it is these differences rather than the similarities that are crucial to a better understanding of the society and its development, and that the persistence of a European concept of feudalism has proved to be misleading. Certain characteristics of Ethiopian society did fit most European definitions of feudalism, however, and help us to understand how an entirely agrarian society stagnated and was unable to advance through technological innovation.

If feudalism is defined in economic terms as a means of production by which a surplus is extracted from the labourers by the 'non labouring' landowners, then it can be said that feudal relationships were prevalent in many parts of Ethiopia. There was undoubtedly a completely agrarian economy in which a vast peasant population surrendered its surplus to the maintenance of the ruling (historically warrior) class and a large, economically inactive priesthood. But the system of land tenure was extremely complex; in Wollo, the area worst affected by famine in 1973–74 there were 100 different systems. There were, however, throughout Ethiopia, two main types of land tenure:

Gult: the equivalent of a fief, another characteristic of classic feudalism — was granted by the church or Emperor to vassals for military or administrative service. Often (but not always) the landlord was absent but had the right to collect tribute in kind and in labour from peasants who lived on the land. It was an all-embracing social and political system, defining relations between classes, with the *gult*-holders having full judicial and administrative authority over the peasants yet with no original right on the land itself. Within the ancient Abyssinian region — the core — fiefs tended to become more or less hereditary, while those in the periphery, the areas conquered by the Emperors, were more firmly controlled by the Emperor. Even within the core areas, however, where *gult* tended to stay within one family, Emperors could transfer the office to other distant members of the family. The complexities of reforming such a system were formidable and had been the concern of many advocating greater equality.

Rist: the system was further complicated because the peasantry was not itself landless. Most peasants had several plots of land (often between 5 and 30) because in most areas the law of primogeniture was not the rule and descendants of peasant landowners inherited a share of land bequeathed. This led to a fragmentation of plots which further increased the difficulties of any attempts to consider land reform. The fact that the pieces of land might lie in different zones (*dega*, *woyna dega* and *quola*) enabled farmers to harvest different crops at different times of year but in many ways was inefficient. Many farmers arranged to have their plots farmed by tenants and many became tenants nearer their own homes.

The peculiarities of these two systems superimposed on one another and the way in which they can be seen to differ from European or Japanese forms of feudalism help to explain the lack of technical progress in basic sectors of the economy. In Europe, lords tended to have direct control over the land as fiefs and, therefore, had clear economic interests in improving techniques. New technology which might require a certain population of users to be profitable, such as a watermill, could be introduced and all dependent peasants compelled to use it for a fee. In the core areas of Ethiopia lords were not bound up with the process of production. With no secure prospect of being able to reap long-term benefits from any investment they tended to pursue a purely predatory strategy, to skim off as much surplus as possible from whatever the peasants produced, however it happened to be produced.

Peasants also had limited interests in technological development as levels of extraction did not stabilise. Levels of tribute gained a certain constancy, but there was always the possibility of further exactions: the support of troops passing from one area to another or even, before the foundation of Addis Ababa, the Emperor and his enormous entourage moving from one province where supplies had been exhausted, to another. The more one produced, it must have seemed, the more was taken away.

In general the peasant class worked the feudal lands of absentee landlords and paid taxes and tithes on their own land to maintain the church and state above them. Ninety per cent of peasant landowners cultivated less than five hectares each and two-thirds of those less than 1.5 ha. The produce from the land not only had to feed the peasant and his family for the year, provide cash for consumer goods but meet the ever increasing demand for taxation as well.

From 1963 to 1973 agriculture was alloted 4.2 per cent of the combined ordinary and capital expenditure of the State (*The Public Sector of the Ethiopian Economy*, Central Statistical Office, Addis Ababa, May 1974). Although external aid to Ethiopia was increasing, the amount allotted to agriculture again reflected the low priority given to it by the government — 3.9 per cent of the total official aid up to December 1970. Of this, less than one-third had been distributed and used.

Such agricultural development as had taken place was mainly directed towards large, commercially-owned farms in the more temperate areas, especially along the Awash river. The priority given to the extensive production of cash crops, such as cotton and sugar in this area, displaced the pastoralist Afar tribe from some of their traditional land, increasing their vulnerability to drought.

The commercialisation of agriculture was a part of the *Third Five-Year Development Plan, 1968/9–1972/3*, which intended to 'induce more foreign private investment and import the needed managerial skills'. Low land rents, exemptions on income, export and import taxes, a high rate of repatriation of profits and very low wage rates were among the inducements which attracted such companies as Handels Verenigens Amsterdam (HVA) and the Tendaho Plantation Share Company.

Several schemes intended to aid smaller farmers were initiated in the southern provinces. Designed and implemented by foreign aid agencies and run by the Extension and Project Implementation Department of the Ministry of Agriculture (EPID), these programmes provided planning, credit, storage and marketing facilities, price stabilisation, extension services and some mechanisation. The Chilalo Agricultural Development Unit (CADU), begun in 1968, was the prototype. The advances in production were impressive but as other results of the programme became clearer the funding and implementing agency involved, the Swedish International Development Agency (SIDA), threatened to withdraw its assistance. Land prices and rents rose, tenants were evicted and many of the beneficiaries were discovered to be outsiders and richer landlords. As soon as an area was opened up by improvements in infrastructure, credit and marketing facilities, landlords began to evict their tenants in order to take over larger scale cultivation themselves or rent land to outside entrepreneurs.

These schemes were mainly confined to the southern regions. In the north, the areas shown to be the most vulnerable to famine, the majority of peasants still tilled their land in the same way they had done for centuries (one observer of that time claimed they had not even advanced to Roman methods). They did use a type of plough pulled by oxen, but made little use of terracing despite the sloping nature of much of the land. An estimated two-thirds of farmed land is on slopes of more than 25 degrees, hence erosion is a major problem. Fifty-two per cent of Ethiopia's land area loses an estimated 2,000 tonnes of soil per square kilometre every year (a 'normal' wet year!), which had been Egypt's net gain in the form of Blue Nile silt until the building of the Aswan dam.

Torrential rainfall during the comparatively short rainy seasons had always been a problem but became more serious as deforestation accelerated. The loss of vegetative cover also exacerbates the effects of flash floods; vast areas of fertile plains are being destroyed as swollen rivers sweep away the top soil. The 1950s and 1960s were decades of comparatively high rainfall and, as the human and livestock populations increased, assisted by rudimentary health and veterinary services, so did the need for fuel, wood for house-building and fencing. Statistics on the destruction of Ethiopia's closed and open forests are varied but less than 4 per cent of total land area now remains in solid stands of virgin forest, compared to 15 per cent in 1955; savanna woodlands, once 72 million hectares, now amount to some 20 million. The increase in the rate of this comparatively recent and alarming depletion is so great that it exceeds the possibilities of the most energetic reforestation programmes.

A destructive cycle set in; the shortage of firewood meant that cattle-dung was burnt as fuel thus diverting the only available fertiliser from the fragile soil. As the soil deteriorated crop yields fell and the demand for extra land to farm, already growing as a result of population growth, became more urgent.

The peasant farmers were completely dependent on unreliable rainfall. Irrigation

91

schemes were limited to the commercial plantations and no traditional systems had been developed. There were no water storage/conservation methods or facilities in common use. In all areas a cultural acceptance of low, unreliable rainfall prevailed. On the Kobbo plain in Wollo, one of the most fertile areas of the whole province, a 'good' rainy season was expected one year in three. In all areas of eastern Eritrea, Tigray, Wollo and parts of Haraghe and Sidamo, all marginal areas inhabited by nomadic and semi-nomadic pastoralists, annual rainfall is so low that a few millimetres a year makes all the difference. The highland areas (western and central Tigray, Eritrea and Wollo, parts of Gondar) are marginal in the sense that average rainfall produces food adequate for an average family to live on with a small essential surplus, given the antiquated methods of production and that no attempts are made to provide additional sources of water. Any factors affecting this precarious balance lead to a shortfall in production.

The political/social system, fragmented farms, antiquated methods, unreliable rainfall, lack of irrigation and erosion had arguably not changed significantly over many decades, but as a result of the rise in population, putting pressure on already overstretched resources, even the traditional fallow system necessary to maintain soil fertility began to be abandoned.

Some agricultural training centres had been established but extension services were quite inadequate to rectify these deficiencies or counter them with improved methods of husbandry, provision of fertiliser or the implementation of any specifically targeted research. This is not to say that the quality of agricultural training and extension was poor. Bearing in mind the quantitative limitations of any such programme starting from scratch, the results in the 1960s were promising, but the impact on a country as large, diverse and beset by problems as Ethiopia was minimal.

To many Ethiopians looking back on recent history, the 1960s and early 1970s were 'the lost years'. A period of relative stability and advantageous weather conditions, the period during which, in many other parts of Africa, newly independent countries were struggling with development issues. Economic and technical assistance were available but not fully utilised.

3. Famine: 1972–74

The 1972–73 drought in the Sahel zone was generally regarded as the worst since 1913; a number of African countries across the continent in the sub-Saharan belt were affected. The human population, livestock and crops of the Sahel countries —northern Nigeria, northern Kenya, Somalia and Tanzania — all suffered, but in terms of human deaths Ethiopia was the worst affected. Estimates vary greatly; but one of the most reliable reports was UNICEF's in August 1973 which gave a figure between 50,000–100,000 from April until August in Wollo province; 65 per cent were farmers (or from farming communities) and 35 per cent pastoralists. The Ethiopian government's Relief and Rehabilitation Commission (RRC) in a 1982 publication gives the total number of dead as about 200,000 in Tigray, Wollo and Northern Shoa.

Ethiopia is on the fringe of the Indian monsoons and experiences two rainy seasons. The mean average monthly rainfall for Kombolcha in Wollo is 26–50 mm in February–April (*belg*) and 100–200 mm July–September (*kerempt*). Both lowland and highland areas are adapted to normal dry seasons and to dry seasons extending into normally wet months.

The effects of the 1973 drought, however, were due to the fact that the rains had been inadequate and their timing deviant since 1968. It is the cumulative effects of unreliable rainfall in these marginal areas that is critical, hence the importance of an understanding of the pattern of seasonal harvests and behaviour in these areas. Subsistence cultivators lack capital to accumulate more than a limited reserve of food; the crop failures of 1972 wiped out any remaining surpluses before the even less adequate rains of 1973. In such circumstances those previously producing cash crops on a small scale consume their own produce and there is therefore less food available in the markets.

As has been pointed out, however, by no means the whole population of an area starves to death in a famine. This was particularly evident in Ethiopia in 1973. In some areas 1973 was the third and even fourth year of drought; peasants had been adjusting to shortages for several seasons selling and mortgaging possessions until nothing was left.

An illustrative case

The nature of famine in rural Ethiopia can be illustrated by the observations of a team from the then Haile Selassie I University (HSIU), now Addis Ababa University (AAU). The team visited Lasta, an *awraja* in north-eastern Wollo in June 1974. (For administrative purposes the provinces of Ethiopia are subdivided into *awraja*, which in turn are sub-divided into *woreda*.) By then the most critical period of the famine had passed but many people were still dependent on relief. The team had ascertained that 25 per cent of the people in the relief shelters in the towns along the main north–south highway had come from Lasta *awraja* and they wanted to gain an overall picture of the situation in order 'to investigate the causes and extent of the famine'. Their survey is quoted at some length, not because it contains any startling conclusions or even useful data, but because it has value as a description by urban based Ethiopians of life in rural areas immediately after the famine. They had expected to see widespread casualties but what they actually saw shocked them more.

> Lasta is virtually a closed area. There is a 120 km track from Kobo (on the main road) to Lalibela, but no all weather road. The first 30 km is in better repair and is used for the transport of grain to a grain store in Tekulesh. During the rainy season most parts of Lasta are quite cut off as there are no bridges across the Tekeze, Ketchine Abebe and other rivers which become impassable in that

season. Last year 17 Muslims from Meqet drowned in the Tekeze after they had been to Lalibela to seek assistance.

Various attempts are being made by the Dutch, the British and the Chinese to improve road services in the area, in some cases using 'food-for-work' schemes. Needy people seem to be making the most of this opportunity to get food although not all labourers are needy. Rich farmers are known to have taken advantage of the system by sending their children and labourers to work on the roads. The only effective means of transport which exists is pack animals; the number of mules and donkeys, however, has been reduced by the drought. The owner of a mule or a donkey is considered rich. He might engage impoverished farmers to accompany the donkey to distant places carrying goods. The earnings of the donkey are shared by the owner and the impoverished farmer.

From the observations of the team the process of deforestation in Lasta is well advanced. There are ranges of barren, sharp edged hills with sparse vegetation. Cultivation and most habitations are on the slopes of the hills as malaria is apparently widespread at the foot of the hills.

The *quola*, or lower area is comparatively warm. The soil of the fields is alluvial and considered fertile. The usual *quola* crops are tef, maize, sorghum, lentils, peas and flax. In a good year the harvest is envied by those in the higher areas. Apart from malaria, drawbacks are the pests *degazza* and *deyri* [which] are so destructive that they have contributed to the worsening of the drought. . . . A severe attack of deyri and the shortage of the small rains this year meant the loss of maize and sorghum seedlings.

The upper-middle part of the mountain range is known as *woyna dega*. It is comparatively cooler and healthier and farmers normally have their hamlets at this level. Similar crops to the *quola* are cultivated. There is one crop a year; the fields are prepared in April/May, sowing . . . in June/July and [harvesting] in November or December. In many areas this year there is no seed . . . and the land is not prepared due to lack of oxen. Last year there was only a partial harvest for similar reasons. It was an improvement on the year before [i.e. harvest of Nov/Dec 1972] but there were many it did not rehabilitate. In addition the yield was considered low by most of the people we interviewed because of the poor soil. The fields on the slopes are unprotected and eroded. Little or no terracing is practised and the rain washes away the top soil and some of the seeds. One should also consider that these fields have been cultivated for hundreds of years.

The *dega* zone starts at about 300 metres. It is cold and windy, there are no plateaux as in some areas. *Dega* crops are barley, wheat, peas and field beans. Ideally, the cultivation time, *belg*, is in February at the time of the small rains with the harvest coming June or July. This year the harvest is poor and sporadic as a result of poor, sparse early rains. The farmers of the *dega* are uneasy.

Health conditions: The Health Officer in Lalibela observes a close correlation between shortage of food and spread of disease. At times of shortage people move around from place to place and often crowd together in certain places. According to the welfare officer malnutrition is widespread. The Health Centre and the two clinics of the *awraja* (Lasta's population was then estimated at 300,000) do not give free services; it is those who pay who make use of them. Impoverished farmers do not seem to make use of them. They can get certificates indicating they are poor but [this] appears to be difficult and time consuming. There are definite deficiencies in the supply of food, only very poor quality onions and green peppers are on sale by way of vegetables ... the only butcher has stopped selling meat because supplies have dried up. At the Saturday market a few sheep and goats were offered for sale at extremely high prices; a farmer who slaughters goats or sheep at the big festivals is considered very rich. It is common for people not to eat more than one meal a day; such people ration their provisions but as the rains draw near these rations are diminishing and the people are worried.

Schooling: There are 13 schools in Lasta, most of them built by the Elementary School Building Unit. The total school population is now 1,698 and there are 123 classes, thus there is an average of 14 pupils per class. This is well below the national average which is 50. At least part of the reason for this is the compound problem of famine, disease and poverty. For example, the school at Debqo had 95 pupils in January; in May [only] 45. The school director reported to the District Education Officer that the children are weak and attacked by diseases. The school at Tekulesh is totally closed. Reports indicate that pupils and teachers could not operate because of the food crisis. Impoverished farmers, understandably, are not interested in modern schooling which has no bearing on their social reality. None of the schools visited took lessons in agriculture seriously. It is the rich and privileged farmers and 'town' dwellers who send their children to modern schools. Farmers want their children to learn reading and writing so that [they] can deal with court cases without the help of scribes. The main purpose is to prepare oneself to defend family land (inherited land) against claimants. Directors reported that most pupils dropped out after they had acquired basic reading and writing skills. At Muja the teachers claimed that people in general and the clergy in particular do not favour the existence of the school there. There is a perpetual shortage of necessary materials.

Social categories and famine: In Lasta the population is spoken of as rich farmers *habtam* and poor farmers, *deha* and the completely poor *mulatch deha*. According to the general opinion of interviewees a rich farmer has at least one ox, a few sheep, goats and donkeys and at least enough grain to feed his family. In the *deha* category a farmer has lost his ox and possibly his other domestic animals, he has no seeds and little grain. He supports himself and his family not from his produce but by other means; he may work for *habtam* to get some grain, he may get money by *arata*, a loan at 50 per cent interest, he may give land away *woledaged* in order to get money and buy grain, he may sell firewood or go to distant places and work.

Some farmers by these means manage to acquire seed; they plough their land manually with hoes. Others may work for *habtam* and thus acquire the loan of the *habtam*'s oxen to plough their own land. Thus some impoverished farmers have rehabilitated themselves. However, many of those who successfully harvest a crop despite *degeza* or *deyri* are then obliged to pay their debts which may be substantial. Their harvest is often not enough to repay debts and see them through to the next harvest. New debts have to be incurred and many farmers are drawn into a vicious circle.

The third category is uprooted and has lost all hope and means of self-rehabilitation. Some have migrated or drifted to the shelters. Some are labourers, servants etc whose only pay is food and lodging. This type is generally excluded from all lists of needy people drawn up by rehabilitation agencies such as EPID [Extension and Project Implementation Department of the Ministry of Agriculture]. No reliable figures could be found for these categories. The *awraja* office has a list of 7,208 impoverished farmers (*deha* and *mulatch deha*) from two of the three Lasta *woreda*. It has no list for the third which is said to be equally affected. The means of registration are highly disputed by all. . . . Some seeds have been distributed by EPID but the screening process was inefficient and there were many complaints about who had benefited from this distribution.

The local administration is archaic, corrupt and highly inefficient. It has been intent upon keeping farmers ignorant of their rights and what is due to them from modern administration. Now *tschikashums* [village headmen] appear to have lost the confidence of their fellow villagers because they have been seen to side with those who have. They appear to have lost some traditional privileges e.g. farmers used to till their land, bring them food and drink from feasts etc. This no longer seems to happen. The administrative machinery, as it stands, seems to perpetuate the famine rather than alleviating it. Farmers are aware of this but remain helpless; in an area where there are no roads, newspapers or radios farmers cannot see alternatives clearly.

The greatest number of deaths came during the rainy season because of the debilitated state of the population and its susceptibility to diseases aggravated by rain — pneumonia, TB, malaria, dysentery. As with the situation in 1984 the critical stage had been reached before any large-scale concerted action to prevent deaths had been taken. As can be seen from the above description agricultural conditions are difficult at all times; inadequate rainfall over several seasons was the immediate cause of the drought but additional factors contributed to the final catastrophe.

Aggravating factors

Socio-cultural factors: Despite a history of peasant rebellions there was, in general, a fatalistic acceptance by peasants of authority; they adjusted to their increasing impoverishment and, never having received aid, did not expect it. Deference and obedience to authority were accepted values; peasants looked to traditional authority figures, both ecclesiastical and political, to define appropriate responses to new situations. If such authorities were to delegate responsibilities it would be regarded as a diminution of their status; to take the initiative was not a peasant's role.

There is even much evidence to suggest that where peasant revolts had occurred they were usually transformed by the local aristocracy into a defence of local interests against centralising encroachments by the Emperor. Peasants would generally consider it a victory for themselves if the interests of the local aristocracy prevailed, believing that any change in the provincial order could threaten their own land rights. The vertical nature of social relationships plus the strength of the provincialism prevented the development of what might be called a peasant-class solidarity.

The authorities from Haile Selassie and the Orthodox Church Establishment downwards did not, in general, appear to see a need for intervention. Haile Selassie had publicly expressed his belief in the maintenance of the status quo and, for example, the role of beggars in society. Local authorities and richer farmers who might have been in a position to agitate for increased aid from the central government or to have provided assistance in the affected areas, are said to have done little or nothing in order to keep some peasants dependent on them. Peasants borrowed money or grain at 50 per cent interest, or released land to them for money or grain. Many peasants became landless and it is doubtful that a special decree in early 1974 to return land to peasants who had been forced to give it up during the famine had its full effect. Landless and destitute peasants were a source of very cheap labour.

It could be added that the peasants' fatalism extended beyond the acceptance of worldly authority. The conservatism, if not inertia, of the Ethiopian peasant has baffled many observers who have failed to understand why peasants resist new methods or ideas even when it appeared clear to the observer that peasant life could be improved. But peasants feel that innovation is ineffectual — they have always been discouraged from making determined efforts to change their environment because they feel that whatever happens it is God's will that really determines events.

The notion that 'satisfaction' — an individual's freedom to behave as he wishes, eat as much as he likes unconstrained by any relationship — was undesirable, pervaded traditional society and was central to the Ethiopian orthodox faith. Fasting was, and is, almost the foremost symbol of adherence, the means by which God constrains sinful human nature, keeps believers up to the mark and prevents the 'satisfaction' that would tempt the faithful to take more than they were entitled to. Famine was seen by many as a punishment inflicted by God because of man's sinful nature. There was therefore no remedy except repentance and prayer. During the famine of 1888–92 the Emperor Menelik publicly led the prayers; in 1974 local government officials are reported to have replied to requests for assistance after crop failures by reminding the petitioners to pray. The idea that God was still punishing the Ethiopians for their sins was by no means unheard of in 1984. Indeed, there were some who believed that persistent political ineptitude was among the major sins. This is not to suggest that prayer has no place, but to demonstrate that the peasants' perception of famine as an act of God had tended to exonerate, for them, the political system.

Administrative factors: In addition to exploitation there was substantial evidence of maladministration. Reports from three separate *awrajas* in Wollo (Lasta, Wadla Delanat and Zobel) confirmed that the *tschikashums* were reluctant to disclose the famine. They were traditional officials who had no government salary but made their living from taxes which they were responsible for collecting. They believed that if they reported the extent of the famine to their superiors their *awrajas* might be exempted from taxation; their incomes would then be depleted or come from outside and be delayed. At one stage *tschikashums* had been directed to collect a special tax from farmers for development purposes. There was general dissatisfaction on the part of the farmers as to where this money had gone; one case was brought against a former *awraja* leader in 1975 for embezzling E$43,000 in this manner. When various attempts were made to distribute grain, clothing and other necessities, local authorities consistently took what they wanted for themselves and/or distributed to those they favoured. They charged money for registering impoverished farmers and were generally uncooperative.

At the national level there was almost total failure to take action until the most critical months of 1973 had passed, even though in September 1971 officials in Dessie, the administrative centre of Wollo province had informed the Ministry of Interior in Addis Ababa of the crisis. Haile Selassie was still held responsible for all major decisions; no one would accept responsibility until there was official acknowledgement of the need for action. Apart from inertia and the more pervasive inability of government ministers and civil servants to take decisions the main reasons for this high level refusal to acknowledge the seriousness of the situation were political. Ethiopia had an international reputation for stability and progressiveness and a position to uphold as host to the OAU. In addition, Ethiopia's tourist industry was becoming successfully established, ironically under such apt promotion slogans as 'The Hidden Empire' and 'Thirteen Months of Sunshine'.

Harsher accusations were later levelled at the authorities amounting to charges of conspiring to allow widespread deaths, particularly among the Afars who were 'difficult' — independent and determined to avoid taxation. Two special courts were set up in November 1974 after the completion of a report by the Commission of Inquiry into Corruption, as part of its investigation into the Wollo famine. The Commission indicted 35 people, some for failing to discharge their personal responsibilities adequately and others for collective responsibility for the famine. It was not possible for any of them to plead ignorance; although Addis Ababa continued to function adequately, with the majority of people maintaining their standard of living, there was constant traffic on the main north–south highway linking Addis Ababa with the towns of Wollo, Tigray and Eritrea. Daily buses passed the *ad hoc* relief shelters in existence at points on this road after December 1972.

In April–May 1973, that is, before the months of highest mortality, staff members of the Haile Selassie I University took photographs in Wollo on a private visit. As a consequence E$80,000 was raised by staff members giving 10 per cent of their salaries in May and June and the students giving up their breakfasts. Efforts were also made by Parliamentary representatives to draw attention to the plight of their constituencies. The presiding chairman in Parliament refused to discuss the issue on two occasions and the Wollo representatives' evidence was dismissed as a pack of lies. Details of the rejection of evidence were later fully recorded in the Commission of Inquiry's report. Details of the Wollo famine are fully recorded in this authoritative document which is still unpublished.

Weaknesses of existing agencies: Despite official refusal to recognise the impending disaster a number of government bodies and national agencies were unable to ignore the problem but their attempts to organise relief were inadequate because their existing resources were so limited and infrastructure so minimal. Without publicity and official mobilisation they had no hope of containing the problem.

1) The Ethiopian Red Cross was first in the field in December 1972 and provided eight shelters in the north and others in the south with some relief provision, medicines and blankets. About 150 Ethiopians and eventually 70 expatriates were engaged. Thousands died in these main road shelters.

2) Ministry of National Community Development and Social Affairs was the only government body which attempted to organise relief, setting up 13 *ad hoc* shelters.

3) Ministry of Agriculture, EPID — Extension and Project Implementation Department — had a network of extension centres and had no excuse for not monitoring the impact of the successive poor harvests. Its attempts at rehabilitation schemes tended to be misconceived, at one stage, for example, it gave loans for oxen where none were available for purchase. It screened farmers for seed but its processes were considered inept, relying on information from local *tschikashums*. Many needy farmers rejected the loans, seed, etc because they knew they would never have the chance of repaying. EPID suffered from lack of transport for the distribution of the necessary inputs and often distributed money where no relevant commodities such as grain and food were available. No one should have been surprised when recipients purchased umbrellas.

4) Office for the Rehabilitation of Children began the Childrens' Rehabilitation Programme in Wollo in April 1973 to help destitute children. It was then part of the Haile Selassie I Foundation. Temporary shelters were established at Dessie and Kombolcha. (Later when alternative funding was provided from abroad various centres providing vocational training were set up. Reunification with the extended family was always a stated priority and case histories of children were built up to facilitate this but some aspects of the programme were criticised for increasing the difficulties of children orphaned during the famine.)

The international response: before September 1973

Before official acknowledgement of the drought the international community could respond only in a piecemeal fashion through missions, international organisations such as UNICEF, and non-governmental organisations (NGOs), such as Oxfam and Save the Children Fund, which had permanent field staff in Ethiopia. It has been said that some of these organisations were threatened with the expulsion of their entire staff if they generated much publicity. There are several examples of relief aid being spontaneously provided by non-governmental Ethiopian bodies and expatriate groups when confronted with the famine. 'Nomadaid', for example, was set up in mid-1973 on the initiative of the Awash Valley Authority, an autonomous public authority set up to control the planning and development of the valley, and FAO and WHO personnel connected with the AVA. They were aware of the drought early and began small scale grain distributions in June 1973. Money was raised through the Mennonite Mission, UNDP and private farmers operating in the mid-Awash Valley. During 1974 their operations extended and they became the main organisers of relief in the area, reaching a total of 36,890 people.

In May 1973 the Christian Relief Committee (later renamed the Christian Relief and Development Association or CRDA) was formed to coordinate famine relief projects and channel aid from foreign donors to agencies working in the drought-affected areas. The originators of this body, which developed into the major coordinating organisation, were the Catholic Secretariat, the Seventh Day Adventists and the Lutherans. The Ethiopian Lutheran church, known as the

Evangelical Church Mekane Yesus (ECMY), was a major Protestant church in the country with a high profile and enlightened attitude in contrast to the established Orthodox Church. (By December 1974 ECMY had raised E\$9,000,000 from within Ethiopia, Germany and Sweden.) These church groups had a network of missions throughout the country and could not ignore what their workers witnessed in these rural areas. They provided relief teams from abroad and individuals such as Father Kevin Doheny, who took it upon themselves to coordinate such relief activities as there were. Gradually, as more NGOs became involved, the weekly meetings were attended by more and more representatives of groups organising their own activities. Between May 1973 and August 1974 the CRDA distributed E\$1.05 million to 17 member organisations already existing in Ethiopia at that time.

International response: after September 1973

The situation changed as a result of the dramatic media coverage of the famine in Europe and North America which discredited the Ethiopian government's 'cover-up' and prompted an immediate flow of funds. Jonathan Dimbleby's documentary film, 'The Unknown Famine', shown on BBC television and elsewhere had a startling impact. For example C\$7,000,000 were raised by Oxfam–Quebec in two weeks after a broadcast. Other journalists, some following up this film, opened up the situation. In particular *Stern* magazine published horrifying photographs of famine victims and launched its own appeal which raised E\$15 million. This funded a German relief operation which included a medical team and road-building operations.

The impact was relayed to Ethiopia as the BBC World Service, Radio Deutschvelle broadcasting in Amharic and the local Lutheran broadcasting station, 'Voice of the Gospel', also broadcasting in Amharic, described the stark situation for the first time. Ethiopian students studying abroad responded to the foreign media coverage by remitting funds and alerting their families. From this point on, relief in the form of grain, medicines, vehicles, cash and personnel flowed into Ethiopia from all over the world through three main channels;

1) Foreign governments: the USA, the USSR, Canada, the UK, Switzerland, Sweden, and other EEC countries, particularly West Germany, gave emergency aid and initiated a variety of road-building, health and agricultural projects.

2) International agencies: UNICEF and UNDP already operating in the country now stepped up their programmes. The World Bank provided a loan of \$10 million in 1974 for rehabilitation projects.

3) Voluntary agencies: many churches and charities launched appeals and channelled funds and materials through a variety of NGOs.

Coordination within Ethiopia

Although the most critical time (i.e. that of highest mortality) was now over, the situation in the existing shelters along the north–south highway was still appalling and the relief supplies now arriving were put to immediate use, but government inaction remained scandalous. Donors complained of bottle-necks building up at each point, outside the ports of Massawa and Assab, on the dockside, at the railheads and in main road towns. Coordination was extremely poor and no government agency was detailed to control relief operations. The government agencies whose functions covered drought relief activities have been mentioned above but the only agency attempting to organise relief on a larger scale was the Ministry of National Community Development and Social Affairs where a Drought Relief Operations Coordination Office was set up.

In early 1974, after growing pressure within Ethiopia itself in the press and on radio, and against a background of the 'Creeping Coup', the Central Office for Relief Organisation was moved to the Prime Minister's office. There was now widespread rebellion within the armed forces and growing public unrest; on 27 February the entire cabinet resigned, On 1 March, Lij Endalkatchew Makonnen, a member of the Shoan aristocracy, was appointed as the new Prime Minister in an attempt to avert even more public disorder. One of his first actions was the appointment, generally regarded in the ensuing months to be a shrewd and appropriate one, of a Relief Commissioner, Ato Shimelis Adugna.

The organisation of the Central Office gained momentum, more competent appointments and secondments were made, including that of a logistics officer, and the growing organisation was once again moved to the Duke of Harar Hospital. Monthly meetings were inaugurated attended by representatives of agencies and embassies. The Central Office did not replace the Christian Relief Committee but once its commitment was demonstrated all grain, transport and medicine were channelled through it. Between March and December 1974 it distributed 112,106 tonnes of grain, built 61 warehouses, requisitioned or was given 195 trucks and landrovers and two water tankers at a total cost of E$12.4 million. There is no doubt that action by the Central Office in Sidamo between April and August 1974 averted a major disaster; the government was so anxious to avoid the tragedy of Wollo that its response was adequate (together with that of other agencies).

A similar operation took place in the Ogaden region of Bale and Harraghe provinces, though the record in Eritrea was different. In August 1974 the Relief and Rehabilitation Commission (RRC) was officially established by a government order which defined the scope of its activities, powers and duties, composition and budget.

The development of the RRC solved some problems; it at least gave foreign agencies a point of contact, and machinery was evolved to meet some of the problems raised by the drought. Many problems, both immediate and long-term, remained, whilst the perennial problems, the unsatisfactory nature of the norm, had merely been highlighted.

The most pressing problem, both immediately and as a constraint on all programmes, was communications which were handicapped by lack of:

1) roads and airstrips; there were only two roads for transporting grain to distribution points; Massawa to Asmara and south, Assab to Kombolcha; one railway from Djibouti–Addis Ababa. There were very few feeder roads despite the proliferation of road building projects;
2) adequate handling facilities leading to bottlenecks and delays;

3) suitable vehicles; 4) drivers; 5) petrol; and

6) cost of petrol — in some cases the transportation costs of a tonne of grain were three or four times the cost of purchase.

Corruption remained serious at some levels; reportedly relief grain was re-exported. Most attempts at rehabilitation involved some form of screening procedure for the distribution of grain, seeds, oxen, tools etc. This remained difficult, especially for expatriates, because many of those in positions of local authority on whom it was still necessary to rely were unreliable.

Information was inadequate and often conflicting. Reporting and monitoring techniques could not be developed overnight especially as effort needed to be devoted to immediate need and estimates of future needs tended to vary. In December 1974 three different estimates were given of Ethiopia's grain requirements for 1975, ranging from 60,000 tonnes to 278,000 tonnes. The fact that at the time only 5,000 tonnes had been committed reflects the rapid shift of interest and concern away from Ethiopia once the immediate crisis passed. Discrepancies in information characterised foreign as well as Ethiopian sources. CRC meetings could become extremely heated as representatives of NGOs (almost 100 per cent expatriate) argued over their interpretation of conditions and needs in areas they all claimed to have visited recently.

There was confusion over priorities and approaches. Despite the influx of funds the financial and manpower resources of all executing agencies were limited. As the need for pure relief passed most agencies moved into some degree of rehabilitation. Usually the local situation suggested obvious and immediate measures which the field team could recommend and implement without recourse to any particular criteria which might have been invoked at a less critical period. It had been discovered that lives could be saved surprisingly easily but the subsistence farmers still had no food, no seed, no oxen, no money and in many cases no land. Hence the problems of immediate rehabiliation were complex. The government's response mechanisms had been inadequate in dealing with the initial crisis. In the absence of fully-developed institutions it was, perhaps, equally difficult to deal with the post-crisis atmosphere of responsiveness.

Ethiopia's relationship with aid donors had broadened and intensified but the new level of commitment was difficult to maintain in the uncertain political atmosphere which followed the overthrow of Haile Selassie. Many development programmes continued: the areas in which work was needed — water control and conservation, agricultural development, forestry, livestock, communications, human and natural resources — were easily recognisable. The need for contingency plans to prevent a recurrence of the famine was recognised as a priority. The framework within which the implementation of such plans might be pursued was, however, shifting, as the Provisional Military Administrative Council (PMAC) established itself and initiated its Land Reform programme. In the aftermath of the drought, when there was a readiness among donors to provide resources and a readiness among the affected communities to accept innovations, conditions were favourable for an acceleration of the development process. For a variety of reasons many opportunities were lost.

4.   The Fall of the Emperor and Emergence of the Provisional Council

Before the Second World War the Ethiopian state organisation was small and decentralised, quite different from the apparatus that had developed under colonial administrations elsewhere in Africa. At the centre were the Emperor and various institutions associated with him, including the all-purpose Ministry of the Pen, the hub of the executive system. In the provinces power lay with the landowning nobility and lesser landowners. More centralised structures developed gradually after the Second World War and a permanent army was established. The growing bureaucracy remained under the control of the emperor. An 'elected' National Assembly was set up in 1955 but not even an official state political party existed. Nevertheless, there was substantial opposition, especially among the provincial nobility, non-Amhara groups, students, the armed forces and sections of the urban population.

Opposition to the monarchy

Sections of the nobility had never accepted the Shoan monarchy's domination. They had supported the Italian invasion but more recently had actively resisted agrarian reform and taxation, especially in Gojjam. In 1974, as opposition to Haile Selassie coalesced, members of the aristocracy were ready to take advantage of his weakness to reassert their power but, like the Emperor, they also misinterpreted the nature of the growing movement now challenging the monarchy. They jostled to seize political opportunities, not realising that the positions they coveted belonged to a system on the point of collapse.

Opposition from non-Amhara nationalities and other ethnic groups was the most evident form of political resistance. This was most effectively organised in Eritrea where regional and democratic rights gained prior to its reincorporation into Ethiopia in 1952 were abrogated. Underground movements developed, first the Eritrean Liberation movement and then in 1960 the Eritrean Liberation Front (ELF). Armed resistance by the ELF began in 1961 and by the late 1960s a large section of Haile Selassie's army was permanently occupied in dealing with their incursions. By 1974, however, Eritrean opposition was much weaker; ELF split in 1970 and a civil war developed between the ELF and the Eritrean People's Liberation Front (EPLF). In 1972 Haile Selassie had reached an agreement with President Numeiry of the Sudan under which the Sudanese–Eritrean border was closed.

In 1960, the year Somalia gained its independence, a small Western Somalia Liberation Front (WSLF) was established in Mogadishu by activists among the

Somalis of Haraghe, which had been under separate British administration from 1941 to 1955. Their sense of separate identity was reinforced by the granting of independence to Somalia.

A more active resistance was also growing among the Oromo people of Bale and Arussi provinces who were progressively deprived of their land by Amhara settlers. A substantial armed revolt by small scale Oromo landowners persisted from 1963 to 1970 with assistance from the WSLF. In 1969 the Somali government imprisoned the WSLF leadership and in 1970 the Bale revolt wavered when its leader was imprisoned. The Bale rebels then broke away to form a new Ethiopian National Liberation Front which aimed to unite all oppressed nationalities in a common movement with a revolutionary socialist programme. This movement was unable to maintain a high level of military operations but was symptomatic of the growing self-awareness amongst the whole Oromo population, especially those resident in Addis Ababa as students or state employees.

The most obvious opposition in Addis Ababa itself came from the students in higher and secondary education. The expansion of the state machinery (the civil service grew from around 35,000 in 1960 to an estimated 100,000 in 1973) necessitated an expansion in education. The record of Haile Selassie's regime in this, as in other respects, was lamentable. In the early 1970s 90–95 per cent of the population remained illiterate and only 8 per cent of those eligible attended primary school. Nevertheless, the little increase in education there was produced a new and influential social category to challenge the aristocrats and landowners who had until then monopolised influence within the state. The new state officials were drawn from the secondary schools (total enrolment in 1970 was 70,000) and the Haile Selassie I University in Addis Ababa (6,000 students in 1974 plus a further 2,000 abroad). Nearly all those educated went into state employment including the armed forces; many of the best secondary school graduates were drafted into the military academy in Harar. By the time of the 1974 revolution there were an estimated 20,000 secondary school graduates in the army and civil service; 4,500 university graduates in all, 3,000 educated in Ethiopia. This number may seem small in absolute terms but in relative terms it was substantial and its effect in undermining Ethiopia's archaic systems should not be underestimated.

The most underprivileged classes in rural and urban areas had little or no access to education but those entering the ministries and armed forces represented a wider section of the population than the traditional nobility. In particular, a substantial number of Oromos had entered the armed forces.

The first signs of student radicalism were in 1960 when sympathy with the abortive military coup was expressed. Student demonstrations in support of land reform followed in 1965. Confrontations continued almost annually and students were killed by police in 1969 and 1971. Agitation for land reform continued and in 1973 students were killed whilst trying to organise provincial protest against the handling of the famine. The radicalisation of the student body was connected to the radicalisation of students abroad in the Ethiopian Students Union in Europe (ESUE) and the Ethiopian Students Union in North America (ESUNA). By the late 1960s the whole movement was generally socialist and strongly influenced by the radical political atmosphere of student politics in Europe and America at that time.

It is easy to underestimate the importance of this student influence but in the absence of any long-established political groupings (particularly socialist) radicalised student groups, closely linked to the emerging civilian political groupings, were vital to the success of the revolution in their interaction with the military and largely responsible for its initial political direction. Because these groupings of the late 1960s were heavily influenced by certain radical political trends prevalent in Europe and North America — the period of anti-Vietnam protest and student riots in much of Europe — a large section of the left lacked any spontaneous, indigenous base. It operated through student activism, resorting to rhetoric and demagogy on the current Western model, claiming to speak for the oppressed but in fact detached from the broader social classes, urban or rural. Because of the speed with which the revolution took place, and the role of the PMAC, any opportunities for interaction between the student activists of the left and other social or political groupings which might have exercised moderating control and guidance were missed. There seems to have been no attempt to combine the socialist intellectual commitment which became commonplace, complete with wholesale lifting of Marxist phraseology by all groups, with any appreciation of specific features of Ethiopian society and political traditions. We may have been spared the thoughts of Chairman Mengistu but the failure of any of the student/civilian forces which contributed to the political tone of the revolution to qualify socialist doctrine in the manner of Tanzania, Ghana, or Zambia, or to devise a 'third' way, left the door open for the hardline, bureaucratic approach.

A split formed in the student movement abroad that was to continue to divide the two main civilian groups which developed as protagonists of the PMAC. The question of nationalities was the main issue dividing the factions; the older generation of students, later emerging as the All-Ethiopian Socialist Movement ME'ISON, arguing that the primary struggle in Ethiopia was anti-feudal and anti-imperialistic and that the question of the rights of nationalities should be solved within that wider context, whilst the younger generation of students, many of whom were of Eritrean or Tigrean origin, stressed the need for national self-determination.

It is important to realise that at the time of the revolution the military was not simply a repressive arm of the state apparatus privileged by its links with the throne. It was part of the very small section of Ethiopian society located in the towns but susceptible to pressure from the countryside and also exposed, through training overseas, to the outside world. Many of the lower and middle ranks had rural backgrounds and were aware of the deteriorating agrarian situation. By 1974, over 3,000 officers had trained in the USA, including Mengistu Haile Mariam. Acute differentials in pay and rank bred resentment among junior officers and NCOs against the dominant aristocratic hierarchy. There was apparently no definite conspiratorial group as there had been in 1960, and the initial involvement of the armed forces in the events leading to the revolution and deposition of Haile Selassie was not part of a coordinated attempt to mount a coup and depose the monarch or even impose reform. The same disquiet at the unresponsiveness of Haile Selassie's regime affecting other sections of the community was, however, present within the armed forces.

Sections of the urban population had begun to organise themselves, notably the Ethiopian Teachers Association and the Confederation of Ethiopian Labour Unions. This was by no means a militant organisation nor was it a substitute for a political party. Most of its members were white-collar workers and it operated under the supervision of the Ministry of Labour. Its concerns were mainly those of direct interest to its members and did not spill over into more general demands for reform in other sectors. Nevertheless, the fact that it had been created after the 1960 coup as one of a number of measures designed to pre-empt further pressure for change is indicative of the growing awareness within the modern sector of the limitations of the regime.

The Creeping Coup

With hindsight one can see that Haile Selassie's monarchy had outlived its time. To some extent external assistance had granted a stay of execution allowing the social and economic forces maturing beneath the surface to be ignored by the government. Two-thirds of Ethiopia's capital expenditure was financed by foreign sources in the last decade of imperial rule, detaching the state from any social or economic base. The regime was neither willing nor able to mobilise the rural surplus for economic growth; rural output stagnated, there was the growing threat of famine, substantial migration of marginalised peasants and a fall in rural tax revenue. Yet no serious reforms to generate domestic income were undertaken, the availability of US support in an era of great power rivalry being an easier option.

In Ethiopia, there was no class to play the social or political role of the bourgeoisie; the small mercantile class was mostly composed of foreign merchants. Thus, any modernising pressures brought about through the impact of external capital were not absorbed by an expanding entrepreneurial class but largely by the expanding state bureaucracy, the civil servants, teachers, students and army officers. These groups, none of whom constituted a coherent political organisation with a programme — let alone a revolutionary manifesto — prior to 1974, nevertheless pushed through a social and political upheaval that can only be termed revolutionary.

Others have detailed the events precipitating Haile Selassie's gradual deposition. The immediate, as opposed to the underlying, long-term structural causes of the revolution were the grievances of certain sections of the armed forces, of students, including high-school students, of teachers objecting to a proposed educational reform, and taxi drivers protesting at a 50 per cent rise in petrol prices following the OPEC price increases. Within a month of the initial mutinies over pay, in January 1974, other military units were joining the protests with political demands including the dismissal of the cabinet. A general strike followed in March with the emergence of the Confederation of Ethiopian Labour Unions (CELU) as an opposition force. Corruption became an issue as the armed forces demanded the arrest and prosecution of certain members of the imperial regime.

The armed forces were granted pay rises, the proposed educational reform was postponed, a commission was set up to investigate corruption. There appeared to be comparative calm when on 28 June 1974 a new body, the Coordinating

Committee of the Armed Forces, Territorial Army and Police, formed by junior officers of the 2nd and 4th Divisions, held its first meeting. The 126 members of the *Derg* — the Amharic word for the concept of a committee of equals — were elected by each of the 40 units in the armed forces or chosen to attend by higher ranking officers, each was below the rank of Lieutenant-Colonel. Mengistu Haile Mariam, a young ordnance officer from the 3rd Division, apparently gave a fiery speech. 'It was a classic case of a body elected in a highly democratic, even haphazard manner becoming a permanent and irrevocable self-perpetuating group.' (Fred Halliday and Maxine Molyneux, *The Ethiopian Revolution.* p. 87).

The Derg's initial programme was not socialist; it took for its motto 'Etiopia Tikdem', roughly translated 'Ethiopia First,' a phrase that had first been used by the *Ethiopian Herald*, the English-language newspaper, in February, and pledged loyalty to the Commander-in-Chief, the Emperor. Clearly, however, this pledge was conditional on its other objectives being carried out. The Derg's 13 point charter concluded, 'The Coordinating Committee believes that this military movement will achieve lasting changes without bloodshed. The culture and history of Ethiopia is unique, so is the nature and course of this military movement.' No doubt many members of the committee had full belief in their continuing support for Haile Selassie once his status was changed to that of constitutional monarch, and public pronouncements temporarily gave the impression that the military saw themselves as the midwives of a new era of reformed civilian government.

By August, however, it was clear that the more radical architects of change among the original members of the Derg were gaining ground. Through a shrewd and systematic propaganda initiative aimed at isolating and discrediting Haile Selassie, they successfully prepared the way for his final deposition on 12 September. The nature of the regime was still obscure, partially because its spokesman was still General Aman Andom, a hero of the 1964 Somali war, who possessed anti-imperialistic credentials. His refusal to agree to the execution of a number of ministers and officials of Haile Selassie's government, generals and aristocrats then in detention, and his conciliatory attitude towards Eritrea led to his murder in November. Shortly afterwards 59 detainees, almost an entire generation of leaders, were shot without trial. A month later the Provisional Military Administrative Council, which had assumed full governmental powers after the deposition of Haile Selassie, issued a policy proclamation in which it introduced the concept of Ethiopian Socialism, meaning 'equality, self-reliance, the dignity of labour, the supremacy of the common good and the indivisibility of Ethiopian unity.'

5.   The PMAC: Institutionalisation and Development

A political revolution had undoubtedly occurred; an imperial regime had been overthrown, many aristocrats had been killed, imprisoned or displaced. The extent of political change in the countryside was negligible but in some areas peasants had occupied the lands of Amhara noblemen and there was an extraordinary change in the country's political climate. During this crucial period the small educated class, strategically placed in the structure of the State, took upon itself the revolutionary aspirations of the underprivileged classes of the old system. By becoming the opposition it paralysed the administrative and repressive apparatus of that system and prevented retaliation. A social revolution was still far off, however, although virtually all political dialogue now took place on the assumption that a rapid transition to socialism must be effected. At the same time there was a sense of disbelief that the historic empire had crumbled with so little resistance. Counter-measures were expected at any moment and a number of radical measures were rapidly introduced in order to destroy the social and economic power of those who might support attempts to reinstate some version of the old regime.

Internal Policies

Early in 1975 the PMAC announced their first measures of expropriation, nationalisation, imposition of state controls and land reform. A measure of mass mobilisation was also involved; peasant associations were to be established to administer the land reform, 60,000 students were sent to the countryside to improve the peasants' living conditions, literacy and political awareness. In the urban areas all nationalised land and expropriated property was to be administered by neighbourhood bodies known as *kebeles*. As was quickly realised, to be effective such mass organisations needed careful handling, but without taking measures to meet the expectations of the urban and rural poor, the PMAC could not have survived.

The PMAC was also under pressure from political parties. At certain stages in its revolutionary programme it sought to establish alliances with the various radical civilian groups, putting into practice much of what they advocated, but no stable relationship proved possible. Paradoxically, the revolutionary transformation involved both the implementation of radical social reforms and the destruction of those groups — the radical intelligentsia and the urban working class — committed to those reforms. Within the Derg itself a battle was being waged between ideological factions; classical Marxist theory was circumvented and replaced with a more Leninist theory allowing the Ethiopian revolution to be effected from above by a vanguard of junior officers from whom eventually Mengistu emerged as leader.

Within a short time the PMAC had presented itself as a radical regime but its initial measures were announced with little preparation. There was considerable opposition from left and right and the PMAC lacked the personnel and infrastructure to administer its measures in either an authoritarian or a democratic manner. The theoretical framework was made somewhat clearer in April 1976 when the text of a new programme, the National Democratic Revolution, was published. As with earlier measures the comprehensive implementation of both the economic and political provisions of the programme were delayed.

In the first place, the PMAC became locked in bitter conflict with the civilian political groups. It clashed with the *zemecha* students in 1975 (all students were despatched to the country-side to participate in campaigns to improve rural conditions), with the Ethiopian People's Revolutionary Party (EPRP) and CELU in 1975–76, and later with ME'ISON and other parties. Democratic decision-making within the Derg had been undermined as power shifted to the hard core of Marxists including Mengistu. He began to consolidate his power and eliminate his opponents within the PMAC and outside. Within the Derg the main disputes centred on how to relate to the civilian opposition forces, and the handling of the Eritrean issue. From July 1975 till September 1976 over 100 members of the Derg and military officials who worked along with it were executed; by early 1977 as few as 20 had survived the purges. The climax came in February 1977 when Mengistu and his supporters shot seven of the remaining leading members, including PMAC Chairman Teferi Banti and others who had been attempting to restrict the power of Mengistu and Atnafu Abate and effect some reconciliation with the EPRP. In November 1977 Atnafu Abate was executed after publicly criticising the use of terror.

The EPRP, which maintained that a Marxist revolution could not be directed by the military but must take place during a period of multi-party democracy, was largely made up of the better-educated middle classes. It had been advocating a programme to which the Derg itself was largely committed, but in September 1976 it made the mistake of launching an assassination campaign against PMAC supporters, particularly *kebele* officials, leaders of the All-Ethiopian Trade Union, a body established to replace CELU in 1976, and political instructors at the ideological training school, (*Yekatit 66* or February 1974). Mengistu responded with a campaign of 'red terror' which for a year took its toll of EPRP members, and many other civilians and students with left-wing tendencies. Amnesty International estimated 30,000 were imprisoned and several thousand killed; some Ethiopians put the figure killed higher.

Secondly, for most of 1977 and early 1978 the PMAC was preoccupied with wars in Eritrea and the Ogaden, which threatened not only its survival as a regime but also the territorial unity of Ethiopia.

Thus the upheaval of the revolution, the internal conflict and the inadequate administrative capacity of the new government meant that no coherent economic policy was implemented in this period. External factors, such as the fall in the world coffee price, contributed to economic decline. In 1978 Mengistu returned from a tour of the southern provinces apparently appalled by what he had seen: the

109

mismanagement of agriculture, peasant resistance to state controls, the lack of official initiatives. A National Revolutionary Economic Development Campaign was launched for 1978–79 and another for 1979–80. In 1980 a much more ambitious 10-year plan was announced. It can be seen that political consolidation was being achieved at great cost. The reforms carried out largely benefited the classes from which the military leaders came. Land reform (see below) strengthened the position of the richer peasants. Provincial power-holders were swept from office, their places gradually being taken by nominees from the centre. A stronger state was evolving with a new system of mobilisation and communication being established, not through ethnic particularism or hereditary position but through political loyalty to the regime in general and the Chairman in particular. Authoritarian and bureaucratic this may be but it has incorporated large numbers of people into the system: over eleven million in peasant associations, half-a-million in the Trade Unions, several million in the Womens' Associations and several hundred thousand in the militia. To some extent the prospect of social and economic development facilitated the mobilisation of such numbers yet, by any criteria, economic progress under the PMAC has been slow.

External relations

Parallel with and relevant to developments within the PMAC and its relations with influential groups within Ethiopia was the improvement of its relations with the USSR. Haile Selassie had been the first African head of state to visit Moscow in 1959; the USSR provided loans to Ethiopia and was involved in the training of Ethiopian personnel. During the 1960s it built the country's only oil refinery at Assab. Any early hopes that Haile Selassie might take up a non-aligned position were disappointed however, and the Russians developed their alliances with Egypt, the Sudan (until 1971) and Somalia, Ethiopia's traditional enemies. They appeared to back Somalia as a strategic counterweight to pro-American Ethiopia and later backed what they saw as progressive developments within the state. Nevertheless, the USSR did not support opposition to Haile Selassie's regime; there was no communist party or pro-Soviet group prior to the revolution. The Russians neither endorse nor actively support the Eritrean movement despite voting against the UN proposal to set up the federation in 1952.

Soviet response to the PMAC was cautious, and the first requests for Soviet military support were rejected, assistance being limited to economic aid and the provision of short courses in the USSR for selected Derg members. The character of the new regime was by no means clear as yet, and the USSR was justifiably suspicious of military regimes which, relatively recently, had repressed left-wing elements in Sudan, Egypt and Indonesia. In addition, the Derg still maintained relations with the USA and Israel. Although the reforms appeared radical, the reckless manner of their implementation appeared to increase the new regime's instability.

After the proclamation of Land Reform in March 1975 *Pravda* warned of the need to go slowly, 'There is still an enormous amount of explanatory and upbringing work to do among the workers, particularly the peasants who must be drawn into administrative and economic activities.' (*Pravda*, 29 March 1975, quoted in Halliday and Molyneux, p. 243.) Again, in May 1976, though welcoming the National Democratic Revolution *Pravda* was cautious: '. . . about 90 per cent of the population live in villages. The great majority of the people are illiterate. The country's per capita income is very low and religious prejudices are still strong. All this demands a careful and realistic appraisal by the authorities . . .' (*Pravda*, 16 May 1975. Quoted in Halliday and Molyneux, p. 243.) The Russians did not wish at that time to antagonise the Somalis and signed a major arms deal with them in 1975.

Relations between the USSR and Ethiopia were seen to improve considerably during 1975 and 1976 and the Ethiopian delegation to Moscow in July 1976 signed the first agreement on Russian military supplies. Delivery was delayed, however, until Moscow was more certain of the Derg's direction. Only with the final emergency of Mengistu as the single leader in February 1977 and the termination of relations with Israel and the USA were the USSR's final reservations overcome. Egypt and Sudan had expelled their last Russian advisers and Somalia was in the process of establishing links with the conservative Arab states.

Both the USSR and Cuba attempted at this time to reconcile Somalia and Ethiopia over the issue of the Ogaden (Somalia's claim to which the USSR had never supported). Missions by both Castro and Podgorny failed to persuade Siad Barre to accept anything less than a transfer of the Ogaden to Somalia. In July the Somali army entered the Ethiopian Ogaden. In November 1977 Somalia expelled all Soviet and Cuban advisers and broke off relations with Cuba. Thirteen days later the USSR began the biggest air-lift of military equipment to any Third World country. In January 1978 Ethiopian and Cuban troops mounted a counter-offensive and by March the Somali forces had withdrawn. It was this war that put the seal on the new relationship between Moscow and Addis Ababa and led to an estimated $1.5 billion worth of military equipment being supplied to Ethiopia between 1977 and 1983. An economic aid agreement and a Twenty-Year Friendship and Cooperation Treaty were signed.

Despite these ties the relationship has not proved stable and continued to be unpredictable. The question of how close the ties should be continues to be unresolved among the top Ethiopian leadership. Soviet pressure for the establishment of a party continued until the formation of COPWE, the Commission to Organise the Party of the Working People of Ethiopia, in 1979. The delay was partly due to the desire of Mengistu and others to prevent those PMAC members most sympathetic to Moscow from gaining control of the new party. It appears that Mengistu now wishes to maintain a distance in the relationship and preserve what he perceives as unique about the Ethiopian socialist revolution. There is also evidence that the USSR is not satisfying the Ethiopians by providing economic aid of sufficient quantity and quality to effect any substantial transformation in its economic structure.

Ethiopia's new constitution

Nevertheless, there has been adverse comment following the publication of the draft constitution on 8 June 1986, suggesting that the image of Soviet socialism is too firmly imprinted on it. Officially, the text was prepared by the Institute of Nationalities in Addis Ababa, established a few years ago. The Institute's draft was submitted to the Workers Party of Ethiopia, which established a special commission to produce a final draft. Discussions on the document were held in all *kebeles* and all PAs, and to ensure democratic participation a referendum was held in January 1987 — a unique occurrence in Ethiopia.

The format of the constitution is similar to the Soviet constitution of 1977, although a significant variation is Chapter 11 dealing with the office and powers of the president. The USSR and most socialist countries of Eastern Europe, anxious to avoid any repetition of Stalin's personality cult, constitutionally distribute power to ensure that it does not accumulate in the hands of one man. The Ethiopian President, in great contrast, will be Chairman of the Presidium, Commander-in-Chief of the armed forces, be able to recommend or appoint directly the Prime Minister, other ministers and judges of the Supreme Court. He can also conclude international treaties as well as issue presidential decrees. Those commentators who see the betrayal of the Ethiopian revolution as reflected in the constitution in terms of the wholesale importation of foreign doctrines, might note that such powerful heads of state are not unknown to Ethiopia and are by no means unusual in contemporary Africa. Even the most respected African presidents have amended their country's constitution to give themselves indefinite tenure; which, in principle, the President of the People's Democratic Republic of Ethiopia will not have. The supreme organ of state power will be the National Shengo (Assembly) which, in addition to determining essential policies, will establish the Council of State, the Council of Ministers, the Supreme Court, and elect the President. The term of the National Shengo, to which deputies will be elected by secret ballot, will be five years, the same as that of the President. To some, however, the legalisation of a one-party state and the return to a constitutionally powerful Head of State formalise the loss of the hard won liberal and democratic rights which seem to have been gained by the original revolution.

The constitution is intended to pave the way for a return to civilian rule. The Workers' Party, described as a 'Marxist-Leninist vanguard party', is to be central to the People's Democratic Republic of Ethiopia (PDRE), a working people's state based on worker–peasant cooperation, with the participation of intellectuals, the revolutionary army, craftsmen, and other democratic social groupings. Its role is to consolidate the national democratic revolution and lay the foundations for building socialism.

The inclusion of villagisation and resettlement in the constitution has caused some comment. As current issues they have important social, political and economic implications and have raised questions as to the Ethiopian government's handling of human rights. Their embodiment in the constitution, however, has led to the conjecture that by adding a constitutional form to controversial matters the government weakens the force of any opposition to either policy. But the preamble of the constitution lays stress on 'the struggle to extricate ourselves [i.e., the Ethiopian people] from a backwardness that gripped us for centuries and to transform Ethiopia into a society with a high level of development . . .', and reiterates that the 'primary concern is development'. In the context of a constitution tailored to the transition that the Ethiopian people are undoubtedly undergoing, the inclusion of Article 10: 'The state shall encourage the scattered rural population to aggregate in order to change their backward living conditions and enable them to lead a better social life', is not in itself out of place. Other articles included in Chapter Two, 'The Economic System', stress the need to ensure the maintenance of the ecological balance, and the conservation and development of natural resources.

On the crucial matter of nationalities, the draft guarantees that 'all nationalities will co-exist in equality,' that particular attention will be paid to 'under-privileged nationalities' and that local government will be implemented. The National Shengo will establish administrative and autonomous regions which will in time be administered by regional Shengos. Rather than avoid the issue of nationalities, the constitution is worded in such a way as to provide for maximum flexibility in the development of policies in this entire area.

In foreign relations the PDRE will 'develop comprehensive relations and cooperation with socialist countries'. There is no mention of Africa, of the OAU; apartheid and racism are not mentioned either, although historically Ethiopia has been associated with African efforts opposing them.

6. Economic Policies and Developments under PMAC: 1974–84

This section aims to briefly summarise developments in the decade between the establishment of the PMAC and the onset of serious drought in the early 1980s. It is intended to cover briefly those areas in which government policies could be said, in a general sense, to have a bearing on development and in particular the ability of the population to withstand drought.

The drought of the early 1970s was the catalyst which brought the imperial regime to an end. Any government which succeeded that discredited one was bound to commit itself to a programme to improve the conditions of the rural population. Any government faced with such a formidable task was up against the existing constraints of mass poverty and economic stagnation in all sectors. No government could have made more than a small impact on the formidable social and economic problems inherited from the previous regime.

The record of the PMAC is mixed; in some areas its policies were well-intentioned, and considerable progress was made, in others its priorities can be questioned. No government can control the climate, and the drought of the 1980s was upon Ethiopia before a fully coherent economic policy had been evolved. But this underlines the urgent problem facing the Ethiopian government arising from the high rate of population growth and falling per capita food production.

The economic situation: overview

In most respects, Ethiopia's economic situation is similar to the depressing picture seen over much of sub-Saharan Africa in the 1980s. With subsistence-oriented production accounting for a high proportion of agricultural output the majority of the population is still outside a modern economy. Slow overall economic growth, sluggish agricultural performance in conjunction with rapid rates of population growth and inadequacies in domestic policies were compounded in the 1970s by external factors: international inflation, rising oil prices and, in the latter part of the decade, a global economic recession, a slowing down in the growth of world trade in primary commodities, and in Ethiopia's case a sharp decline in the price of coffee and a low level of aid commitment.

During the decade ending 1982–83 Ethiopia's GDP grew at an average rate of only 2.2 per cent in real terms compared with a population growth rate of around 2.5 per cent. In the aftermath of the revolution the armed conflicts and internal challenges were serious constraints on economic growth. Production in the commodity producing sectors declined or stagnated up to 1977–78. The government made a concerted attempt to revitalise the economy in 1978–79 and 1979–80. New *zemetchas* were launched, aimed at increasing industrial and agricultural output, distribution services received increased budgetary allocations, industrial activities resumed around Asmara and favourable weather conditions contributed to better agricultural output. GDP grew at about 5.2 per cent and 5.5 per cent respectively in these years. Ethiopia's external current account deficit and the government's overall fiscal deficit both remained below 5 per cent of GDP.

In 1980–81 to 1982–3, however, the economy suffered setbacks. The growth of real GDP slowed to 2.9 per cent p.a. in that three-year period. Persistent drought returned. There were capacity constraints in industry, stagnation in building and industry and a very low level of total investment because of severe constraints on domestic resources and a failure to attract external investment.

From late 1982 the government attempted to arrest the economic decline by launching a ten-year plan with revised strategies. In January 1983 Chairman Mengistu, in his speech to the second COPWE Congress, emphasised the importance of revitalising agriculture through guaranteed producer pricing, the diffusion of improved technology, the need to restore confidence among private entrepreneurs in small scale industry, and the need to attract foreign investment and technology to develop Ethiopia's natural resources. Measures were introduced aimed at promoting joint ventures between foreign investors and Ethiopian public enterprises. Proposals were made to simplify and rationalise the system of direct and indirect taxation. Despite this evidence of increasing government awareness of the problems, economic recovery was necessarily slow. There were severe constraints imposed by the lack of finance, foreign exchange, domestic savings, shortage of trained manpower and a continuing lack of confidence among private businessmen. All this apart from the devastating effect of the drought itself.

Balance of payments and terms of trade

Ethiopia's balance-of-payments deficits have been consistently below the sub-Saharan African average throughout the decade but in 1981/82 the deficit increased to 5.2 per cent of GDP and in 1982–83 to 7.1 per cent, reflecting deteriorating terms of trade. In 1980–81 the export price of coffee dropped some 25 per cent below the 1979–80 level causing a 17 per cent decline in coffee export earnings. The continued high dependence on coffee export earnings is a major weakness in the trade structure. The export of pulses, previously another major export crop, reached a record level in 1973–74 but has since declined.

The abolition of some of the rents and taxes that were paid in kind seems to have allowed farmers to increase their own consumption and decreased the surplus available for marketing. The PMAC has claimed this as an example of the enlightened reforms it has implemented, it being preferable for subsistence farmers to have more to eat than be forced to part with their surplus. This is an improvement on the previous situation but a different policy of incentives and inputs might have increased total production allowing both increased consumption and a marketable surplus.

Imports, though tightly controlled, increased in 1981–82 and 1982–83. Imports of consumer goods declined but there was an increased flow of food and other commodity grants.

At the end of 1982 Ethiopia's external debt stood at $1,028 million, equivalent to about 23 per cent GDP. This relatively small figure reflects the low volume of concessionary external resources available and the concessionary nature of transfers. Until the recent drought Ethiopia was amongst the lowest recipients of official development assistance with about $6 per capita in 1981–82 as compared to about $20 per capita in sub-Saharan Africa as a whole. The debt service ratio began to increase (11 per cent in 1982–83) as export earnings decreased and larger debt service payments fell due. Compared to many countries Ethiopia has manageable debt service obligations as yet but the problem could increase unless ways are found to expand export earnings. With the exception of certain issues of compensation, Ethiopia has a good reputation for repayment.

Land reform

Of all the reforms enacted, the most important and radical was land reform carried out within six months of the PMAC coming to power. No legal ownership of rural land was henceforth permitted; only a 'possessory' or 'usufructuary' form of tenancy. In the south much of the previously subjugated Oromo peasantry seized land, in some cases killing the owners. In the north where the *rist* system prevailed there was initial resistance in Tigray, Gojjam, Begemdir, parts of Wollo and Shoa and among the Afars. Nevertheless, the initial consequences of the reform appeared substantial. With good weather prevailing, production in the peasant sector rose slightly in the first year. As peasants were relieved of landlords' demands, rural incomes rose by as much as 50 per cent according to some estimates.

By 1978 there were 28,583 Peasant Associations (PAs) established on a minimum area of 800 hectares with between 200 and 400 family members each incorporating 7.3 million households. The task of each association was to allocate land to members, adjudicate disputes, promote a range of social and economic services, act as a channel for the transmission of government (and later party) programmes and generally to mobilise the rural population for development. Service Cooperatives (SCs) were to be set up to procure the inputs for between three and eight Peasant Associations and market their surplus. By 1978 there were said to be 343 of these, linked to a system of peasant defence systems. By 1985 the number had increased to 3,946 but only about 25 per cent were registered with a corporate status permitting them to borrow from banks. They are expected to operate consumer retail shops for members.

A number of problems hindered the smooth growth of PAs however, some actually caused by those who benefited from the initial reforms. The PMAC had no administrative apparatus to initiate far-reaching reforms, and for the measures to succeed the support of the peasants was essential. Substantial powers were handed to the PAs themselves. Tenancies given to peasants gave them effective autonomous control over their own plots for the first time. Beyond establishing an upper limit on tenancies (ten hectares), the decree of 1975 had not specified how the land should be distributed. Inevitably, as the central regime could not supervise local redistribution policies in all areas, those peasants who had been in a somewhat privileged position prior to the reform received most land. Government instructions were defied, and overall, the richer peasantry not only gained a disproportionate amount of land but by ensuring that they controlled the new PAs, their credit, equipment, inputs and their distribution, continued to exploit the poorer peasants.

Given the radical nature of the nationalisation measures, it could be argued that one opportunity lost was the possibility of the imposition of improved land management. As nationalised land was distributed to PAs a greater commitment to such measures as terracing, the rotation of grazing areas and the establishment of village fuel-wood areas could have been demanded.

The achievements of PAs should not be underestimated but there are great divergencies among them, partly because of the nature of their structure. Each PA is a corporate body having jurisdiction over a geographical area, its own natural resources and its member families. Each member pays an annual membership fee and is expected to make special contributions for literacy campaigns, local infrastructural activities and political and social activities. It is also common practice to provide free labour once a week. The leading organs are the general assembly, the executive committee, inspections committee and the judicial tribunal. Whilst the general assembly is the final decision-making body, it meets only periodically and rarely plays an assertive role. The elected executive committee, headed by its chairman, performs the day-to-day functions and has access to governmental authorities at *woreda* level.

Few countries can claim to have achieved the creation of such a widespread network of grassroots organisations but so far they have not had their hoped for effect in generating self-development and mobilisation. They lack trained cadres with the expertise and competence to lead them to initiate their own programmes.

Hence there is still much inertia as they simply await government directives. The long years of subordination and subjugation in a feudal setting, illiteracy and isolation, have tended to make the general membership apathetic and passive rather than assertive. General assemblies are often badly attended and used by those who have assumed leadership as a rubber stamp. Although the old feudal structure was discredited in times of drought and uncertainty, the relationship between landlord and peasant often functioned in the classical feudal reciprocal fashion. The replacement of this with a viable communal and cooperative society requires more than periodic lectures on ideology from government officials.

The first attempt at a *zemetcha* when students were sent into the countryside to mobilise the peasants to implement the reforms was not a uniform success. In places students clashed not only with landlords but also with police and state officials. Students recalled to the towns were critical and suspicious of the PMAC's policies and fuelled the conflict about to break out between the PMAC and its civilian opponents.

No longer forced to sell their produce by landlords who had controlled the marketing system, the newly powerful peasants were able to consume more of their product, which reduced the food available for the urban market. This, coupled with the strain of conflict on the country's inadequate transport and distribution system, led to shortages and higher prices in the towns between 1976 and 1979.

The newly established state farms did not make up this shortfall, despite receiving the greatest proportion of agricultural investment. The total area under cultivation fell immediately after the reform, partly as a result of some land from large farms being transferred to PAs but also because of the disruption of the existing management systems. By 1978 grain production at 600,000 tonnes had fallen by 300,000 tonnes from the 1975–76 level.

Part of the response to the decline in economic production in all sectors, the Economic Development Campaign of June 1979, involved a new phase of land reform. This laid the foundations for a programme of producer cooperatives to be implemented in three stages. In the first stage, *malba*, tenancies were to be limited to 2,000 sq. metres and means of production to be shared; in the second stage, *welba*, tenancies were planned to be limited to 1,000 sq.m. with the means of production owned by a cooperative; the final stage, *weland*, abolished private tenancies over land and created a collective structure whereby about 2,500 adults farm about 4,000 ha. of land.

Decades of abuse of the peasantry and neglect of rural production had left peasant society inward looking and resistant to change. Despite the success of some PAs this conservatism does not change overnight. The basic unit of production in Ethiopia is still the family whose attachment to its own land and implements must be respected. Officials now stressed the dangers of forcing the pace of these reforms. Nevertheless, overt opposition to them appeared; clashes in Sidamo resulted in the deaths of 150 peasants. By 1980 only 40 producer cooperatives existed, mainly of the *malba* variety. There are others under consideration and policies are still based on this approach.

The response to this new phase of land reform reflected two of the contradictions in the programme which have not yet been resolved. Firstly, despite attempts at ideological education, the PMAC is experiencing the social contradictions that have occurred in many countries which have attempted the transition to socialism. It cannot arbitrarily remould social relations irrespective of traditions and culture. The early view held by the PMAC was that the people themselves would see that the 'non-capitalist' approach was the best way to improve living standards and any reversals would be due to imperialistic intervention or counter-revolutionary activity. It is now acknowledged that social, tribal, and religious factors exist within the society and will continue to affect progress in the period after the dismantling of the old social order, despite mass education campaigns and the creation of the Workers Revolutionary Party. There are obvious indicators that the PMAC has not yet come to terms with this inevitable characteristic of a society in political transition and has not yet dealt successfully with peasant farmers, who do not behave in accordance with its plans, whether it uses coercive or non-coercive means.

Secondly, the economic, infrastructural and geographic constraints inherited by the PMAC were so great that it is doubtful whether it could have provided the level of inputs necessary as a corollary to radical land reform measures to ensure a marked improvement in peasant agriculture without a very different allocation of the resources at its disposal. The inadequacies of the service cooperatives had led to disillusionment on the part of many PAs. Particularly with the return of drought in 1980–81 and 1981–82 in Wollo, Gondar, Tigray and Eritrea, the credibility of the PMAC's approach was at a low ebb.

Agriculture and forestry

The agricultural potential of Ethiopia is often spoken of, and its realisation is synonymous with any improvement in the standard of living of the vast majority of Ethiopians. There are relatively large areas of fertile and virgin land in the south and some central areas of the country. Of an estimated 80 million hectares of agricultural land only 12 million hectares are used for crops or fallow. Weather conditions are not equally volatile in all regions. There are about 31 *awraja* (mostly in Shoa, Gojjam, Arussi, Gondar, Sidamo, Wollega and Keffa) out of a total of 102 which have about half the country's fertile land and where the pattern of rainfall is relatively stable. These high potential areas contain nearly 60 per cent of the PA membership (and probably peasant population) produce about 54 per cent of cereals, over 90 per cent of grains procured by the Agricultural Marketing Corporation (AMC) and account for nearly 95 per cent of fertilisers used by the peasant sector.

The satisfactory growth of agriculture is critical not only for the improvement of the food situation but for accelerating the growth of the GDP, of which agriculture accounts for nearly 50 per cent, as well as 90 per cent of export earnings. Production data especially for food crops are not very accurate (although this has improved since 1981–82 with the introduction of better statistical methods) but Ethiopian national accounts show an average growth of agricultural value added of about 1 per cent a year during the decade ending 1981–82. Between 1971–72 and 1977–78 droughts and internal turmoil affected output. In the five years beginning 1978–79 real growth averaged about 2.5 per cent p.a. but only in 1979–80 and 1982–83 did the rate of agricultural growth exceed the rate of population growth (estimated at 2.7 per cent). This poor performance cannot be entirely explained by unfavourable weather, the limitations of natural environment and the disruptions caused by the revolution and internal conflict. Government policies have had an effect, especially in the areas of farm organisation, extension and pricing policies.

Smallholders organised into PAs account for 94 per cent of cultivated land and over 90 per cent of output: most food crops — cereals, including tef (which accounts for one-third of cereal production and half the area allocated to cereal production) as well as pulses, oil seed and coffee and virtually all livestock. The land used by state farms producing cotton and sugar for export and internal consumption, grain intended primarily to supply urban needs and vegetable products for some agro–industries, is relatively small (204,196 ha) and output similarly so but not the proportion of resources allocated to them. The government's policy of augmenting urban food supplies and building up surpluses through the expansion of state farm food-grain production has been a costly experiment. Estimated production of cereals increased annually but actual production and delivery to the AMC consistently fell short of these targets. Costs of production are so high that these farms incur heavy losses despite the substantially higher prices (between 20 per cent and 50 per cent higher than those received by peasants) paid for their grains by the AMC.

The government is aware that the state farms are not performing adequately and has tried to attain financial viability by reducing overhead costs, better maintenance of equipment and reviewing mechanisation policies. After criticism of management policies, the Ministry of State Farms is currently reorganising its staffing structure. There is evidence, however, that the government is also aware of the more fundamental economic issue of whether resources devoted to the state sector could yield a higher rate of return if used in alternative ways, such as raising productivity in the peasant sector.

Increasing crop yields on rain-fed areas can come about only through the increased use of high-yield seed, improved fertiliser and appropriate husbandry. The successful introduction of new inputs and technology is dependent on a well-trained and highly motivated network of agricultural extension workers and a complementary policy of price incentives and supply of consumer goods.

The concept of a minimum package agricultural programme based on the provision of fertiliser, improved seeds and farming practices was introduced by a number of agencies after the 1972–73 famine, particularly the IDA-financed Minimum Package Project. Projections based on the optimal use of these inputs claimed an increased yield in cereals of 100 per cent; application of fertiliser alone could raise yields by around 50 per cent. Fertiliser use in the peasant sector did increase from 1973–74 to 1979–80 but, as the price of fertiliser almost doubled in the years 1980–81 and 1981–82, its use sharply declined. Simultaneously, prices paid by the AMC for maize, sorghum and tef were reduced slightly making the use of fertiliser unattractive.

Although small intermediate technology projects have demonstrated alternatives to the use of chemical fertilisers, in some areas the problem of rapid deterioration of fragile top soils has become so acute that it can be tackled only by the combined use of fertiliser and agronomic guidance. It is noticeable that fertiliser use did not decline so sharply in areas in Shoa and around Addis Ababa, where farmers were able to sell their grain on the open market and were not dependent on selling to the AMC at relatively low, fixed prices.

Adequate varieties of improved seeds have not yet been developed, and supplies of improved seeds to farmers did not increase. Out of a total production of 22,000 tonnes of improved cereal seeds in 1981–82 less than 4,000 tonnes were supplied to peasants. Many of these seed varieties are a decade old and have lost much of their yield potential and disease resistance. Without adequately improved seed the impact of fertiliser is lower. The price of 'improved' seed is double the price of grain.

There was some expansion in the area covered by extension services but there were no corresponding increases in manpower and financial resources. As a result, relatively inexperienced and inadequately trained extension staff have been thinly spread over large areas. Of 15,000 staff now involved in provincial agricultural services, fewer than 2,000 have had at least two years agricultural training and another 2,500 have had as little as a few weeks training in addition to nine months practical experience. The extension workers, called development agents (DAs), are also expected to spend their time on other community activities and spend only approximately 25 per cent of their time on fieldwork. Many of them are expected to provide a full range of advice, covering animal health, plant protection, farm supply services (seeds and machinery) without a full back-up staff of specialists. The lack of operating funds has also severely reduced their effectiveness.

The government's agricultural pricing and marketing policies did not provide adequate incentives to expand production and marketed output of grains. An estimated 20 per cent of the total food-grains consumed in the country are marketed, out of which nearly 70 per cent is handled by private traders and the rest by the AMC. About 85 per cent of AMC's domestic procurement, which increased from one million quintals in 1978–79 to over 3.5 million quintals in 1981–82, is made in the three major surplus regions, Gojjam, Shoa and Arussi. Private traders are required to sell all their grain purchases from Arussi, Gondar and Gojjam and 50 per cent of their purchases from other regions at about Birr five above the producer price. Farmers and traders are not permitted to transport food-grains out of these regions. Restrictions on inter-regional transportation have led to inter-regional price differentials and adversely affect consumers by pushing up prices in areas where there is a deficit but keeping down prices in surplus areas, thus dampening incentives. The expansion of marketing supplies and the development of an integrated national market have thus been hindered. Pricing is thus only part of an integrated approach that could be improved. AMC itself has hardly broken even, despite falling prices paid to the producers. This is partly due to the higher prices paid to state farms and the relatively low price at which most of the wheat was sold.

Coffee is not only prominent in Ethiopia's exports but is also an important consumer item; domestic consumption is estimated to absorb more than half total production. In the face of declining world coffee prices the government is (like other coffee-dependent countries) faced with the dilemma of trying to maintain coffee tax revenues at as high a level as possible without, at the same time, depressing incentives to coffee producers to the point where the country's long-term export prospects are endangered. The government has been trying to extend its control over coffee production, which has traditionally been carried out by smallholders with a low-level of proper cultivation techniques. So far, attempts both to increase production in the modern sector and maintain peasant production have met with limited success. Coffee-berry-disease has been prevalent for some years and efforts to distribute seedlings of disease-resistant varieties have been limited to state farms and cooperatives. Because of the imposition of restrictions on labour movements the traditional seasonal migrations from northern areas to the coffee-growing regions have not taken place. Once again extension services, required to demonstrate the effectiveness of weeding, pruning, mulching etc are inadequate. Investment in facilities such as purchasing stations, pulping factories, rural roads and transport, warehouses and washing stations has been limited. There has been negligible private investment in such facilities since the effective nationalisation of a large section of coffee marketing and the take over of the washing stations by cooperatives. The government introduced a revised pricing policy in 1982/83 in the hope of revitalising peasant production.

As with the need for improved farming techniques, the development of irrigation and water conservation measures to minimise the impact of droughts was acknowledged after the 1972–73 famine and a proliferation of water provision projects, including wells, dams, tanks, ponds, hand-dug wells, and spring protection, resulted. As in most African countries, irrigated agriculture has a small place in the Ethiopian economy and the traditional peasant agriculture is rain-fed, hence the logic of the resettlement programmes in which communities are moved to better-watered lands.

Both voluntary work campaigns and food-for-work campaigns have been used to construct wells and tanks by the Ethiopian Water Works Construction authority. Between one and two million unskilled workdays per year have been generated. Both manual and mechanical pumps are installed but both types have been subject to breakdowns, so it is estimated that 50 per cent of pumps are out of order at any one time. Throughout the country there have been many attempts at labour-intensive irrigation programmes but full details of their construction and maintenance have not been compiled. This is an area where efficient communal action, prevented in the past by fragmentation of land, has been seen to be effective.

About two-thirds of the land cultivated by peasant farmers is on slopes of more than 25 degrees, most of it in the hills and gorges of the heavily populated central highlands. Here, any water conservation and irrigation measures must be linked to erosion control. The implementation of such measures, including terracing, tree planting, gully damming, the provision of stone-faced ditches to protect the terraces and divert flooding water into feeder canals, demands hundreds of man-days. The organisation involved must be over a wide catchment area and often requires reapportioning land to take account of terracing and tree planting.

The Soil and Water Conservation Service reported that from 1977 to 1984 highland farmers in PAs planted 500 million seedlings and constructed 700,000 km. of terraces. This was one of the largest anti-erosion and food-for-work programmes ever undertaken. (WFP's evaluation report noted that 30 million voluntary workdays were used in connection with reafforestation and soil conservation activities in the period 1982–85.) The peak of the effort coincided with the drought and many seedlings died. Many farmers have yet to see the evidence of how water can be utilised by the conserving terraces. Where trees have grown, however, springs which have not been seen in years flow and enthusiasm is maintained. It is reported that the programme has not run into problems encountered elsewhere in Africa where peasants have allowed trees to die to enable them to get more food by planting replacements. The Ethiopian peasant has seen the impact of deforestation and erosion and needs little convincing. He was fully aware of the damage wrought by allowing oxen on to slopes planted with seedlings — officially closed to grazing — but no other vegetation was available.

With devastating soil erosion and only 3–4 per cent of its area covered with forests, Ethiopia is faced with the immense task of restoring the forest and the soil. Since the overthrow of the old regime, institutional and other changes have led to the establishment of four major forestry production systems; Farm Forestry, Community Forestry, Soil Conservation and the State Forestry.

Farm Forestry: Each farmer is encouraged to plant seedlings around his house to be harvested for domestic energy and construction material. The main trees used are Eucalyptus species; farmers produce their own seedlings or get them from the community forestry nurseries.

Community Forestry: Community Forestry Department was established in the 1970s and is a major producer of trees and plantations. It provides technical advice, seedlings and equipment whilst farmers provide labour through their PAs.

Soil Conservation: (see above) Terracing and planting are being complemented by 'eye-brow' terracing and closing-off land for grazing; schemes are also evolving to introduce zero-grazing.

State Forestry: During the 1970s the State Forest Development Department became increasingly aware of its need to promote rural development and became involved in remote areas where there were often no social services. Often the first government agency to enter an area, it has thus become engaged in building and running clinics, forest projects involving establishing villages with schools, drinking-water and electricity.

Despite the extension of forestry services the capacity of the organisational structure to cope with the demands upon it is limited. Due to lack of financing, poor logistics, limited management and supervisory skills, plantation and maintenance operations have become inefficient. A vast number of man-days are spent in establishing plantations but, because of lack of supervision, proper seed deliveries and logistical problems, the survival and success rate are unnecessarily low; averaging 40 per cent.

In 1975 there were eleven graduate foresters; the situation has improved considerably but the lack of skilled manpower has hindered attempts to both expand and consolidate the programme. Whilst this means there is a limit to the volume of technical and financial assistance that can be absorbed, that level has not yet been reached. All operations have been dependent on the eucalyptus species and although some attempts have been made to grow seedlings from the churchyards of

Ethiopia, where the old indigenous trees grow under protection, there has been a lack of experimentation and research.

During the eleven years, 1974–85, a total of 9,432 km of rural roads were built. This represents an average of 857 km per year (and includes the years of famine during which there was a slight acceleration). Construction methods and costs vary widely depending on road standards, construction techniques and terrain. The Ethiopian Transport Construction Authority with 4,713 km, the RRC with 1,789 km, and the Ministry of Agriculture (335 km) have built roads with more mechanised equipment. Others, built on the voluntary work basis, are constructed more cheaply because of the absence of structures, drains etc.

Manpower

Compared to many countries in Africa, Ethiopia has had a well-educated bureaucracy from pre-revolutionary times. Many well-qualified personnel in all fields have left the country since 1974, however, and the large number of expatriates who filled positions in education and business has also diminished. These gaps have been filled but there has been a tendency to promote less experienced nationals. In addition, many of those educated prior to the revolution (and one must not forget Ethiopia's extremely small educational base) were killed or silenced during the revolutionary turmoil. The EPRP recruited most successfully from university and high school graduates; the purges of 1976–78, therefore, had most impact on the educated classes. Having silenced the EPRP, the PMAC imposed military supervision on ministries and instituted a process of political education for civil servants and the staff of public enterprises. Whole ministries were required to participate in public discussions or outings to the countryside to heighten political awareness. Not only may the success of these initiatives be doubted but seen to be counter-productive. Often, the more politically aware and dynamic civilians who supported fundamental change were exposed and dismissed. Those who remained were often the less active who found it easier to accommodate to the situation and on no account speak out or take initiatives.

The government's success in the implementation of all economic programmes depends on the availability of adequate numbers of professional, managerial and technical staff. Government ministries, public and semi-public corporations make requests for recruits from a Central Allocative Committee. Judging from the requests for manpower not filled there are shortages of skilled personnel in virtually every field: engineers, accountants, managers, administrators, economists and specialists in agriculture, in particular. These shortages result from a high wastage rate in tertiary education, partly because of poor secondary education, lack of adequate equipment and facilities in tertiary education, inadequate orientation of the higher education system towards science and technology, lack of coordination and standardisation of special training programmes and a low return of trainees from abroad.

Unlike many African countries, government expenditure on education and training is very low. This does not include the expenditure on the literacy campaigns and other activities such as the construction of primary schools through community schemes. Since 1976–77 the proportion of GDP devoted to education has been between 3 per cent and 3.5 per cent a year. From 10.4 per cent to 15.3 per cent of government expenditure has been on education but at the primary and secondary levels over 90 per cent of this is on salaries, leaving very little for school materials and supplies; at the secondary school level, where vocational and technical subjects are particularly important, this low expenditure is critical.

Health

The health of Ethiopians is among the worst in the world. The causes are rooted in poverty; the high mortality rates and generally poor levels of health are not so much fatal diseases as conditions such as malnutrition, or diseases which in Europe or North America would be easily treatable: respiratory infections, measles, diarrhoea. Many serious diseases still prevalent in Ethiopia have been virtually eliminated elsewhere by hygiene or cheap injections. Improved diet, health care and sanitation could eliminate these diseases in Ethiopia and the rest of Africa, too. A study by the Ethiopian Nutrition Institute (ENI) in 1980 showed average calorie intake to be at or below two-thirds of requirements in seven of the eleven regions studied, the worst being Tigray with 57 per cent. These averages hide wide variations within the regions.

According to World Bank reports, infant mortality is as high as 145 per 1,000; for every 100 born 15 die before their first birthday and a further 10 before their fourth. Mothers not only bear many children but frequently die in the process; maternal mortality is estimated at 20 per 1,000.

Once again Ethiopia's striking geographical diversity affects the livelihood of its population; malaria does not occur in Addis Ababa which is high and cool, but the watered valleys at lower altitudes, those in which there is potential for agricultural development, harbour malaria and bilharzia. These diseases are increasing as new settlers and new agricultural programmes create breeding sites for water-related vectors and thus transmission rates build up. Meningococcal meningitis occurs seasonally in some northern areas; venereal diseases are widespread resulting not only in the ill-health of this generation but congenital syphilis for the next; leprosy is still prevalent, particularly at high altitudes.

Whilst health is generally poor, the vulnerable groups, as elsewhere, are mothers, unborn and newly born children, but Ethiopia has special problems. Illicit abortions lead to sepsis and an increasing number of deaths; 20,000 women are estimated to die of septic abortion each year. It is also estimated that 10 per cent of pregnant women are at risk from being exceptionally young, from poor nutrition, anaemia, malaria, multiparity and obstetric disproportion. Health services are available to only 40 per cent of women and even then utilisation of these services is low. Most women have no ante-natal care; risks are not identified and women have too far to travel if things go wrong. Over and above these risks and poor nutrition there is the normal work-load of most Ethiopian country women which leads to low birth weights and premature labour. The incidence of intra-uterine infection another cause of perinatal death, is as high as 15 per cent. After the revolution some efforts were made to resettle some of the thousands of women engaged in prostitution in Addis Ababa (estimated to be around 100,000 in 1977) but prostitution as such has not been prohibited or restricted.

From the beginning, the revolution stressed the importance of the emancipation of women, and measures have been taken to achieve greater equality. There is a network of women's associations for the mobilisation of women, and opportunities for greater participation of women in socio-economic development exist. There is a long way to go, however, despite considerable evidence of women's increasing awareness of their rights and improved status.

At times of famine women and little girls were always fed last thus ensuring that the highest death rate at such times applied to females. Sex inequalities in sustenance are found in many societies (Amartya Sen; *New Society*, October 1983). Under the old land-holding system landlords preferred men to work their fields; if a husband died a woman was often forced to resort to beggary, prostitution or some form of servitude. Land reform was intended to benefit women equally and undoubtedly has in many areas. PAs were intended to support the changing position of women but it is not known to what extent customary and traditional values reassert themselves at times of crisis.

The main diseases affecting children have been mentioned; 60 per cent are estimated to be undernourished. Permanent childhood disability is another problem. The National Commission for Children estimates that, of a total disabled population of three million, 1.4 million are children disabled by blindness, deafness, paralysis, injury and mental retardation, many of which are preventable. An increasing number of children are stranded as a result of the death of their parents, often the result of war and migration.

Health care

The PMAC inherited a health service concentrated on urban centres; mainly Addis Ababa and Asmara, leaving 80 per cent of the rural population without access to health care. The government is committed to 'Health for All by the year 2,000' and has started to extend services with priorities to maternal and child health. Within the 10 year plan it has laid out plans for health, nutrition and population growth. Despite a recent extension of overall coverage from 20–43 per cent, however, the present distribution of health facilities still reflects the earlier emphasis on urban centres and curative health services. For more than 50 per cent of the population their only resource is the traditional healer.

The government plans to set up a new system based on PAs with advice from the Women's Association at that level. A Community Health Agency and a Traditional Birth Attendant are to receive training to serve about 2,000 people. At *woreda* level there is to be a Health Station for a population of up to 10,000, staffed by three Health Assistants who will receive 18 months training at a regional school. At *awraja* level there is to be a Health Centre serving a population of 50,000, staffed by a nurse or health officer in charge, two to four nurses, one or two sanitarians, and other assistants and technicians. A number of Medium or Rural Hospitals are planned, with surgery facilities, and a Regional Hospital in the capital city of each region. Referrals are to come from lower levels and receive full services in surgery, paediatrics, obstetrics and gynaecology and act as training hospitals for their particular region. Referral hospitals will be in Addis Ababa and one in Jimma. Provision of this coverage is at present beyond the government's financial and manpower capacity even though expenditure and the number of trainees have been increased.

7. Regional Political Issues

Eritrea

In its human and political dimensions the issue of Eritrea's secession from Ethiopia has become a tragedy of great proportions in which no simple attribution of responsibility is possible. The precolonial (i.e. pre-Italian) relationship between Ethiopia and Eritrea is open to interpretation by both sides. The Ethiopians point out that the highlands of Eritrea, with the province of Tigray, were at the centre of the first Christian kingdom; the Coptic Church and the Tigrinya language retain their dominance so that there is still virtual cultural unity with Tigray. In the minds of the Ethiopian rulers, past and present, Eritrea is not a marginal, distant province, but the 'Sea Province', their gateway to the sea.

Eritreans, on the other hand, argue that over long periods of recorded history their region was separate, either because no effective central government functioned or because all or part of the region was controlled by other powers: the Turks, Egyptians, Italians. Both sides attempt to argue from historical precedent to establish the legitimacy of their current position. In reality no distinct and united area corresponding to Eritrea was at any time an independent entity prior to colonial times; an Ethiopian entity did exist but the extent and centre of the Christian kingdoms varied considerably over the centuries.

The establishment of Eritrea as a separate united province was a result of the imposition of Italian rule. Unlike Ethiopia, Eritrea is typical of most modern African states in that territorial boundaries and growing national consciousness date from the colonial period. Eritrea's case differs in that the boundaries imposed by the colonial power separated it from areas which, although ethnically similar, remained independent. By the time the colonial period had ended, however, not only had Eritrea forged a separate social identity but had also experienced, under Italian and British rule, a level of economic development and democratic freedom not found in the rest of Ethiopia. In addition, the source of central power in Ethiopia had shifted from Tigray to Shoa and the Eritreans found themselves governed, not by the same Tigrinya-speaking group, but by their historical rivals, the Amhara. The rise of Arab nationalism had also influenced the Muslim half of the Eritrean population.

A guerrilla struggle began in 1961 but by 1974 was at a low ebb. It was soon apparent that the Derg would not accept the idea of full independence; all Eritrean groups, despite their in-fighting, are committed to nothing less and have shown no willingness to compromise. The ELF and the EPLF launched an offensive against Asmara in 1975. There were those within the Ethiopian command in Eritrea and in the PMAC itself who began to doubt the wisdom of the uncompromising policy in view of the cost and of the clear determination of an increasing number of Eritreans to oppose it. In July 1976, the military administrator of Eritrea, Brigadier General Gyetachew Nadew, came to Addis Ababa for consultations and, having apparently disagreed with Major Mengistu, requested a plenary session of the PMAC to review the situation. He was killed in his home by soldiers, and no attempt was made to assess the possibility of alternatives to brutal and expensive military action.

By 1978 the EPLF had reached near victory and had gained conspicuously more support from the civilian population because of the Ethiopians' intense military retaliation. A series of negotiations failed and the Ethiopians embarked on another heavy assault but were unable to make a clean sweep of the province. A military stalemate existed until the EPLF launched a new offensive using a more mechanised army. In March 1984 they won a significant battle using tanks and armoured vehicles overrunning 100 km of the Ethiopian front, thus breaking the encirclement of its main base, capturing fuel and ammunition and the small port of Mersa Teklai. This development has ruled out any short or medium term victory for either side and implies an indefinite continuation of the same costly war.

The PMAC has to pay for nearly three-fourths of Soviet military aid. Ethiopian spending on defence and internal security rose from 14 per cent of total government spending in 1970 to 21 per cent in 1976, an estimated 30 per cent in 1979 and 45 per cent in 1983/84; recent estimates put it at above 50 per cent.

Compulsory conscription was introduced in 1983 and the army grew to 306,000 in 1984, comparable to the armies of major European powers. Attempts to avoid conscription have led some of those eligible to avoid major towns and government centres. Some are reported to have taken refuge in the Sudan.

Probably over 100,000 Ethiopian troops were killed in the period 1976/84. Some defeats, the destruction of the 'Peasant Army' in 1976, the failure of the 'Red Star' campaign, involving 15 divisions advised by Russian military experts in which around 40,000 troops were killed in 1982, and the fighting on the Sahel front in 1984, when 3,122 prisoners were reputedly captured by the EPLF, have contributed to demoralisation and dissent within the army.

The PMAC inherited the problem from Haile Selassie's regime, which provided almost no mechanism for demands at the periphery to be met by action at the centre. Despite apparent acquiescence in many areas, not just in Eritrea, ethnic contradictions lay just below the surface of political life, for local and ethnic loyalties remained more powerful than loyalty to the centre. Under Haile Selassie a precarious equilibrium had existed but as the old system crumbled ethnic movements took on a new life.

Intent on integration and centralisation of control, the new government would not make concessions. The language of its Nine Point Peace Proposal for the

Administrative Region of Eritrea (May 1976) was conciliatory, recognising the rights of nationalities to self-determination and the unity of the Ethiopian struggle against 'feudalism, imperialism, bureaucratic capitalism and all reactionary forces'. Behind the faultless rhetoric was a refusal to admit that there could be ethnic and national conflicts requiring attention. There was no acknowledgement of any right to secession or even a suggestion of what autonomous powers regional government might be given.

A proposal for limited autonomy for nationalities was put forward at the first Workers's Party Congress in September 1984, but appears not to have been followed up with substantive proposals. The new constitution acknowledges the right of nationalities and refers to autonomous regions. The PMAC continues to refuse to countenance complete separation, however, for three main reasons: Eritrea is seen as an historically integral part of Ethiopia, it provides access to the sea, and to grant full independence could have disastrous implications for the rest of multinational Ethiopia. In addition, as the Ethiopian government is increasingly hard-pressed to diversify its narrow export base and enhance its foreign exchange earnings, it is looking to the exploitation of the country's mineral deposits. The potential for the discovery of minerals in economic quantities is higher in northern Ethiopia where the most extensive areas of pre-Cambrian rock exposures are to be found. Coal, iron ore, copper, potash and salt are among the minerals known to exist in Eritrea. Although no economic quantities of petroleum have been discovered, the presence of oil and gas in the Red Sea has led to hopes that further exploration may lead to the discovery of economic deposits.

The wastage of resources has been universally deplored. During the period prior to the drought, Ethiopia was in no position to administer the Eritrean region, which shares the same problems of inefficient agriculture. Rainfall in the province has been poor for eight out of the 14 years 1970–84; drought affected large areas in 1980, 1981, 1982, and 1983 but in many areas the war had a more serious effect on food production. By early 1984 the Khartoum office of the UNHCR reported 300 people daily fleeing from Ethiopia to join the 300,000 Eritreans and 150,000 other Ethiopians already in Sudan. Ethiopian aerial bombardment caused agricultural work to take place late at night, livestock were a deliberate target of raids over EPLF-held territory. Massive assistance is now needed to reverse the devastation of the province's agriculture. In 1984 about one million people were in need of food relief. An ironic aspect of the conflict has been the apparent self-reliance, resourcefulness and dedication of the Eritrean people in building up industries and infrastructure, training and educating their communities.

Tigray

The province of Tigray, lying between Eritrea in the north and Wollo and Gondar in the south, but bordering the Sudan in the west, has a Coptic Christian population of around five million. It can be divided into three main areas; the western lowlands, traditionally sparsely populated because of the high incidence of malaria and water-borne diseases but with rich, fertile soils; the central highlands, heavily over-populated and susceptible to minor climatic variables, and, the eastern escarpment and rift depression, mostly inhabited by the nomadic Afars. The history of resistance is quite different to that of Eritrea; Tigray is the major example of Haile Selassie's policy of allowing considerable autonomy to certain provinces with a high degree of regional or national feeling. Thus, resistance began in a conventional form after the military assumed power, when former governor *Ras* Mengesha Seyoum organised a Tigrean Liberation Front. The formation of such movements under a traditional leadership against a revolutionary central government might have been anticipated on a greater scale.

The TLF later merged with the conservative EDU, but in 1976 a new, more left-wing faction recruited from the younger intellectuals emerged, the Tigray People's Liberation Front, calling for an armed struggle based on the thoughts of Mao Zedong to establish an independent Tigray province. The TPLF's support for the EPLF may account for its success; from 1976 onwards the TPLF received logistical support from the EPLF and in 1980 intervened on the side of the EPLF against the ELF. Its strength has grown from a few hundred guerrillas to several thousand and it has been able to carry out what to the EPLF is its most important function: the harassment of the Ethiopian military passing through Tigray province up to the capital, Mekele, and then on to the Eritrean capital, Asmara. Claims in mid-1980 that 70 per cent of the province had been 'liberated' were exaggerated but it did appear that the guerrilla force was gathering support.

Factors underlying the resistance were not, in the first instance, nationality based and have never reflected a widespread adherence on the part of the whole population to Maoism. The land reform was originally seen as an interference in regional, ethnic and social structures, which in Tigray are relatively homogeneous. In addition, it was perceived as yet another idea of the despised Oromos, its main beneficiaries, who were seen as the instigators of the revolution. The Eritrean issue was another factor because 'The Peasant Army', again largely made up of Oromos, was allowed to live off the land whilst traversing Tigray.

Since 1975 the Ethiopian government has mounted seven large military campaigns in Tigray to counter the expansion of the TPLF, but they have been counter-productive: the aerial bombardments including cluster and napalm bombs and the use of sophisticated Soviet-supplied armaments have caused widespread destruction of homes, crops and livestock and the displacement of 100,000 people from the western region, which was the TPLF's economic base. The TPLF has become another 'hidden' movement whose success depends on civilian support. Like the EPLF the TPLF has set up a complete *de facto* alternative administration initiating its own land reform, Social and Economic Department to extend infrastructure, health care and road building. Food production under the TPLF is said to have increased by 200 per cent and agricultural cadres have been trained to assist in irrigation, ploughing and soil conservation projects. The first congress of the TPLF (1979) pledged to extend its activities into the towns; at the second congress (1983) a United Democratic Front, a collaborative movement of all anti-government forces was formed. The TPLF claims to control 85 per cent of the province.

Part 2:
Famine: 1982–86

8.   Brief Chronology: 1979– March 1984

David A. Korn, United States Chargé d'Affaires in Ethiopia, in an article on the recent famine, 'Ethiopia: dilemma for the west' published in *The World Today*, the magazine of the Institute of International Affairs writes, 'a prudent and concerned government would have needed nothing more than to rise from bed each morning and look at the sky to realise, by the summer of 1984, that Ethiopia was in trouble.' Mr Korn was in Addis Ababa at the time and we must assume therefore that, like many of those dealing with Ethiopia, he had found it difficult to appreciate the complexity of Ethiopia's growing seasons and the adverse effect of seasonality upon the poor. Whatever was happening in the skies anywhere in 1984 was irrelevant to what was already happening on the ground. What was happening in the sky in 'the summer of 1984' was relevant only to the *next* harvest but, whatever the quality of the *meher* rains, the majority of those affected by the famine had already reached or were reaching the point at which emergency food aid was necessary if they were not to die.

Two of the most crucial lessons of the famine of the early 1970s appear to have been forgotten. However poor and malnourished, people rarely die of starvation as a result of the failure of one harvest. It is a succession of poor harvests that signals danger. Secondly, there are seasonal patterns of food shortages, high food prices, indebtedness, higher incidence of diseases and other adversities that can be observed each year. The ability of a poor rural population to hold out against this multiplicity of difficulties is considerable; they are inured to the hungry season, which in Ethiopia corresponds to the main rainy season. All those who are prudent and concerned may well look to the skies (in the appropriate place — the skies in Addis Ababa are not an adequate monitoring service for the areas between 300 and 1000 km north where drought was most prevalent) during the wet season for it is then they begin to gauge the success of the next harvest, *meher*, to be gathered in November–December.

To all professionals concerned with monitoring food availability, the most critical period, especially for those sections of the population most at risk, comes at the beginning of the long wet season, whether or not the rains during that season are adequate. As will be seen, this picture in Ethiopia is further complicated by the *belg* rains that can produce a smaller crop, which is often expected to tide the population of the northern provinces over the worst period, and by the variation in rainfall which can produce different qualities of crops within one region.

The development of a disastrous famine in 1984 must, therefore, be seen against the succession of poor rains and inadequate harvests in the four years after 1980. Because of altitude, latitude and other factors, rainfall in Ethiopia is by no means uniform, and areas in the same region may have a different incidence of rainfall in the same season. Obviously, however, the regions of Ethiopia most prone to drought are in an area of marked seasonal rainfall and the more marked the seasonality, the less reliable the rainfall during the wet season.

In many areas the 1979 *belg* and *kerempt* rains were poor. In 1980, in Tigray, Eritrea, Wollo and Gondar and parts of northern Shoa the pattern was again abnormal. In Tigray the *kerempt* rains were only 30 per cent of the 'norm'. The Relief Society of Tigray (REST) estimated that 50 per cent of all livestock owned by pastoralists in the eastern part of the province were already dead by March 1981. Forty thousand people migrated from the central highland areas to the more fertile western areas. Sidamo was also affected in the latter part of 1980. The RRC estimated (March 1981) that 12.38 per cent of the rural population would experience food shortages as a result of poor harvests in 1980.

In 1981 yields were again low in many areas after inadequate and irregular *belg* and *kerempt* rains. In some areas hailstorms destroyed standing crops late in the *kerempt* season. By February 1982 there were shortages in many northern areas as a result of the 1981 shortfalls. In April the RRC stated in its document. 'Assistance Requirements for Populations Affected by Drought and Man-made Disasters' that 'an estimated 5,494,100 population is currently facing food shortages as a result of the failure of the . . . rains during the last Meher season. . . . This total includes 3,058,500 drought affected and 1,651,000 war-displaced people.' The 1982 *belg* rains again failed in many areas. The *kerempt* rains were the worst since the early 1970s. In Tigray province no crops were harvested in many areas. This was mainly a result of the poor rains, but also reflects another factor observed in 1975 when only half the land normally cultivated was sown despite the adequate rain. As drought persists the vicious circle of no seed and no oxen sets in, but even if there is some seed farmers hesitate for fear it will not rain at all. There was at least a one month delay in the first rainfall anywhere in the summer of 1982; in some areas seed was retained and remained unsown as the incidence of rain failed to conform to any familiar pattern.

From December 1982 with poor harvests in many areas the first signs of a major famine, even then the result of several seasons, could be seen. Between October 1982 and spring 1983 400,000 migrants passed through REST checkpoints although there was no accurate registration. Migrants were directed to suitable villages in the west of Tigray for absorption. People from Wollo and Gondar province began drifting into Ibenat. In December 1982 Save the Children Fund (SCF) set up a feeding centre for malnourished children in Korem, Wollo province. Between 300 and 400 children were cared for that month, by April 1983 the total figure had risen to 35,500. Children were selected for special feeding by the weight-for-height method; after measuring weight and height the child's weight as a percentage of the ideal height can be calculated.

In December 1982 about one-third of the children arriving in Korem were below 80 per cent, when the risk of mortality rises quickly. This figure rose to nearly one half as the months passed. Some arrived weighing 70 per cent of their proper body weight; there was little hope of any arriving at all if they were below that weight. By January the RRC estimated that 3,423,000 people were affected by food shortages as a result of insufficient or untimely rain and pests during the main season. A further 1,600,000 were also affected by the continuing destructive civil war in the northern provinces, giving a total of 5,023,000 at the beginning of 1983 with no hope of sufficient food to last through it. By March the Ibenat shelter had 7,000 people, Korem 24,000 and Makelle 30,000.

In April 1983 there was a joint UN Appeal (UNDRO, WFP, UNICEF, WHO) for relief assistance for one million people from 13 regions for eight months. Throughout the next few months people continued to come to the shelters located on the main roads but it was not possible to distribute in the rural areas where undoubtedly many others were suffering. The Ethiopian government estimated that only one million of the total in need were accessible and appealed for the provision of new vehicles and help with the rehabilitation of existing vehicles.

The weather did not return to normal in 1983; the usual pattern of mid-June rains followed by ploughing and seeding was disrupted as the *belg* rains were short and late. There was some migration back to their own land by families who had migrated to Western Tigray, and an uneven return by some of those in the shelters and those who had migrated into Gondar from Wollo. The main *kerempt* season began on schedule but the rains were spread over a shorter period; soil moisture, although sufficient in some areas (particularly west and south) began to decline. Some crops developed to the point of seed formation and then dried up for lack of moisture. In Tigray, Eritrea, east Gondar and Wollo the rains stopped too early to ensure continued plant growth.

In the northern areas, therefore, there was clearly going to be another major shortfall. Many of those who had been destitute before the *kerempt* rains had not planted because of inadequate provision of seeds and tools. In Gondar and Wollo the shelters began to fill up again. In September 1983 the RRC forecast that there would be food shortages in the four northern provinces of Eritrea, Gondar, Wollo and Tigray. Many with a knowledge of the cumulative effects of poor harvests did in fact predict catastrophe in 1983.

An estimated 400,000 people were displaced in Tigray and became wholly or partially dependent on relief assistance and help from the community already settled in the western lowlands. Many were continuing their westward migration into the Sudan. By late 1983 400 a day were crossing the border. REST established and administered 17 reception centres. In Eritrea, independent relief workers observed the effects of drought; the RRC estimated that yields around Asmara were less than one-sixth of the average. Tragically, the SCF team working in Korem were taken hostage by the TPLF in April 1983 and did not resume their operations until December 1983 when 2,000 malnourished children were accepted. By this time the picture to those with a knowledge of these areas prone to famine was clear. The Christian Relief and Development Association (CRDA), the successor to the CRC, held monthly meetings in Addis Ababa in which reports from those in the field were relayed and minuted; diplomats and representatives from UN agencies were present at these meetings. On 7 November 1983, representatives from the private American agency Catholic Relief Services (CRS) reported on a visit to Makelle, predicting a 90 per cent crop failure for that season.

These were the warning signals, available, acknowledged, their message understood by many professionals in the field, in the capital and elsewhere. Even the media was aware long before the extraordinary impact of television coverage later in 1984. In summer 1983 Jay Ross, the experienced African correspondent of the *Washington Post*, reported on his own visit to northern Ethiopia and quoted the estimate of Trevor Page, senior Emergencies Officer for the World Food Programme (WFP), that between 50 and 100 children were dying daily in northern Ethiopia. In one village he visited he reported that 150 children had been buried in April and May. He quoted Major Dawit Wolde Ghiorgis, Relief and Rehabilitation Commissioner, as saying that unless there was enough international assistance thousands of people would stream out of the mountains seeking food. 'It will take years to rehabilitate them.'

The Ethiopian situation was bad but it was part of a much larger problem affecting many parts of Africa. Overall monitoring of the continent was in progress, and warnings supporting the fear that 1984 would see many people acutely short of food were issued from several international agencies.

It is pointless to discuss when the much greater toll in human life became inevitable but there were several months when it would have been possible, with coordinated effort, to have averted the full disaster of 1984. Berhane Gizaw, then Head of the Early Warning and Planning Services Department at the RRC said, 'We allowed them to exhaust their resources during the bad years of 1982 and 1983 and then left them to face the crisis of 1984 in that state.' (Quoted in Peter Gill, *A Year in the Death of Africa*, p. 26.) In Korem (only one of the relief camps) the monthly death toll up until March 1984 was under 100, but in April the camp recorded 854 deaths. By October 1984, the month that BBC television showed the Visnews film of the famine, over 100 people were dying each day. Yet, with the known history of successive crop failures, given no large-scale intervention by government, voluntary or international agency, it should have been obvious that this would be inevitable.

It is one thing to say that it should have been obvious to experts by early 1984 (and was to many), quite another to acknowledge that very little had been done by October 1984. The Ethiopian government, the international agencies, the NGOs, the media had the knowledge; the resources to prevent disaster existed, but clearly the ability to link the knowledge with the resources did not. As Ian Carruther's depressing observation on Ethiopia and elsewhere concludes; '. . . knowledge is not a sufficient condition to generate feasible avoiding action or preventive measures.' (Quoted in Chambers, et al).

9. Monitoring Systems and Contingency Mechanisms

The Early Warning System (EWS)

There is a broad consensus on the type of data that are useful to give warning of impending famine and alert those in a position to take timely averting action: rainfall data, crop monitoring, data on seeding and planting, data on population movement and specifically rural/urban migration; local stock movement, rising local food prices and falling prices of livestock and other assets which people anticipating famine try to sell, nutritional status of children and other vulnerable groups. The collection, collation and dissemination of this information is a different matter.

The importance of an 'Early Warning System' was realised after the famine of the early 1970s and the RRC incorporated an Early Warning and Planning Services Department (EWPSD) into its organisational structure. The EWPSD comprises three divisions, one of which is concerned with collecting and analysing information on emerging crop failures, one with assessing the impact of disasters at field level, and one with planning resettlement schemes. Information is based on *woreda*-level reports submitted by local officials and PA leaders and collected by *awraja*-level supervisors of the Central Statistical Office (CSO). Reports are produced regularly, the most important usually being issued about September by which time crop growth should be well underway and harvests can be predicted with some accuracy.

Although the EWS was successful in reporting the extent and seriousness of crop failures, it, like some NGOs and the International Disaster Institute, was not consistent in its interpretation of the relative seriousness of the consequences of crop failures in particular areas. Relief aid was requested for areas which showed extraordinary resilience, whilst later others which had not been regarded as priority cases suffered. It seems unfortunate that the 'extraordinary' nature of these rural groups remarked on by independent observers should have led to a lack of credibility in the RRC by donors who were sceptical of the estimated number of people in need. In retrospect, however, it is noticeable that in some cases governments and agencies which later accused the Ethiopian government of secrecy and complained of the difficulty of getting accurate information were also those on record as disputing the information made available to them at the time.

The shortcomings of the system as it stood at the beginning of the 1980s reflected under-manning, under-funding and the difficulty of confirming estimates. Meteorological and satellite information does not give enough precise information to be very useful in a country as diverse as Ethiopia, although all concurrent information of this nature, such as that available to the FAO, supported the picture as presented by Ethiopia. The National Meteorological Services Agency (NMSA) contributes regular reports on weather conditions during the rainy season to the EWS. Unfortunately, although there are over 1,000 weather stations in Ethiopia, only 20 regularly reported to NMSA, which is not an adequate number to give an account of the state of soil moisture conditions in the numerous micro-climate zones of the country.

Overseas support for the RRC's programmes was withdrawn by the USA and the UK in 1979. Although its performance from then on was undoubtedly hampered by the constraints mentioned above, it continued to function, aided by the UNICEF, and was generally regarded as reasonably efficient. The irony of the situation in which Western aid donors having demanded and helped to create a scientifically based early warning system, then ignored it, was pointed out by Mr Taye Gurmu, then deputy commissioner of the RRC at a conference on the EWS held in August 1984. 'There is clearly a defined objective in the production of its [the EWS] figures and reports and that objective is action on behalf of those affected by food shortages. If action does not result there is little point in the system itself.' (Quoted in Peter Gill, p. 36). The reasons for the lack of response to the RRC's figures will be looked at more closely in the next section, but in retrospect they were not discredited. These figures may have appeared to be subjective but they did not contradict any other properly interpreted information available at the time.

Emergency food stocks

For an EWS to be effective it must be linked to a system of food provision for distribution to those areas in need. The RRC has a Relief Aid Service Department which, acting on initial data from the EWS, determines the distribution quota for each *woreda*. The department makes enquiries in the RRC regional offices, requesting additional information on local conditions. Local officials, including *woreda* administrators and PA officials, are required to obtain firm information on the numbers at risk and to identify sites for distribution centres. Tentative lists of requirements for food and other relief commodities are passed to the Aid Coordination Department. There is an accepted procedure for the formation of an administrative structure to supervise commodity distribution.

The ideal functioning of the system would logically depend at this stage on the existence of a stockpile of food of all appropriate types. Plans for a Food Security Reserve in Ethiopia were first mooted at the time of the last big famine. Instead of relying on mobilising the international community afresh during each crisis, the food would be kept in storage for use in an emergency. Having been seriously canvassed in 1975 and commended by the FAO in 1979 the idea was accepted. The initial stockpile was to be 60,000 tonnes rising to 120,000 tonnes. The UN (WFP) would contribute the first 12,000 tonnes and monitor the build up of the stockpile for the first four years, by which time they said 'the full grain reserve would be established'. If the plan had been carried out there would have been 120,000 tonnes of grain on hand, more than was committed by donors to Ethiopia in the first nine months of 1984. The UN's 12,000 tonnes were delivered in 1982 but there was no follow up.

The lack of buffer stocks is also clearly an indictment of Ethiopian agricultural policy, in particular the efficiency of the state farms. The AMC gave 60,000 tonnes to the reserve in early 1984 but this was a loan to be repaid with donor commitments to the RRC when received. It must be conceded that the concept of buffer stocks is a complex one. There have been stock-control problems in some areas where the pre-positioning of stocks for potential famine areas has taken place (Niger and Kenya). Moreover, some donors prefer to give food aid for relief and rehabilitation efforts rather than low-profile reserve stocks. Fearing adverse effects on world grain markets, some governments, the USA in particular, have not supported strategic grain reserves. It might be thought, however, that the knowledge that the plan to establish stockpiles had not been effective would have added credence and urgency to the appeals of the RRC when they asked for extra requirements.

10.   The Poor Response: March–October 1984

March 1984: the RRC's 'Assistance Requirements'

At a seminar on Food Aid and Emergencies held in December 1984 at the Institute of Development Studies, University of Sussex, the 'two-phase' approach found much favour. With disaster looming one does not start with time-consuming and difficult assessments leading to lengthy international discussions but with rapid action, preferably coordinated and carefully arranged in advance on a stand-by basis. The quick action provides breathing space during which a better assessment of total needs and logistical problems can be made. This 'two-phase' approach is yet another mechanism that we can see, with hindsight, might have been successfully applied to avert the worst effects of the famine in Ethiopia. Even if no coordinated or coherent approach had evolved earlier, this would have been the most appropriate approach to adopt in March 1984 when the RRC made its plea for assistance at a meeting of donors.

The RRC had published several reports on the food needs of drought-affected areas prior to 1984; in January 1984 it published a synoptic report of the previous *meher* harvest. On 30 March 1984 it issued its request for emergency food aid to cover the rest of the year. In March of any year a full assessment of the previous year's main crops is possible and there are also indications of whether the small, *belg*, rains are likely to provide a 'bridging' crop. The RCC was thus able to calculate how much food assistance would be needed for the population at risk until the next main crop harvest at the end of the year. Although several donors' meetings are convened each year this was a vital one, and despite some statements since made to the contrary, it seems clear that the tone of the meeting indicated that the RRC perceived an emergency and were attempting to bring it to the notice of the donor community. Seventy representatives of international and domestic donors attended. A video of Western television coverage of conditions in Wollo earlier in the month was shown with an RRC commentary. The Commissioner, Major Dawit Wolde Ghiorgis, gave a speech mentioning the certain death of oxen, and therefore an inability to plough during the next rainy season; the need for financial help to improve transport, and a specific warning on human deaths. Donors requested clarification on the level of government food stocks and questioned the capacity of ports to handle large quantities of aid.

The document given to all donors, 'Assistance Requirements 1984', dealt in an unemotional but quite specific way with the details. First it established the current situation: 'At the moment only three months after their harvest in some cases, people have been forced to depend on outside sources of grain assistance.' Consecutive crop failures had led to:

> large scale suffering because drought always affects the section of the population least prepared to face it, i.e. the marginal and subsistence farmers . . . the only alternative left to the country is to appeal for international assistance to bring relief to the population until such time as weather conditions improve and full agricultural production commences once again.

Estimates of the number of people affected in different regions were given; 1,790,830 out of 2,500,000 in Wollo; 1,300,000 out of 2,504,800 in Tigray. The conclusion of the report was not in doubt:

> Ethiopia is facing a potential disaster of considerable magnitude in which this year around one-fifth of the country's population will need assistance in some form or another. If those affected do not receive relief assistance the consequences will be frightening.

The warning could not have been clearer. It was delivered by the organisation whose place it was to deliver it to those whose reason for being in Addis Ababa was to receive and respond to such messages. Why then did it bring so little response?

Why was the response so poor?

Statistics

There are two aspects of the statistical confusion referred to by some agencies in their attempts to explain the reasons why the RRC's request did not meet with an adequate response. In the first place there were certain inconsistencies in the figures relating primarily to the inclusion in the total figures of those at risk in Eritrea and Tigray. The compilers produced overall figures for these two provinces but in all supporting documents (available to all donors) it was acknowledged that there were no formal reports for either region. It was stated that 5.2 million people were affected and that 912,000 tonnes of extra emergency grain was needed. However, it was then acknowledged that the handling of the full amount with the present limited transport resources would be difficult and, therefore, the amount requested was reduced by 50 per cent to 456,000 tonnes. Of this 33,500 was to be contributed by the AMC and the RRC held 44,000 tonnes. The deficit was 378,500 tonnes. This apparently arbitrary reduction of the full estimated needs, on the grounds that handling would be difficult, gave rise to unjustified scepticism.

Secondly, there was the more general argument that the RRC's commodity accounting and statistical methods left much to be desired and therefore any statistics it came up with were to be treated with caution. The fact that they then halved their own estimate weakened their own case still further in the eyes of some donors. The irony of this is that there was clearly no deliberate statistical fudging; the intention behind halving the estimate was to increase rather than decrease credibility by attempting to be realistic about the logistical situation.

'Crying wolf'

There is no evidence that the RRC at any time in the 1980s requested assistance that it did not need. Nevertheless, a feeling that there was an element of 'crying wolf' appears to have existed among some donors. There were two reasons for this; firstly, the drought was cumulative, the situation deteriorating overall but not uniformly. In some areas crops had failed successively; in others there had been slight improvements but not enough to arrest the downward spiral completely. As stated elsewhere, because of a number of different factors, difficult terrain, lack of infrastructure, funds, manpower, and civil war, a comprehensive indication of exactly where and when crop failure was leading to starvation was never made. The RRC told donors that people in certain areas needed assistance and if they didn't get it they would die; they did not say exactly who and where. As mentioned above they were not the only ones to have underestimated the extent to which people had managed to postpone complete destitution by the disposal of their assets, including their homes, to buy food. Secondly, the reluctance of some donors derived from the feeling that the country, whilst apparently continually appealing for help, did nothing to help itself in terms of increasing the inputs to peasant farmers, gearing agricultural policy to provide marketing incentives and improving the efficiency of state farms. There seemed little understanding of the organisation problems faced by the government; in the meantime people starved.

Perceptions

Perhaps both the former two sections — 'Statistics' and 'Crying wolf' — should be grouped together under a broader heading: perceptions, or mutual misperceptions. We now know that donors were not faced with grave statistical inaccuracies. Fieldworkers in Ethiopia appreciate the difficulties of data collection and collation. It is easier to find quotations demonstrating the relative strengths of the RRC compared to corresponding bodies in other countries than to find substantiated criticism, yet the reluctance to give the organisation the benefit of the doubt at the most critical time did exist and was crucial.

Staffing at all levels had some bearing on this. The Ethiopian government has a staff assignment rather than staff recruitment policy. In the field the level of motivation and aptitude of some RRC workers was adversely remarked on by some expatriate workers. The fact that the RRC usually sent a junior representative to the monthly inter-agency coordination meetings of the CRDA in Addis Ababa has been widely commented on. However, whenever senior representatives of the RRC met diplomats, foreign government officials or senior agency representatives, they were confronted with antagonistic questioning of the accuracy of their assessments and accusations of corruption and ineptitude. It is not surprising that lower ranking officers were delegated to bear the brunt of the general criticisms of their government. This may seem frivolous but it is related to another point which had some bearing on the donors' perceptions of the RRC.

Ato Shimelis Adugna, the first Commissioner of the RRC, was universally respected. His successor, Major Dawit Wolde Ghiorgis, had an unenviable task as the Ethiopian government representative with the highest profile among Western donors; personifying the precarious balancing act of the Ethiopian government — allied to the USSR but appealing to Western donors — Commissioner Dawit's main fault (until his defection to the USA) appears to have been his manner, which was clearly thought inappropriate in one asking for aid. The implication is that not only do donors have to be told the facts, but told them by someone with a suitably deferential and supplicatory personality.

The perceived inadequacies of the RRC and failure of successful interaction between the RRC and agencies in Addis Ababa apparently persisted throughout the period March–December 1984. A study of 'Emergency Preparedness in Ethiopia' made by the International Disaster Institute reported on a 'widespread lack of confidence in the RRC among international agencies and voluntary agencies', but the RRC's next report on the situation 'Review of Current Situation in Drought-Affected Regions of Ethiopia: July 1984' was again clear and, given the resources available and lack of outside support, it is difficult to see where the organisation can be seriously or justly faulted. By the end of July, when their stocks had been depleted except for 8,000 tonnes in Eritrea, they had distributed 86,000 tonnes of grain and 6,000 tonnes of supplementary foodstuffs in four months. The Commission had begun the period with a deficit of 19,000 tonnes owed to the AMC. During the four-month period the RRC had received 15,000 tonnes from imports, used its 44,000 in stock and the rest was from 'stocks not originally earmarked for relief both from AMC and state farms'. Obtaining the grain from other government agencies, as well as shifting 86,000 tonnes, were both events critics would have said were unlikely.

Too many countries

If the RRC's requests were not detailed enough or adequately corroborated at a micro-level, they were supported by a wide range of reports and analyses at a macro-level, but again what might have been interpreted as confirmation of their needs seems to have weighed against them. The Global Information and Early Warning System of the FAO, set up in 1975, uses satellite technology to predict problems; the METEOSAT of the European Space Agency provides information on cloud cover, and the American LANDSAT monitors vegetation patterns. Thus FAO was able to predict drought in Africa and did so from the beginning of 1983 but on a continent-wide basis, initially naming 22 countries with 150 million people at risk. The calculations used are based on crop years which vary in different parts of Africa and so the list itself varied between 21 and 24 countries. Whether, in fact, the selection of countries on the list owed as much to diplomacy in Rome as to actual scarcity in Africa, it blunted the impact of the appeals made to the donor community. Ethiopia was not sufficiently highlighted until after the media had taken up the cause.

There were a number of other warnings of the situation affecting Africa; at the 99th Session of the International Wheat Council in November 1983 warnings were given about the deteriorating food situation in the Sahel, including Ethiopia. The UN Economic Commission for Africa again stated 150 million Africans would face hunger and malnutrition in 1984. The 38th UN General Assembly ended with a call upon the international community 'to undertake effective and timely action' and the UN Secretary General held a press conference 'expressing great concern' about the worsening situation. In January 1984 this was followed up by meetings between the UN representatives of individual African states and potential donor nations. There was some response to this; the US government, for example, announced an additional $90 million for Africa.

Shortly before the RRC's own appeal in March 1984 the World Bank issued a warning that Africa was facing a food crisis and that four countries, Ethiopia, Chad, Mozambique and Burkina Faso, had only enough food in stock to last for four months. The justification for the presentation of aggregate figures and blanket reporting on the emergency must have been the hope of extracting large scale donations. The overall reports — 150 million people facing starvation — provided a completely inaccurate picture of what was happening in Africa. Whereas in some areas of the afflicted states crop production was normal, the picture given was one of an entire continent equally stricken by distress. Public opinion saw only inefficient and chaotic conditions characterising the African continent and failed to realise that some nations were at that time making strenuous and fruitful efforts to improve their economic position and policies. A result of the undifferentiated approach was to deflect aid from those areas which were severely affected.

WFP/FAO estimates of needs

The appeal of the RRC in March could have been the opportunity for this Africa-sized problem to be narrowed down and an examination of the Ethiopian case made. Whereas the initiative could have been taken by any agency, small or large, at this point it must be assumed that under the present regime it was more difficult for the smaller agencies — churches, NGOs, diplomatic missions — to act (see below). If the major international donors had wholeheartedly supported the RRC's appeal at this point the situation could have changed.

The UN agencies in the field, UNDP, UNICEF, UNDRO, FAO, WFP had the advantage of having an overall view of the continent's needs and the detailed Ethiopian picture. They had been reporting on the situation for several years; in 1980 an UNDRO inter-agency and multi-donor mission had visited Ethiopia. As a result the UN General Assembly had appealed to members to increase their assistance to Ethiopia. In 1982 another multi-agency UNDRO mission had visited

Ethiopia and commented on drought in the north-central and eastern parts of the country. Again the UN General Assembly endorsed the mission's findings and requested the UN system to continue to provide assistance (December 1982). UNDRO Sitrep (situation reports) in March, April and May 1983 spoke of conditions comparable to the severe drought of the 1970s; in June it noted the immediate need for more spare parts, truck tyres, etc, to improve transport facilities for emergency food distribution. In October UNDRO gave updated figures on those affected by drought in the northern areas. In February 1984 it announced the termination of its involvement in the drought areas whilst UNICEF announced it would accelerate and concentrate its activities where possible.

The FAO Global Information and Early Warning System gave reports on crop shortages in January, April and June 1983 when it reported widespread famine conditions in Wollo, Gondar, Eritrea and Tigray, and again in August. In September this report gave an overall satisfactory report on crop conditions, but in November this optimistic view was qualified as in the four seriously affected areas the rainfall, though better than 1982, was still below normal and it was known that many of the population had not been able to carry out normal agricultural activities. In February 1984 the report was yet more specific; although crop conditions had been normal, in many parts of the country the final shortfall in the worst affected provinces was worse than in 1982 and serious shortages were expected to persist for another year.

All the information collated by UN agencies within Ethiopia for the significant years prior to 1984 contributed to a picture of repeated crop failures or shortfalls affecting the same communities, many of whom (more than one million people) had already resorted to relief shelters. Their own forecasts for 1984 predicted total cereal production as 'below normal and less than domestic requirements' (FAO Special Report January 1984), whilst more detailed reports showed a dire picture in the north. Clearly, there was no hope of immediate rehabilitation and the population of the affected regions was yet again bound to be dependent on food aid transported into their home areas.

The main UN source of food aid in normal circumstances is the World Food Programme. WFP was set up in 1962 by the UN and the FAO. It is supervised by a 30-nation body, the Committee on Food Aid Policies and Programmes (CFA) which meets twice yearly in Rome to approve and to 'evolve and coordinate short-term and longer term food aid policies. . . .' WFP's main aim is to stimulate economic and social projects by using food aid in development projects. Up to 1981 less than 20 per cent of its resources had been distributed as relief. WFP resources come from over 100 countries in the form of food, cash or shipping. The USA is the largest contributor of food and the EEC and Canada are also important donors.

The WFP status report of 22 March 1984 'Food Aid Deliveries to African Countries affected by Food Emergencies' gave figures for food pledges for Ethiopia until the end of 1984. These included food for ongoing schemes and it would seem only 7,810 tonnes were intended for emergency use. It also said that the AMC had 240,000 tonnes in reserve for the south of the country, but this was in fact normal national requirements and did not represent either a reserve or emergency stocks. This confusion over the intended use of grain already pledged, plus the status of reserve stocks implicit in the WFP status report, persisted for some months. To the sceptical reader the figures seemed contradictory and did not appear to support the RRC's figures or their sense of urgency.

In February, a joint FAO/WFP four-man mission from the Office of Special Relief Operations had been dispatched from Rome with a brief 'to evaluate the food supply situation and logistic problems related to the mobilisation of food within Ethiopia'. This external mission worked with the RRC as it produced its own report and had access to the Ethiopian field staff of the relevant organisations. Had the mission endorsed the view of the emergency held by the RRC and some of its own personnel stationed permanently in Ethiopia, it would have had considerable impact on the urgency with which the donor community responded. Although it seemed to agree with many of the RRC's findings, it failed fully to endorse its conclusions. The RRC had calculated the country needed 900,000 tonnes of grain but launched its appeal at half that figure. The FAO/WFP report, while mentioning the large figure, appears in its conclusion to cut it yet again by almost three-quarters so that the UN-backed appeal for the whole of 1984 emerged as 125,000 tonnes.

Dr Kenneth King, the resident representative of UNDP and UN Disaster Relief Coordinator in Addis Ababa, had apparently attempted to convince the mission of visiting experts that their figures were wrong and their assumption that logistics was an overwhelming problem which one should not even attempt to overcome was ill-founded. In May 1984, about when the FAO/WFP report was published, Dr King was interviewed for a British Independent Television documentary 'Seeds of Despair' in which he said:

> And I'm not talking about figures, what we're talking about is lives. 125,000 tonnes would be a 1/7th, 14 per cent, which means we're condemning by a stroke of the pen 86 per cent of the people who are affected to, if not death, then to a sort of half life, to a life without food over long periods. This I cannot accept.

Apart from Dr King, most of the UN staff in Rome and Addis Ababa appear to have been influenced throughout the rest of 1984 by this report. It is clear from several of the actual written reports that the effects of cumulative crop failure were never understood. This is supported by the opinion of Berhane Gizaw, head of the EWSPD, who reported a conversation with the FAO mission during which he tried to convince them that the peasants in the north had sold all their livestock and possessions and had nothing left. A mission member replied, 'You've been telling the world of this problem in 1982 and 1983 but we've not seen the people dying like flies yet.' (Quoted in Peter Gill, p. 50.) This calls into question the value of visiting missions if their expertise, in overriding the balance of opinion of those in the field, leads to such miscalculations.

It also highlights a key problem facing all those attempting to deal with an insidious, creeping famine — the need for a clear definition of what constitutes an emergency. What criteria should be used to assess the extent of the problem and the ability of a country to cope with it? Surely not the mass death of those affected. That may be inevitable in the event of a flood or an earthquake but the phenomenon of numerous deaths in time of famine takes months, if not years, to materialise.

Considerable thought is now going into the more careful definition of an emergency and into the creation of effective mechanisms through which the international community can respond rationally to the key indicators, so that next time it will not be left to the BBC to decide when an emergency begins and ends.

Another significant source of misunderstanding was the status of the grain held in stock by the AMC, despite the RRC's explanations. The distinction between normal stocks available for purchase in cities and for the provision of the army and emergency buffer stocks was not appreciated. By June 1984, when there was no grain available in Ethiopia for food distribution, the distinction became clearer but by then time and opportunities had been lost. It should have been clear to donors, despite their distaste for the regime, that normal urban demands and those of the armed forces were unlikely to take second place. It would be naïve to believe that any government, whatever its political complexion, could afford to make its army and urban population go hungry in order to feed the rural poor. As noted above, some stocks were made available to the RRC.

The underestimation of the capacity of the port of Assab to receive and clear incoming grain was the third area in which the report's conclusions were mistaken and unfortunately influential. Grain losses had occurred at the ports of Assab and Djibouti because of inadequate inland transport resources between 1974 and 1977. An emergency transportation unit of 150 Volvo trucks and trailers provided by UNEP/WFP/ILO in 1977 dramatically increased the capacity to move both relief supplies and the WFP's regular food aid (linked to projects), but during the 1970s the offtake from the port of Assab had remained below 100,000 tonnes a year.

There had been problems over the question of the priority of relief commodities arriving in Assab during 1983, but these had been resolved and there were government and RRC assurances that all ships carrying relief supplies would receive priority handling. From its previous experience WFP asserted that the total capacity of Assab and Massawa was no more than 1,000 tonnes per day. The argument seemed to be that as Ethiopia could not import more than 365,000 tonnes a year there was no point in trying. When the grain finally arrived in large quantities and efforts were made to resolve the problems, Assab alone discharged more than 2,000 tonnes a day and when necessary geared up to deal with up to 3,000. Port handling equipment was supplied by the British Overseas Development Administration. The problem of the port being a security zone was also overcome. However, the FAO/WFP report, compiled by external experts, seems to have had a very negative effect; in addition, changes of personnel within Addis Ababa during this period seem to have led to a continuation of the complacent approach.

No complacency remained within the UN agencies by the end of 1984, and during 1985 WFP's operations and reporting techniques were not only greatly improved but pivotal to relief operations throughout Africa. Distinctions between what food had been committed and what had actually arrived, what was for emergency use and what was designated for on-going food-for-work programmes were carefully made. During the crucial months of March till October 1984, however, the information from Rome (FAO/WFP) continued to be dangerously misleading. In July, the FAO reported that 230,000 tonnes had been received or was in the pipeline. On 6 August the RRC reported that it had received only 34,000 tonnes of relief grain since its March appeal. Governments and other agencies, faced with such discrepancies, believed the UN agencies rather than the Ethiopian parastatal agencies, but the former were wrong. In August an WFP representative in Addis Ababa still maintained (to an Oxfam visitor) that there was sufficient grain in the country or on the way. By September, however, the WFP's unconvincing presentation of food aid statistics at a CRDA meeting was greeted with ridicule.

11. Failure of Other Potential Donors

The USA

The USA is the biggest donor of food aid worldwide, accounting for about 50 per cent of Western donor disbursements in cash terms in 1980. The US food programme comes under Public Law 480, the Agricultural Trade Development and Assistance Act, popularly known as 'Food for Peace'. The law was passed by Congress in 1954 and has since been amended on various occasions. The objectives of the law are to expand international trade, to develop and expand overseas markets for US farm products, to alleviate malnutrition and hunger in the world, to encourage economic development and improve food production in less developed countries and to advance the objectives of US foreign policy.

Once the American public had roused its government to respond to the crisis, spokesmen for the administration could plausibly claim that they had shouldered their customary burden. Over one million tonnes of US relief food was delivered to Africa during 1985, of which more than 300,000 was for Ethiopia. Aid was to be strictly non-political; Peter McPherson, then head of USAID, said in March 1985 in a *Washington Post* article that, 'The US motto has been "A hungry child has no politics"'. The State Department in April 1985 concurred: 'The US has not allowed political differences with any governments to weaken its determination to have assistance reach those in need. We are the largest donor to Ethiopia a country whose Government had been openly hostile to us for several years.'

The extent of the US contribution in 1985 is not in dispute. One wonders, however, who is rewriting history when one reads such articles as that of David A. Korn:

Throughout the summer of 1984 . . . not a word was spoken publicly by top Ethiopian officials . . . about massive famine or unusual drought. Later, after international media had exposed the extent of the crisis the Ethiopian government and its Relief and Rehabilitation Commission began to rewrite history claiming that they had not ignored the drought and famine but had simply underestimated its extent and that when they did sound the alarm western donors were derelict in responding.

In 1977 the USA suspended all aid to Ethiopia on the grounds that it was concerned about the violation of human rights under the military regime. In 1984 economic assistance was still barred on a number of grounds. Title II of PL 480 is intended to allow food relief to pass through political barriers, but from 1982 USAID has placed a restriction on this by refusing to channel food through the RRC. This restriction was relaxed in November 1984 when Peter McPherson reached a new formal agreement with RRC Commissioner Dawit.

Ethiopia did receive some emergency aid from the USA through American charities operating in the country, particularly CRS which had been active since the 1972–73 famine. CRS received food aid to distribute in feeding centres for pre-school children and nursing mothers in Addis Ababa and Dire Dawa. It became aware of the mounting crisis but also that the US relief entitlement to Ethiopia was being reduced. In 1980 Ethiopia received 83,000 tonnes, in 1981 24,000, in 1982 6,000. According to US budgetary proposals to run from October 1983 Ethiopia was to be phased out entirely. CRS attempted to prevent this and, beginning in December 1982, made proposals that food should be made available to support a new programme CRS wished to start in Makelle, Tigray. Eight hundred and thirty-eight tonnes of food was required to be transported to Ethiopia at a total cost of $397,000. This request was approved in May 1983, five months later, at a time when NBC had just announced its intention of filming the drought areas, and Jay Ross's articles on the famine in the *Washington Post* were being published. Other journalists were applying for visas to follow the story. When CRS applied for another 4,500 tonnes to expand the Makelle programme in July 1983, the request was granted in nine days.

In August 1983 a USAID team spent two weeks in Ethiopia and recommended an additional 15,000 tonnes. Also in August an eight-man Congressional team visited Ethiopia and concluded that thousands faced 'imminent death unless there was an immediate increase in American and international relief assistance to Ethiopia'. In October, CRS made a further application for 16,000 tonnes to feed 35,000 families and 14,000 destitutes in Tigray and Eritrea for nine months. In December another USAID mission visited Ethiopia and recommended that this 16,000 tonnes should be approved immediately. In January 1984 USAID told CRS it would be receiving 8,000 tonnes. In Ethiopia CRS filled the gap with food diverted from its permanent programme and 5,000 tonnes donated by the Canadian government and 2,000 tonnes from the Mennonite Mission group. The regional CRS Director told the House Sub-Committee on African Affairs:

> The drought of 1983 will stretch into 1984. Thousands will die. Somebody will count them. Somebody will survey the results of relief efforts. Most will criticise but after all the papers have been published and the books written what will anybody learn. History teaches little to bureaucracy. But let's keep on trying.

There were undoubtedly bureaucratic reasons to account in part for the delays. USAID asserts that it had faith in the CRS channel and it does not appear that there was any real belief in the prospect of the aid being diverted improperly. The most probable grounds for withholding emergency food aid must still be political; the main contention being that by providing relief to a Soviet-backed regime the USA was enabling it to concentrate resources on the wars which it fought to retain its power. The General Accounting Office reporting on its investigations into the US response to the Ethiopian famine (April 1985) affirmed that the

> US knew that a potentially serious food shortage situation existed in the northern provinces in 1982. . . . Many officials within the US administration argued that donated food was saving foreign exchange for the Ethiopian government and those savings increased its capacity to import military and non-essential goods and concentrate its funds on the war effort in the northern provinces. This concern remains open and is frequently debated, but the US policy to feed hungry people is currently overriding this concern.

Peter Gill's interpretation of this last sentence in his book *A Year in the Death of Africa* is that for a period in 1983 and 1984 it was not.

Through a succession of political manoeuvrings on Capitol Hill, involving the US Administration's policy in Central America, the issue of increasing foreign assistance to Africa became entangled with that of increasing military aid to El Salvador and to the 'Contras' of Nicaragua. Senator Danforth, who had brought the government's attention to Africa's needs, contrived to get the measure providing a US$90 million supplement through, but an additional $60 million was not passed until four months after the Senate had originally voted for it. USAID was unable to spend it within that fiscal year and it was added to the larger amount later committed for 1985.

No longer having its own personnel in Ethiopia, USAID was dependent on visiting missions and the advice of other experts in the field. Like others, they chose to credit the FAO/WFP with the most accurate picture of what was happening, although they undoubtedly did receive alarming reports from other sources. A few days after receiving the RRC's report in March, the US Embassy in Addis Ababa was concerned enough to recommend that the USAID should carry out its own survey. This was undertaken but it was concluded that, although the situation should be monitored, no extra food aid should be given. In August, USAID was quoting from the FAO/WFP report to a recently formed Select Committee on Hunger to support its position that Ethiopia's shortages were in check. USAID did not mention the RRC's own calculations of Ethiopia's needs, and also supported the FAO/WFP's position that people's needs must be measured in relation to the perceived capacity to supply them. Believing, up until September 1984, that the target was 125,000 tonnes, USAID also confused the figures on pledges with what had actually arrived. In mid-September the situation changed: an American voluntary relief worker told the US Embassy in Addis Ababa that he had never seen a situation as bad as that in the north and his view was corroborated by a senior Western Ambassador who told Americans that about 900,000 Ethiopians 'will have died' of malnutrition and related diseases by the end of 1984. At the same time, private agency officials in Washington reported to Peter McPherson that they could not handle the quantity of aid required to meet the emergency and that arrangements must be made with the Ethiopian authorities.

The EEC

The EEC is a substantial donor of food aid but its programme has often been criticised for being exceedingly cumbersome. This proved to be the case throughout its response to the Ethiopian (and African) famine, remaining so even after it responded to the sustained burst of publicity in the autumn of 1984. Prior to this, like the USA, it did not make the most of opportunities to offer extra aid. This was partly due to the prevailing conservative attitude to all aid programmes and the particularly hostile attitude towards the Ethiopian regime. In addition a succession of allegations in the press and by individual politicians claiming to have evidence of corruption and the diversion of EEC food aid to the Ethiopian army or even the Soviet Union, definitely contributed to the cautious and reluctant approach. The EEC representatives eventually satisfied themselves that there was no significant substance to these allegations but their publication damaged the chances of preventative action. The prominence given them also illustrates the bias of the European press and politicians against the Ethiopian regime. Many in the field confirm that corruption and division of relief food is far less prevalent than elsewhere, for example the Sudan, but stories from other places do not receive the same prominence.

The EEC's existing aid programme included major infrastructural projects and a food programme which was unashamedly not simply humanitarian but one of 'the alternative measures of satisfactorily dealing with unsaleable supplies'. During recent years the EEC agricultural commodities policies (purchase of surplus production at guaranteed prices, export subsidisation, storage costs, destruction of surplus products) accounted for an average share of two-thirds of the EEC budget. The total cost of EEC food aid to developing countries worldwide in 1984 was less than one-third of the cost of storing all surplus products in 1983. In 1981, 40 per cent of EEC development aid funds was spent on food aid but these funds are actually spent on the non-marketable grain surplus. The price of this grain is higher than world market prices; thus not only is at least 40 per cent of the aid budget channelled back into the EEC system but the amount of grain purchased with those funds is less than could be purchased on the open market. The bulk of the existing food aid to Ethiopia was for use on development projects. The EEC was not alone in its preference for 'food-for-work' programmes which did not build up 'food dependency', but it clung to this idea rather longer than was desirable in a time of emergency.

According to the EEC Audit Office the average delivery period between the allocation of food aid and its arrival at its destination is 419 days for wheat and as many as 578 days for butter oil. These lags enabled Brussels' officials to claim that their response in 1984 had been better than in 1983 and that the delays in the arrival of pledged food were eventually to Ethiopia's advantage, as the food plugged a vital gap in September/October 1984 when stocks were at their lowest and the emergency had not yet reached the world's attention. In a limited sense these interpretations are true but they cannot counter the conclusion that until public opinion affected European leaders the EEC's response was inflexible and ungenerous. The figures cannot hide the fact that at the vital time there was very little, if any, *extra* assistance.

In May 1984, Commissioner Dawit toured Western capitals in an attempt to follow up the requests of 30 March. He had submitted a large request for extra assistance to the EEC, including 115,000 tonnes of grain, 15 tonnes of milk powder and 2,500 tonnes of butter oil. Allocations had been made before Commissioner Dawit arrived: Ethiopia was to receive 18,000 tonnes of grain for food-for-work schemes. The extent of the EEC's response to Dawit was to agree that this could be used for emergency purposes plus an extra 1,400 tonnes of milk powder and 300 tonnes of butter oil. It was this shipment which was distributed in September and October 1984. By late August 1984 the European grain harvest was being heralded as a record-breaker, yet neither the EEC nor the British Overseas Development Administration reacted generously to Oxfam's initiative to organise an emergency shipment of grain. In August 1984 Marcus Thompson, an Oxfam Disaster Officer visited Ethiopia partly to take over for a period whilst the Field Director was on leave and partly to decide how best to spend a large sum of money which had been received from a Disasters Emergency Committee Appeal in Britain in July. The alarm of the RRC and voluntary agencies was successfully conveyed to Marcus Thompson who suggested a one-off shipment of 10,000–20,000 tonnes of grain (a quite unprecedented step for such an agency). Both the ODA and the EEC said there was no grain available for such purposes.

The non-governmental agencies

The actions of Catholic Relief Services and Oxfam, Norwegian Church Aid and Redd Barna, the Norwegian Save the Children Fund, in their shipment of grain demonstrate what was already the case but becoming increasingly obvious as the crisis developed, that the NGOs were more responsive and more flexible than the governments of the major donor countries. Nevertheless, these small organisations acknowledge important shortcomings in their own response.

The aftermath of the famine of the early 1970s had produced a feeling that rehabilitation moving into development projects would eventually prevent famine. The optimism engendered by that approach had faded for a variety of reasons, but the belief that long-term development was the priority remained firmly entrenched. The NGOs were understandably so intent upon pursuing their own development targets, a difficult enough task beset by the constraints such work in Ethiopia entailed, that they did not perceive the potential extent of the emergency. Possibly there was a feeling on the part of some NGOs that their fund-raising rationale was based on the idea that such disasters could be averted by constructive response, that is, by development programmes, and that to acknowledge the crisis was to acknowledge failure.

Linked to this is the fact that emergency relief operations and development programmes are conducted under different conditions of funding and staffing and in the case of most NGOs there were no contingency plans for moving from one to the other, nor was their structure apparently flexible enough to allow the personnel involved to take the responsibility of changing gear. Most expatriate development workers are specialists in a particular discipline: agriculture, health, irrigation. It is not their brief to take an overall view. Evidence, for example, of extremely poor nutrition was available to a number of agencies, but this was not treated as an indicator or linked to crop cycles and harvest potential.

Although liaison/coordination existed it was not organised in a way which provided an overall view, summary or projection of future conditions. No comprehensive picture was built up. It is understandable that those in the field were fully stretched in the management of their own activities but a more comprehensive policy on information sharing among those organisations linked to the CRDA, might have produced a more unified response earlier. As it was, a telex signed by 18 member organisations, adopted and distributed by UNDRO, the office of the UN Disaster Relief Coordinator in Geneva, provided an appraisal of the affected population and their needs, and appears to have had some effect on major donors one month before media coverage finally galvanised the international community into action.

There is no doubt that the atmosphere in Addis Ababa was not conducive to high-profile dynamic action, but the example of the September telex suggests that opportunities for thoughtful initiatives existed. In this context the harassment endured by the Ethiopian Evangelical Church of Mekane Yesus since the revolution is relevant. A Protestant church linked to the Lutheran World Federation with a wide network of mission stations and a proven ability to organise relief activities and promote response in others had had senior headquarters staff imprisoned. Its experience of having to live under the conditions imposed by the regime may have prevented this organisation from fulfilling a wider role.

Reaction to Ethiopian government actions

In March 1984, the Ethiopian government formed a high level committee of six ministers, chaired by the Minister of the Interior, to monitor the situation and with the power to mobilise extra resources. It was this committee that authorised the purchase of grain from government stores for use by the RRC for relief purposes. In June, Colonel Mengistu opened the 10th Ministerial Session of the World Food Conference, held in Addis Ababa. He said, 'Ethiopia is currently suffering from the severe drought that has hit most African countries, and conditions are becoming worse even now.' But, in general, the failure of the Ethiopian government to be seen to treat the famine as the greatest priority clearly had a negative effect on donors. The Ministers involved in the special committee, and Commissioner Dawit himself, conducted themselves energetically, but they were not members of the Politbureau which resolved major policy issues.

The time, money and efforts spent on the celebration of the 10th Anniversary of the revolution has been heavily and justifiably criticised. Even members of the RRC were required to practice marching and banner waving. This was viewed with anxiety not only by expatriate observers but also by government staff. The anniversary of the revolution, which owed so much to the catalytic effects of the last famine and the previous regime's failure to publicise and prevent it, fell, with tragic irony, during the month when the predicted deaths were reaching their peak. Journalists and aid workers were prevented from travelling during part of August and September. The performance of the Ethiopian government cannot be excused. Nevertheless, the alarm had been raised long before August 1984.

12. Action at Last: An Accelerated Response

The improved response from September 1984

In August the situation deteriorated greatly in the northern provinces; in Korem 400 people were estimated to have died during the month. Many international agency personnel were away for their summer vacations. Nevertheless, by the end of the month many still in the country were extremely troubled, and significant efforts were made to bring the emergency to the attention of those who could assist, even before the disaster became world news two months later. A variety of coordinated initiatives were taken; a special committee of representatives of WFP, the EEC, the Canadian government, CRDA and ICRC was set up to look into the logistical difficulties of distributing more relief food. At its special meeting on 17 September, CRDA members decided to send a telex expressing deep concern at the gravity of the famine and the desperate shortage of relief food to the UN, all governments and other donors. On 28 September, they followed this up with another appeal to the UN and governments for immediate help to prevent 'hundreds of thousands of people from dying'.

By October, 100 people were dying in Korem every day. UNDRO called a meeting of major donors and some NGOs at which methods of stepping up international relief efforts were discussed as well as increased support for the distributive efforts being made by the RRC. Having published its '1984 Meher Season Production Prospect Supplement' the RRC estimated that 7,326,370 people would face food shortages as a result of 1984 crop failures.

At a donors' meeting on 8 October it stated that the estimated food requirements for the next 12 months would be 1.127 million tonnes of grain, 94,000 tonnes of supplementary food and 27,000 tonnes of oil. The Ethiopian government was to provide cash for 60,000 tonnes of locally purchased grain and 100,000 tonnes of commercial imports. Commissioner Dawit told the meeting, 'Taking into consideration past experience of unmet requests and appeals we have been obliged to reduce our requirement for food by 50 per cent thus making the attainable amount 624,310 tonnes'. The Ethiopian government announced the establishment of a National Committee for Relief and Rehabilitation.

'Where monitoring failed the media succeeded'

As the agencies within Ethiopia finally switched into emergency gear, the donor community outside Ethiopia was prompted into desperate action by the shock engendered by horrifying films of the starving. It may be noted that there had been responsible newspaper coverage of the impending disaster before the competitiveness of the British television companies produced its hard-hitting shots in October. On 23 October the BBC main evening news showed a film of famine in Ethiopia. On 25 October Thames Television showed its documentary film 'Bitter Harvest'. By ensuring that the public of the USA, the UK and other nations (the BBC stated that the Buerk/Amin film was later shown by 425 of the world's broadcasting organisations with a total audience of 470 million) were made aware of the extent of the human tragedy this television coverage forced Western governments to acknowledge their responsibilities, although various expedients were clearly employed to ensure that very little *additional* expenditure was incurred. Similarly, the UN agencies perceived they must take extraordinary action to restore their tarnished image.

By the first week in November, 20 fixed-wing aircraft and 30 helicopters from the UK, USA, USSR, FRG, GDR, Italy and Libya were involved in airlifting supplies from Asmara, Addis Ababa and Assab to central distribution points, primarily Makelle and Axum. By December, about 5,000 tonnes of various relief commodities had been airlifted. Between October and December donor governments or organisations agreed to provide the RRC with a total of 181,486 tonnes of grain and 15,369 tonnes of supplementary food (having been urged to provide 521,428 tonnes). By December only 5,651 tonnes (3.1 per cent of the total commitment) had arrived but, fortunately, outstanding pledges of 85,359 tonnes of various foods were received from abroad. The port of Assab successfully handled these amounts.

On 6 November, the UN Secretary General appointed Kurt Jansson as Assistant Secretary General for Emergency Operations in Ethiopia (EOE). The UN, as has been seen, already had several agencies represented in Ethiopia which had between them a mandate to deal with many aspects of the famine. There was, in addition, UNDRO, which had already become involved. This body, especially set up to 'mobilise, direct and co-ordinate the relief activities of the UN system and co-ordinate the assistance with that given by other inter-governmental and non-governmental organisations', had failed to accept and make known the urgency expressed by the RRC in its own reports. Possibly it was not given the staffing, funding or attention required for it to meet the needs imposed by the emergency. Similarly, throughout 1984 the UNDP representative, who was the senior UN representative in Addis Ababa, was not given contingency funds or staff to tackle the increasing problems.

During the build-up to, and on occasions during, the famine, rivalries between the various UN agencies and their personnel verged on the scandalous. Like many governments, however, the UN now had to be seen to be responding to the crisis, and to attempt to recover from the opprobrium of having failed for nine months to take the lead while being in the best position to do so. The appointment of Kurt Jansson enabled the UN to get off to a fresh start. He brought a new staff with him and successfully began to gain the confidence of the Ethiopian government, the RRC which had become very disillusioned with the major donor agencies, and other organisations in the field. From December 1984 until May 1985 food was distributed at a rate of 45,000 tonnes a month; more than four times what the UN had previously judged to be possible. Six weeks after Kurt Jansson's appointment as his representative, the UN Secretary General created a new office to which he was to report, the Office of Emergency Operations in Africa, OEOA.

The management and ability of Kurt Jansson galvanised the organisation of the emergency action, aided by an enhanced commitment on the part of the Ethiopian government; on 3 October 1984 the Politbureau considered the situation and formally declared the drought a priority. Each member of the Politbureau was made responsible for a specific issue and directives were issued to ports and to each level of the government. Taxes on incoming shipping and the internal purchase of commodities were waived. Special grants of Birr 80 million were approved and it was reported that mass organisations and individuals within the country had raised Birr 2.5 million. In early 1985 Colonel Mengistu addressed the nation on the crisis on television and radio. He announced that luxury imports, primarily cars and textiles should be banned. There was to be a strict petrol rationing and no private motoring on Sundays. All Ethiopians were to contribute one month's pay as a 'famine levy'; farmers were each to give 100 kg of grain. If necessary all should be ready to give of their time to help establish the new resettlement areas. (Staff and students of higher education establishments were required to do this in mid-1985 at the end of the academic year.)

There was also an unprecedented flow of funds and food from individuals and private organisations. Even by December 1984 cash and goods in kind totalling Birr 4.9 million had arrived in Ethiopia. Public contributions to non-government organisations in countries outside Ethiopia were to continue at an amazing rate for many months. 'Compassion fatigue', though often mentioned by politicians, did not set in. This was partially due to the efforts of Bob Geldof and others who organised spectacular fund-raising events; the Live Aid concert alone raised $70 million. Bob Geldof is an extraordinary person with an almost recklessly fundamental approach to the scandal of human beings dying of starvation on one part of the planet whilst others live in plenty on another, but there is no doubt that he was able to appeal to a public growing more aware and sensitive to the issues. To some extent this was due to the media coverage but the fact that the public response was not a nine-days wonder but an enduring concern revealed a new sense of responsibility among the people of the richer nations. The public response was also an indictment of 'official' reaction; an expression of the anger and frustration felt by those who believed governments were not representing the true level of concern for social and economic issues relating to the Third World.

At this global level the impact of the media was extraordinary, although many deplored its sensationalising approach and its failure to take advantage of the opportunities to educate and analyse. It is true that the combination of public opinion, the rivalry of the BBC and independent television, together with the unique structure of the BBC, enabled the Ethiopian famine to remain news in the UK for an unprecedented length of time. By giving the Buerk/Amin story the lead on its main news programme on two consecutive nights, with the items of eight and seven minutes (two minutes is the normal length), the BBC maximised the impact of a story which might otherwise have been quickly forgotten. What should be realised is that this process was fairly arbitrary. There is no guarantee that humanitarian stories will always be given such prominence. October 1984 was a relatively uneventful time in Europe, there were no important stories already commanding the headlines. Of equal interest is the powerful influence of the press at a national level within countries prone to drought, as noted by Amartya Sen.

India, he points out, has not had a famine since independence; given the nature of India's political system and her relatively free press she is unlikely to have one. As soon as there are a handful of deaths from malnutrition the press spreads the news and generates political disquiet. Under this pressure and the challenge of opposition parties the government cannot afford to fail to take action. In this way famines have been averted in India even though food output per head is still low. The government in fact has not overcome persistent undernourishment but cannot escape taking counter-measures at times of famine. These involve storage and distribution of food and generating purchasing ability through employment programmes. In contrast, China, which has a greater commitment to tackling the problems of constant malnourishment, has suffered major famines with great loss of life. There is no 'political early warning system' as in India, where newspapers and critical politicians demand immediate action and even changes in policy. There were many factors contributing to the magnitude of the disaster in Ethiopia, one of them may have been the absence of a free press to mount pressure on the government.

Ethiopian resettlement policies

A controversial aspect of the response to the emergency was the Ethiopian government's decision to implement a large resettlement scheme. In Ethiopia resettlement of people from drought-prone areas in the northern provinces has been a feature of government policy both before and after the revolution. The government's decision to mount the programme during an emergency, without adequate planning or support services, together with the fact that it could be perceived as being related to regional political considerations, led to criticism from many donors and international sources and a refusal to allow food aid to be diverted to resettlement areas.

During the period in which resettlement was carried out, there was little effort on the part of critics to understand that resettlement might be a long-term necessity and to distinguish between this and the implementation of the scheme during the emergency. After some initial hesitation some agencies decided that the half million people who had been moved deserved some assistance. They have taken the line that the people cannot be moved back and must be helped to realise the full potential of the new start. The problems of starting from scratch are formidable, but where agricultural and medical help has been offered, resettlement schemes are showing substantial progress. In an attempt to elucidate some of the issues that have led to continued criticism, the next chapter includes a longer discussion on the resettlement programme.

Developments in 1985

Throughout 1985 the crisis persisted and the RRC was faced with vast and competing needs. including famine in areas of the southern provinces. These could not be fully met because of inadequate food and transport resources. In Wollo. 9,000 tonnes of grain was distributed each month against an estimated requirement of 35,000 tonnes. The RRC was receiving about 24,000 each month, so Wollo was getting about one-third of the relief supplies available to the Government.

In March. the UN held a major donor conference in Geneva. Four months later the OEOA calculated that $1.17 billion had been pledged in food for the whole of Africa. but unmet food-needs were still put at $500 million. Pledges of non-food items, seeds, tools, pesticides, etc. amounted to $112 million. The resistance on the part of some major donors to meeting the development, as opposed to emergency needs, especially in the case of Ethiopia was considerable.

Within Ethiopia emergency airlifts became vital to providing food for remote areas. At the beginning of 1985 the two RAF Hercules and their crew had their tour of duty extended until June. then till September; as a result of further public pressure they stayed until December. Together with the Polish Air Force flying Russian helicopters the RAF dropped 7,000 tonnes of food during the first six months of 1985 into areas inaccessible by road, and distributed another 12,000 tonnes by landing the food. The cost of keeping them in Ethiopia was shared by the ODA and the Ministry of Defence; by the end of December 1985 the share of the MOD was about £12 million. This represented the only additional expenditure sanctioned by the British government during the entire famine emergency. The rest of the cost of the RAF operation came from the previously fixed overseas development budget.

In a report published in May 1985. the House of Commons Foreign Affairs Committee expressed the view that it was unacceptable that almost the entire cost of the UK's response to the crisis should be met from the previously agreed Overseas Development Budget. The Overseas Development Administration has a contingency reserve of £55 million from which most of the additional funds provided during the African emergency, including those channelled through the EEC, came. Over and above that figure. contributions to the emergency programme were at the expense of the normal programmes.

The achievements, if they can be called that, of the emergency were to contain the problem. Within the relief camps the death rates were gradually reduced; in Harbu, Wollo, for example, where 2,612 out of 7,200 people died between 29 October 1984 and the end of January 1985, only a few were dying each day by mid-1985. In the Korem camp more than 100 people were dying each day in October 1984; this number rose before the end of the year but had been reduced to about 20 each day by mid-1985. Fifty-two thousand people remained in the camp. but food supplies throughout the period amounted to less than 1,700 calories a day per person. There was never enough to be distributed to enable people to return to their homes and start planting. Rehabilitation could not begin until people were back on the land, but provision of seed, tools and fertiliser was still inadequate.

Because of the seemingly inevitable lags and delays food and some agricultural inputs arrived in greater quantities in the second half of the year; often too late to be of use during the planting season. Little or no response was made at that time to provide the necessary food aid or agricultural inputs for those who had been transported to resettlement areas.

Developments in 1986

The situation in 1986 improved considerably; the number of people needing food aid, approximately 6.5 million, remained almost the same as in 1985, but gradually shelters were phased out and, because of the improved transport situation, food was distributed to people in their home areas. Between October 1985 and mid-1986 more than 170 heavy duty trucks arrived from donors, including 100 from Italy. The UN established a new transportation unit, The World Food Programme Transport Operation in Ethiopia (WTOE), comprising 250 vehicles, including some from Band Aid/Live Aid and USAID. This had to deal with a new facet of the emergency when the Djibouti–Addis Ababa rail link was severed by a collapsed bridge.

The RRC estimated that 1.34 million tonnes of emergency food aid was needed for 1986 but, owing to delays in the arrival of 1985 pledges and the publicity which focused on the continuation of the crisis, there were no gaps in provision as there had been in 1985. A total of 785,200 tonnes of grain and supplementary food for relief and related activities was pledged for 1986. The main 1985 harvest was one-third greater than 1984 but still below normal. The tendency persisted for NGOs to distribute more relief grain than the RRC. Of the total food assistance, 518,200 tonnes was acquired and distributed by NGOs.

The rainfall during the two major seasons was much better than the previous year in most parts of the country. In many areas the *belg* rains were abundant, resulting in good crops where they had been planted. Significant exceptions were in Gondar, Gojjam, Eritrea, Illubaber and Wollega. In collaboration with NGOs the Ministry of Agriculture distributed 28,000 tonnes of seed and two million hand tools to take full advantage of the *kerempt* rains leading to the main *meher* harvest. Though better than 1985, the amount and distribution of the main rains were unfavourable in many parts of the country. Excessive rain and hailstorm damage were widely reported; some areas experienced dry spells in July and August and the rain ceased early in some northern areas.

Because of the length of time there have been shortfalls in production, it has now become difficult to define 'normal' production. In its Early Warning System Synoptic Report, '1987 Food Supply Prospects', published in January 1987, the RCC Early Warning and Planning Services define 'normal production' as the average production for the period 1979–83, and stress that this does not mean self-sufficiency. Overall national production for the *meher* harvest was indicated as about 12 per cent below normal.

In areas where the nomadic population lives, pasture and water availability improved; the number of livestock remained far below the minimum required. Restocking in most areas, particularly Eritrea, Tigray and Wollo, was difficult because of lack of animals to be bought.

Throughout the year despite a shift from relief activities to development, the need for relief persisted. With the acute emergency over, however, new arguments arose over allocations. CRS, for example, faced with the need to continue food programmes, found its allocation of food aid cut by the US government as it reduced its commitment. Having received 51 per cent of the US total commitment in 1985, CRS was to receive 41 per cent of a smaller amount. Despite an earlier decision to phase out its operation by the end of 1986, however, USAID remains in Ethiopia, convinced that the sheer precariousness of the situation merits their continued presence.

Developments in 1987

The precarious nature of the situation can be demonstrated by considering the expected needs of those vulnerable to famine, as described at the RRC's regular donors' meeting held in Addis Ababa on 15 January 1987. Two separate estimates for the new food aid requirement for 1987 were given; that is, in addition to any carry-over of relief food from 1986, commercial imports or regular food aid programmes.

The RRC's Early Warning and Planning Services Department considers food availability at *woreda* level in an attempt to identify those areas and populations unable to produce enough food to supply their needs and whose access to markets will be impaired for a variety of reasons. Having considered the results of the *meher* harvest in detail according to crop and region, the EWPSD gave an estimate of the number of crop growers and nomads who would be likely to require assistance in each region. The total was 2,500,000 (1,838,950 croppers and 661,050 nomads). The total food assistance for this number (grain, supplementary food and edible oil) was estimated to be 409,203 tonnes. This figure did not take account of refugees who had returned to the country, Sudanese refugees fleeing from the disastrous situation in southern Sudan or any requirements of the resettled population.

An FAO crop assessment mission made detailed studies of crop production region by region. Applying the aggregate figures for the whole country (FAO reported the production of cereals to be 7 per cent above the previous year but 4 per cent below normal pre-drought levels) to an average ration of 435 grams of cereal equivalent per head per day for a population of 45.59 million people, a deficit of approximately 600,000 tonnes of grain was revealed. (It should be noted that the figure of 435 grams is below the accepted UN norm of 500 grams).

This food balance sheet methodology is clearly less sensitive in some ways than methods aimed at locating the pockets of people in need. Nevertheless, as an indicator of the overall deficit situation, it can be useful in determining the dimensions of the food aid requirements.

The treatment of this divergence in the estimated total requirements of food assistance revealed a very different approach on the part of the international community. In his statement at the donors' meeting, Michael Priestley, UN Resident Coordinator and Chairman of the UN Emergency Prevention and Preparedness Group (successor to the Special Office for Emergency Operations in

Ethiopia (EOE)) proposed that the RRC appeal should be treated as the absolute minimum level of assistance.

The significance of both figures, those produced by the EWSPD and the FAO mission, is that they presume the *belg* crop will be normal. Given the unpredictability of rainfall patterns in recent years, it can be seen that, once again, if rainfall is appreciably deficient, an immediate reassessment of the situation will be necessary. Any appreciable deficiency in the main season rainfall in the near future could put 10–15 per cent of Ethiopia's population directly at risk of starvation.

Part 3:
Efforts at Consolidation of the 'Positive' Consequences of the Crisis

13. Wider Responses

After an inexcusable delay, the stark crisis in Ethiopia and other countries produced an unprecedented response in the international community and also among African governments and people themselves. The negative effects of such a disaster are irreversible: loss of life, physiological and psychological damage to the susceptible sections of the surviving population, loss of livestock, ecological damage and the displacement of peoples. Other negative effects such as the decline in exports and damage to on-going projects may be of a relatively temporary nature. There is the possibility, however, that certain benefits may accrue if opportunities are grasped. There is no doubt that such opportunities were lost in the aftermath of the 1973–74 famine. Many of the development and economic strategies of the past decade have lost credibility. Not only was the situation in 1984–85 far worse, but the message was clear; droughts will recur and famines with them unless a greater and better coordinated effort is made to attack the basic causes.

In particular, there appears to have been a great deal of rethinking among African nations. Whether their apparent willingness to tackle the deep-rooted problems will continue and whether it will be matched (and encouraged) by the international community remains to be seen, but the signs that a new seriousness is affecting attempts to create self-sustaining societies in African are strong.

The African response

In 1980 the Lagos Plan of Action, setting out a strategy for accelerated and self-reliant economic development, was adopted at an OAU summit meeting but instead of steady progress the next five years witnessed a continuing deterioration, so that at an OAU summit meeting in 1985 African leaders were confronted with an unprecedented economic and social crisis. African economies had been severely affected by the deep, world-wide recession, penalised by deteriorating terms of trade and unfavourable methods of commodity pricing, the burden of debt-servicing and natural disasters. The leaders did not, however, omit to mention 'domestic short-comings' and were unprecedentedly critical of the failures of African governments, in particular their lack of action in the implementation of the Lagos Plan. It was acknowledged that had the aims of this Plan been incorporated

163

into national policies the effects of drought and world recession could have been mitigated.

The 1985 OAU summit adopted a 'Priority Programme for Economic Recovery' which had five broad aims: to accelerate the implementation of the Lagos Plan; to improve the food and agricultural situation; to alleviate the burden of external debt; to create a platform for common action; to deal with the effects of South Africa's policies of destabilisation of the frontline states.

Under each of these headings the OAU summit recommended a number of steps at national, regional and international level. There was no attempt to disguise the magnitude of the effort necessary to implement the 'priority programme'. The Lagos Plan is ambitious and leaders are aware of the strength of the combination of factors which have rendered past attempts at such plans ineffective. There is a level of determination brought about by the severity of the current crisis which may prove effective if the momentum can be maintained, for all the issues are recognised to be long-term, relating to greater economic self-reliance and economic integration.

Although none of the 'priority programme's' broad aims is new there is a stronger emphasis on the need for better national management. Not only is the old pattern of development strategies being re-examined but also the patterns of cooperation. It is recognised that aid is not a panacea, whether in an emergency or in the long-term, as it is no substitute for sound internal policies effectively implemented. This was the prevailing consensus at a number of international conferences, in particular the North–South Round Table discussions of March 1986, 'Beyond the Famine: New Directions in Development', held in Nairobi and Khartoum. The new direction was towards government policy changes and local solutions, with the emphasis on an increase in agricultural production through a better deal for the smallholder.

The World Bank

Whereas African opinion is by no means unanimous on the appropriateness of many of the economic measures which have been urged or forced on African countries in the past decade by multilateral lending agencies, the World Bank in its April 1986 study, 'Financing Adjustment with Growth in Sub-Saharan Africa 1986–90' states that many African countries are now making significant progress in reforming their economies, but declining exports and investment threaten to undermine the progress. Total capital flows to low-income African countries are declining whilst the debt burden is serious and growing.

The study emphasised that 1986 was to be a year of opportunity for Africa to build on progress and for donors to help ensure the progress with more financial assistance. It estimated that at least $11 billion a year in concessional flows during 1986–90 will be needed. For low-income African countries to finance a minimum level of imports and to service existing debt, the region will need about $35.3 billion per year for the next five years. Allowing for expected proceeds from Africa's exports, and known aid commitments, a gap of about $2.5 billion remains. The World Bank suggested that additional bilateral aid agreements could bridge the gap by a combination of both additional fast-disbursing aid and debt relief. It emphasised that 'no donor country should be a net recipient of resource flows from any African country undertaking credible economic reforms'.

Although these large figures illustrate the dimension of the problem, they do not show that not all countries will be treated evenly. The figures demonstrate the likely shortfall of aid from the donor community. This reflects a growing hostility on the part of the USA, the UK and some other nations towards UN organisations. It also reflects a tendency on the part of the USA and these same allies to be more critical of African governments and more selective when considering aid commitments. Thus some multilateral organisations, even though committed to the type of programmes essential to the progress of the smallholder, are being restricted by inadequate funding, for example, the International Fund for Agricultural Development (IFAD). Countries such as Ethiopia, which are not committed to market oriented policies, will be constrained by lack of bilateral aid. The current Three-Year Development Plan (1986/87–1988/89) acknowledges a need to increase the inflow of foreign loans and assistance. A special committee is studying ways of increasing the availability of such lands, but any proposed are unlikely to affect the underlying reasons for the low level of technical assistance to Ethiopia.

The UN Special Session on the critical economic situation in Africa: 27–31 May 1986

The concept envisaged by the African leaders and endorsed by the World Bank was a new 'compact' for the continent, in which international donors complemented the new efforts being made to fully mobilise and utilise domestic resources and entered into a new partnership. A special session of the UN General Assembly was called to discuss future progress. It was believed that the unprecedentedly united voices not only emphasising self-reliance, food production, environmental management and popular participation, but also acknowledging the failings of structural rigidity, misplaced priorities, bureaucratic ineptitude and official corruption, would meet with a sympathetic response. There was an understanding that the session was not concerned with detailed pledges but nevertheless the end result, despite an apparent absence of confrontational politics and a unanimous acceptance of the principles of an international programme to improve Africa's economic situation, was a disappointment to representatives of African governments.

The OAU paper had said:

> Even if all the domestic resources being mobilised to finance Africa's Priority Programme for Economic Recovery (APPER) are used in servicing debt, the African countries will still not be able to meet all their debt obligations, let alone have the resources left to finance APPER. Therefore the central issue is what the international community does in alleviating the debt-service obligations of African countries.

This central issue was addressed only in general terms; no specific measures were considered. The USA and Japan in particular, rejected the idea of discussing the debt issue, relegating it to the fora concerned, such as the IMF, World Bank and

GATT. The international community resolved to supplement Africa's own financial efforts through 'intensified cooperation and substantially increased support', but made no definite commitments of either money or action.

Perhaps no more could have been expected and the consensus expressed does represent the beginning of a new era in North–South relations. However, seen against the winding down of emergency aid in the countries still affected by famine and its after effects, and the shortfall in non-food aid requested for rehabilitation purposes, the results were not encouraging.

The donor–recipient relationship

As someone noted at the Nairobi Round Table conference: 'aid fatigue exists on both sides'. Yet the relationship between the aid receivers and the aid givers must continue. Appraisal of the performance of donors and governments during the crisis has led to a number of areas being considered in need of reform. Some of these have been addressed at the UN Special Session, some have been acknowledged by aid agencies themselves, others were considered at the plethora of post-famine conferences.

1) Donors present their aid, even at times of greatest emergency, through a barrage of baffling rules and regulations. The UN recommended 'an evolution of procurement policies and administrative procedures which would improve delivery of product inputs.'

2) More consideration should be given to indigenous competence, expertise, experience and local conditions, particularly local techniques and equipment. This exhortation to 'buy talents and products locally' was linked to the point that local knowledge is too often and too easily underestimated by both expatriates and central governments.

3) To ensure a greater impact for aid projects there should be more effective coordination of aid. Some countries believe they should be more selective about aid, not simply because much bilateral aid is perceived as politically motivated but also because their own development criteria should be more clearly defined and aid more stringently judged to be in accordance with it. In this respect technical assistance should be more responsive to local needs and priorities. This approach could be developed so that unneeded and lower priority projects could be phased out and funds diverted to economic recovery programmes.

4) To attempt any of the above effectively, African states should improve their own surveillance, monitoring and evaluation capabilities so that quality improvements can 'yield' more from limited financial resources.

5) More account should be taken of recurrent and local costs when new programmes are introduced. Measures to assist in meeting recurrent and local costs of on-going projects should be considered where these have proved worthwhile, rather than the inception of new ones.

6) Some initiatives should be taken to bring African money and highly-trained Africans home. The political and practical difficulties of this would be enormous but as a joint exercise it might present an effective low-cost programme. Low risk

bonds, which entail no questions as to the source of the funds of the purchasers, can be designed, and bilateral agencies and foundations might be asked to encourage skilled Africans to come home by paying air fares and some resettlement costs. An amnesty programme could be as effective as paying for more training.

7) Low income countries do not present obvious investment opportunities but a climate of commercial reliability can be created in order to foster domestic and international investment.

Many of these guidelines are seen to be means of improving the efficiency and impact of development assistance without greatly increasing their financial targets. Although eventually the African countries may seek to demand 'higher-cost' solutions, they now seem to be seeking agreements with donors on low-cost solutions. The rationale of the current 'low-cost' approach is that it will serve to revise the donor view of recipients as inefficient, soaking up whatever is given to them. Donors will not be pushing recipients in different ways but will stand back to allow the recipients to ask for what they really need, having reviewed their situation. Whereas increased realism and efficiency cannot be bad, it is worth noting that there does not seem much alternative to this approach. The percentage of GNP devoted to official development assistance is falling in several of the major donor nations: the USA, the UK, Italy and Japan. In most others it is static. In only the case of Norway is it currently 1 per cent, in most it is below 0.5 per cent.

14. Possibilities for Action in Ethiopia

By revealing limitations in both national capabilities and international coordination and responsiveness, the recent crisis has created a climate in Ethiopia in which new efforts to deal with the overall problems of development can be made. A great many programmes and projects are already at the planning stage or underway. Whilst there is no clear dividing line in the type of activity — all are concerned to improve the livelihood of the rural population — there are two main objectives: firstly, to deal with the more immediate effects of the famine by building up the resources and the resilience of those individuals affected; secondly, to lay down a more secure path for future development.

In the first area there remains a need for food aid in the short and medium term to avoid hunger and starvation in the areas which cannot recuperate from such a devastating famine in a matter of months and to expand food-for-work-programmes for infrastructural projects. Equally important for immediate recovery is assistance with the means of recovery: seeds, tools, pesticides etc. The RRC has prepared detailed projects to rehabilitate different groups; the population

167

of the shelters, the orphans, peasant farmers in drought-affected areas, those on resettlement schemes, pastoralists and returning refugees. An outline of the needs of the second area is given below.

Food production

Policies should be aimed at an increase in the level of food production in order to achieve three linked objectives: 1) the self-sufficiency of individual farmers; 2) the production of a marketable surplus by individual farmers to provide a cash income as well as a contribution to the total available surplus; 3) the creation and maintenance of security food reserves at regional and national levels.

To ensure these three objectives, the promotion of technical improvements and the distribution of inputs is required. Although in the long-term national self-sufficiency may not be realistic, in the short-term the majority of the population will remain dependent on their own production. The primary aim of production will still be consumption. Yields must, therefore, be increased through improved seeds, better varieties and the introduction of new crops. Improved ploughs and the wider use of fertilisers have already been experimented with in some areas. In specific regions and in some settlement schemes a comprehensive approach to improving production, including the introduction of new food crops which increase the variety of foods eaten, thus improving the diet, has been successful.

The existing extension service, with comprehensive support services, must be extended and maintained. This must be responsible for introducing improved methods of husbandry and elminating post-harvest losses.

Efficient marketing of surpluses should be linked to producer incentives. In 1985 the import parity prices (at the official exchange rate) for maize, sorghum and wheat were respectively 80 per cent, 50 per cent and 45 per cent above the AMC farm-gate procurement prices. There is now a large body of evidence indicating that supply response to price in Africa is as high as elsewhere. Years of bias against domestic producers has contributed to stagnating agricultural production but price incentives to producers have a range of effects beyond increasing output. For example, more capital is attracted into agriculture, technical improvements are made and, in the longer term, the farming community remains on the land. If there are incentives to produce a surplus there will also be incentives to care for the land and thus prevent its degradation. Incentives must, in fact, be interpreted in the broadest possible way rather than as economic dogma; they should include secure and efficient transport and marketing systems, timely payment for crop deliveries, and availability of consumer goods in rural areas. The consolidation of land reform and improved security of land tenure should also be considered from the producer's point of view; uncertainty over the future of the land has a discouraging effect upon the individual farmer.

A great deal of work has already been done by the Ministry of Agriculture, the World Bank, FAO and IFAD to create a policy framework and devise programmes for accelerated agricultural growth. Increased importance is attached to peasant production in the current Three-Year Development Plan. Within this framework there is still room for a greatly enlarged programme of international assistance which can be channelled along the existing institutional lines reinforcing and complementing the government's plans for broad-based development.

For satisfactory meat and dairy production and to improve the quality of livestock, similar procedures and incentives must be followed and provided.

Soil and water conservation

Increases in agricultural production can be realised and maintained in the rain-fed areas only if soil and water conservation measures are practised and reafforestation energetically pursued. The task facing the country exceeds the capacity of existing governmental organisations. Nevertheless, high priority is attached to programmes aimed at environmental regeneration and conservation-based agricultural development. Prior to and during the years of drought PAs and other mass organisations were mobilised to build terraces, plant trees etc. In many cases, investment in both financial and manpower terms was not fully realised partly because of the drought but partly because of lack of supervision and maintenance. Support, in the form of logistics, equipment, seeds and training, to ensure the improvement and consolidation of existing programmes is necessary. The growing awareness of the importance of conservation measures can be exploited. In resettlement areas it is important that the same process of degeneration, an inherent danger where a large number of people are clearing forests in preparation for intensive agricultural activity, is not allowed to begin. Opportunities for permanent employment in all aspects of this area can be explored.

Forestry

The potential of forestry as an instrument of rural development has already been recognised. Many opportunities for the implementation of projects which would fit into the existing framework of forestry production systems have been established over the past decade. As with soil and water conservation, programmes exist which are in need of consolidation and improvement. There are a variety of suitable projects; small fuelwood plantations closer to towns; firewood and industrial plantations in settlement areas, aimed at meeting energy requirements in the longer term; rehabilitation of degraded forests; consolidation and expansion of the community forest programme. The idea of involving women in such forestry projects as the running of plant nurseries, is under consideration.

Health

Throughout the emergency period the Ministry of Health, the RRC, WHO and other agencies providing health care attempted to maintain a holistic perspective. Food, shelter, water, clothing and an attack on the root causes of famine were, and still are, viewed as priorities, even to be put above medical and health services. The Ministry of Health is a member of the Politbureau Co-ordinating Committee but the coverage, accessibility and utilisation of health services is limited even in 'normal' times. As all those participating in the emergency become involved in rehabilitation, whether of those returning from the shelters to their home areas or to resettlement areas, the first concern remains food distribution.

To help ensure that available resources are being used in such a way as to have a long-term positive impact on the health and disease status of as many people as possible, the Primary Health Care approach has been adopted as a framework in which to develop and expand health services and activities. This approach must be based on a fair distribution of resources, community involvement, preventive measures, appropriate and affordable technology and a multi-sectoral approach to health problems. The provision of the following are priorities; education about health, nutrition and disease; safe water and basic sanitation; immunisation; appropriate treatment of common diseases and injuries; provision of essential drugs; an effective referral system; family health care and the involvement of basic health workers. As so much of Ethiopia remains dependent on traditional practitioners and practices, ways in which they could be integrated into the system could be studied.

The provision of clean water within reach of dwellings must be a priority but in view of the extent of the problem it can be tackled only over the long-term. Whilst 32 per cent of the urban population has access to clean, drinkable water, the proportion in rural areas was estimated in 1982 to be only 4.3 per cent. For the country as a whole it was estimated that the nearest domestic water source was over one kilometre away from 45 per cent of communities in the dry seasons and 27 per cent in the wet seasons. During the dry seasons 75 per cent of rural villages faced a serious shortage of water and more than 50 per cent were exposed to the hazards associated with the unhealthy nature of the water they habitually used. Women and children have to spend long, arduous hours fetching water and wood. Ongoing programmes are said to have an annual capacity of installing water supply systems for up to one million people (the figure was 300,000–400,000 a few years ago) using boreholes (capital intensive), spring protection and development, farm ponds, tanks and hand-dug wells. There would be opportunities to provide increased resources to expand this scheme or promote water-supply schemes in the context of other projects.

Diversification of rural economic activity

Non-agricultural activities should be regarded as part of the long-term anti-famine strategy. In the medium and longer term, as and when agricultural incomes rise and can be sustained, there is a large potential demand for a wide range of consumer goods, building materials, improved agricultural tools, transport and other services. At present the small-scale manufacturing and handicraft sector is relatively small and concentrated around towns and cities. Non-agricultural activities are widespread as part of the traditional pattern of subsistence; yarn, cloth, pottery and wooden utensils are produced in many homes. Within many local communities the potter, the weaver, the carpenter and blacksmith run their small enterprises. Traditionally, however, the range of occupations and products is limited owing to lack of mobility, low incomes, the relative isolation of much of the population and the low level of technological innovation.

Resettlement policies and villagisation

To the Ethiopian government it appears self-evident that many of the policies mentioned above will be easier to implement if peasants are congregated in villages or settlements rather than in scattered homesteads.

The recent resettlement scheme was a government initiative aimed at moving those most affected by famine to more promising areas in the south and west. Over time there has been considerable spontaneous migration out of Wollo and Tigray and also movement to more favourable sites nearer to the migrants' old homes.

Traditionally, highland peasants cultivate the plateaux tops, and considerable 'resettlement' has taken place as erosion and population pressure force them to move downhill. The potential of these lowland areas is limited, however, by malaria, tsetse fly and water-logged soil in some valleys.

Various forms of resettlement have been and are supported by a number of donor agencies that concur with the government's pragmatic view that resources sufficient to rehabilitate the degraded highland areas so that they can support even the present level of population can never be provided. The World Bank recommended a resettlement scheme in 1971; during the 1970s the FAO cooperated with the Ethiopian government on a comprehensive study entitled 'Highland Reclamation', a study in which they concluded resettlement was a valid option.

Undoubtedly the most comprehensive and up-to-date study of soil and resources in the Ethiopian highlands, however, is 'The Ethiopian Highlands Reclamation Study' (EHRS) produced jointly by the FAO and the Ethiopian Ministry of Agriculture. Over 30 working papers on a wide range of issues relating to the degradation of soil in the highlands and to policies to combat further degradation were produced between 1983 and 1985. The study details the alarming trends in serious soil erosion and divides the highland areas into three broad agro-ecological zones: the high potential perennial crop zone (HPP); the high potential cereal crop zone (HPC); and the low potential cereal crop zone (LPC). The LPC zone covers almost all highlands in Eritrea, Tigray, Wollo, northern Shoa, eastern Gondar and parts of Haraghe and Bale. About 60 per cent of the most serious erosion is in the LPC zone, which has the largest history of population settlement, de-vegetation and erosive cropping. A greater proportion of its soils is derived from more erodible materials, on more erodible convex slopes.

The zone has short plant-growing periods resulting in thin vegetation and slower natural rates of soil formation. By the year 2010 degradation could destroy the farmlands of some ten million highlanders, 15 per cent of the population, 60 per cent of which live in the LPC zone. Within the lifetime of today's children over one-third of the highlands could become incapable of sustaining cropping, while the population could treble. 'In such circumstances nature is likely to impose its own checks by ever more severe and more frequent crop failures arising from the combination of continued degradation and periodic droughts'. (EHRS. Executive Summary, p. 8.)

To check and reverse the degradation process a conservation-based 'Development Strategy' has been devised. But given the level of technology and poverty, to expect a fast change in land use is unrealistic. Despite criticism of old resettlements, the study (p. 21) acknowledges that:

171

Resettlement is necessary in order to provide breathing space for reclamation and even conservation to be effective in the most densely populated and degraded areas, especially the LPC zone. It is estimated that considerably more than 150,000 persons annually will need to be resettled or preferably 'migrate' voluntarily if present population growth and degradation trends continue. Such rural–rural resettlement/migration also provides a means of expanding crop lands and thus production in presently underutilized areas of the HPP and HPC zones.

There is also evidence to suggest that one impact of the land reform measures of the mid-1970s was to slow down the spontaneous migration process. As all peasants now had the right to land the movement ceased of those forced out of tenancies or whose claims to land had become so small as to become inadequate. In addition, it was often difficult to leave one Peasant Association and join another. Thus, population pressure was building up in the highland areas without the natural outlet of spontaneous migration.

In November 1984, believing itself to be justified by the above considerations, the government decided to execute a resettlement scheme designed to rehabilitate 1.5 million people most acutely affected by famine from Wollo, Tigray and northern Shoa, by moving them to under-utilised areas of the country where they would receive land and immediate necessities to enable them to start a new life. The first phase moved 552,641 people, mostly to Illubaber, Keffa, Wollega and Gojjam, and smaller numbers to Tadele in Shoa and Gondar. The RRC Commissioner invited some representatives of the NGO community to visit some of the resettlement areas for the first time in January 1985. Some of the areas they viewed showed that considerable progress had been made but other reports were highly condemnatory and the whole scheme came under intense criticism from many donors. Certain accounts of the transport of the settlers described brutal mistreatment, the splitting up of families and claimed the scheme was not run on voluntary lines but amounted to enforced deportation.

There is no doubt that the Ethiopian government had hoped for external assistance with the scheme, which was viable only if considerable inputs were provided at each settlement. In his review of December 1984 the Relief Commissioner had outlined the alternative plans and detailed the assistance requirements, ranging from heavy land-clearing, water-drilling and road construction equipment and tractors to hoes, blankets and kitchen utensils. The massive criticism eventually led the government to suspend the scheme in mid-1985, conceding that serious mistakes had been made in its implementation. Its intention was to consolidate progress up to that point before extending the scheme.

There is agreement on the lack of preparation and preliminary studies. Site selection procedures were seriously inadequate. Evaluations of a former resettlement programme criticised the site selection procedures. But the expertise required, not only in the major fields of agriculture but also in social anthropology, health, ecology and infrastructure, was simply not available. Now there is a growing realisation that investment in site selection and planning can be less costly than the failures that follow hasty decisions by a high-level team flying hurriedly around the western parts of the country. The main problems turned out to be absence of drinking water in some chosen locations, and flooding and water-logging in areas near Gambella. In addition, the black, clayish soil covering many areas chosen as resettlement sites — the Metekel area of Gojjam, the Gambella plain and areas around Metema in Gondar — has limited agricultural potential.

There were no basic services at many reception centres. The journey, whether by road or aeroplane (transport was provided by the Russians) was arduous, and many people were unfit due to the effects of three to four years of famine. Families did become separated, not because of deliberately harsh treatment, but because of poor logistics and inadequate planning. The programme began with genuine efforts to recruit people on a voluntary basis but these deteriorated in places where officials were under pressure to meet quotas set by the government.

The question of the use of force and the voluntary nature of resettlement is undoubtedly the main issue that led to the international condemnation of the Ethiopian government, resulting in a lack of support for the resettlement policy at the time when aid was needed. The government's policy, as stated in an RRC press release, listed four criteria by which Peasant Association leaders, local administrators, and RRC staff should register settlers: the willingness of heads of families to be resettled; to bring along their dependants; to be engaged in agriculture; and their physical fitness.

At the regional level, however, other criteria were added. Regional administrators thought it appropriate to select families whose *meher* crops had failed completely, or were in debt and unable to repay, or cultivating slopes above 30 degrees. Others included people who had migrated to a feeding centre.

The voluntary nature of the government's criteria was further modified in the eyes of some of those making the selection at the local level by the fact that the government allocated quotas to each administrative level regarding how many people should be moved. Zealous administrative officials undoubtedly tended to disregard the voluntary aspects of the criteria in their attempt to meet the quotas.

Until the better rains of 1985 there were unquestionably many who went voluntarily. Regional authorities in Tigray and Shoa had ceased to select settlers by September 1985, very few still wanting to go. In Wollo, settlers were still being selected, but once the rains began there was great reluctance to move. It should be remembered that, despite the changed nature of the authority, peasants in the highlands are unlikely to resist authority. Perhaps it is only possible to say that a peasant is resettled 'voluntarily' when migration is seen as the last resort.

Another allegation of the resettlement programme's critics was that people were taken away from the security areas so as to decrease support for the rebel forces. As mentioned above, the Low Potential Cereal Zone (LPC) covers the highlands of Eritrea, Wollo, Tigray, northern Shoa, eastern Gondar, and parts of Hararghe and Bale. Almost 90 per cent of the settlers come from these areas and more than 70 per cent from areas not considered to be security areas; 63 per cent from Wollo, 18 per cent from Shoa, 15 per cent from Tigray, and none from Eritrea. If the crop-growing *awrajas* most affected by food shortages in the years 1981 to 1985 are considered, a complete correlation with the origin of settlers in the 1984–85 resettlement scheme is shown. All settlers came from *awrajas* in the top third of those affected by crop shortages. None of the *awrajas* in which people were resettled were in the top third of the list of those affected by food shortages. It should be added however that more than half the country's *awrajas* (50) have been affected by famine at some time since 1958.

Another source of criticism was the issue of the separation of families. Although this undoubtedly took place, the issue is far more complex than might at first appear. Investigations have shown that, in many cases, the separation which occurred and may well be lamented by those now in resettlement areas, was countenanced by members of the family. For example, it was often agreed that children should be left with their grandparents while the parents, or a surviving parent, went with the older children to the resettlement areas. For many this was viewed as a temporary separation, some members of the family would experiment, others would 'wait and see'.

On other occasions, members of the family did not agree; a husband, for example, might join the scheme, leaving a wife with other relatives from whom she was unwilling to be parted. Family reunification becomes costly and complicated. In late 1985 an effort by the ERCS/ICRC to unite families was only partially successful. Of 79 cases of separation involving 145 people, 50 cases were traced, but of these only in six cases were the people willing to move in order to be reunited with other members of the family.

The government's decision to opt for a consolidation period was due to the decline in the number of voluntary settlers, the lack of assistance as a result of adverse publicity, and unforeseen problems arising in areas destined to receive the majority of the settlers according to the original plan. During this period of consolidation there has been some reconsideration on the part of a number of donors. Studies carried out by those with first-hand experience of the resettlement sites, particularly an evaluation team commissioned by the Irish voluntary organisation, 'Concern', to consider its involvement in two settlement areas in Wollega, Jarso, and Ketto, have clarified some issues and dispelled some of the disinformation surrounding the projects.

Between 1976 and the recent drought two main types of settlement scheme, involving 40,000 people, had been implemented by the present government. These were of two main types: low-cost settlements, where settlers were allowed to cultivate their land individually, with the minimum of assistance and little central supervision, on the agricultural estates nationalised during the land reform process; and special settlements, established in sparsely populated areas, which followed a producer cooperative model. The low-cost settlements have become more productive with higher yields per hectare, more self-sufficient and more self-reliant than the special schemes, despite the greater input of resources and extension services.

The main reason for this appears to be the failure of mechanisation — in particular, the extensive use of tractors — to increase food production. Not only are many tractors out of action at any one time because of lack of fuel, spare parts and qualified personnel, but the yield per hectare is not proving sufficient to justify their cost.

A second reason for the relative lack of success of the special scheme lies in the nature and organisation of the producers' cooperatives. Their introduction involves complex social innovation entailing a great deal of overall direction from party cadres. Evidence suggests that this saps the individual enterprise and initiative of the farmers, resulting in a continuing dependence on the supply of inputs from outside and on the cadres for decision-making.

Nevertheless, the majority of the settlements in the most recent programme are of this type. Villages of approximately 500 families have been erected in clusters in the areas of Gambella, Assosa, Metekel, Metema, Jarso, Kello, and Anger Gutin — all lowland areas under 1,500 metres. In these areas the growing period is much longer and the rainfall much higher than in the areas from which the settlers came. There is a high level of technical inputs with the introduction of mechanised farming and irrigation and the creation of new social and physical infrastructures. In contrast, a smaller number of settlers have been integrated into existing Peasant Associations in more densely populated areas of the highlands of Wollega, Illubaber, and Keffa.

In some of the new settlements the problems associated with mechanisation have already arisen and some flexibility in the extended use of oxen has been shown. No consistent policy appears to have emerged, however, on the degree and speed at which PAs and Service Cooperatives will be strengthened to take over management of their own affairs from the officials who have organised the initial phases of the resettlement operation. Representatives from all relevant Ministries — Agriculture, Health, Education, and Construction — officers of the RRC as well as cadres of the WPE have cooperated in the setting up of each settlement. The magnitude of the operation necessitated this approach, and the mobilisation of students, party workers and the existing communities in the location of settlements to clear land, build huts and generally prepare for the settlers was impressive, but the time has now come for a transition from the campaign basis of the settlement to normal agricultural development.

Perhaps the most serious challenge facing those involved in the schemes, however, is to develop a farming system based on practices different from those which have turned large parts of the country into unproductive, degraded hillsides. The resettlement scheme took place during an emergency, and the scarcity of resources persists. It is easy to see why short-term needs take procedence over long-term considerations, but the same exploitative methods are employed at most settlements for clearing and cultivation which ultimately made it necessary for the settlers to leave their old homes. Erosion is already clearly visible in a number of settlement areas. There is little to suggest that government staff or settlers have got beyond paying lip-service to the need for soil conservation. Where NGOs have become involved in support for settlement schemes, there is some recognition that immediate measures must be introduced to intensify the use of land already cleared rather than extend the cropping area. Substitutes for the timber being used to build stores and homes are being sought.

The other area in which anxiety has been expressed for the long-term success of these schemes has been the impact on the existing populations of the settled areas. Certain statistics show how great this has been in some regions; the newly settled population now constitutes 10 per cent of the population of Wollega, 24 per cent of the population of Assosa *awraja*; 3 per cent of the population of Gojjam, making up 38 per cent of the *awraja* of Metekel; 16 per cent of the population of Illubaber making up 85 per cent of the *awraja* of Gambella, and 26 per cent of the *awraja* of Gore.

Most of the integrated settlements are in the area of highland peasants, most of Oromo origin. Some settlers are ethnically Oromo but the majority are Amhara or Tigrean. The achievement of moving 95,000 families into 866 PAs in these areas in one year should not be underestimated, especially as in both 1985 and 1986 famine touched the western areas of Wollega, Illubaber and Keffa. In the long-term, however, there is a need for tribal assimilation, which will be made easier if the social and technical services initially tending to favour the settlement community are provided equitably to both settler and host community. The integration problems affecting the lowland areas are very different, for there the indigenous tribal people are distinctive groups of semi-nomads who have already been pushed towards marginal areas. There is no evidence that existing agricultural land has been taken away from local populations, but as those groups — the Anuak, Nuer and others — move regularly and are dependent on fishing, gathering and hunting, large permanent settlements inevitably threaten their traditional way of life.

It would be difficult to believe that the progress made in the settlement areas could have been achieved without a willing and motivated work-force. In several areas a food surplus has been produced after two seasons; protection of water supplies and medical services have improved the health of the population. Many problems remain, but an increasing number of international agencies and NGOs subscribe to the view that the half-million people who have been moved deserve assistance to realise the full potential of their new start. Their contribution in technical resources and expertise may not only assist in the fight against malaria, tsetse fly, soil erosion and water-logging, but may also help create a climate in which all those involved, including the relevant Ethiopian authorities, can contribute to a positive discussion on how settlements can be successful.

The separate policy of villagisation has also led to criticism of the government. In the current Three-Year Plan the objectives of the new initiative to congregate peasants are, 'the creation of a conducive situation which would facilitate the dissemination of improved agricultural technology, provision of other basic socio-economic services by the government and also the improvement of the land use practices of the peasants'. Such an objective, given the nature of the problems, should certainly be treated as a serious option. Once again, it is the implementation of the policy which has raised questions.

The process of moving peasants to newly constructed huts in rows has been carried out clumsily and in many cases the supply of services to the reluctantly congregated peasants has not followed. The reasons for such a policy are, therefore, not clear to the peasants, who see nothing positive to set against their list of complaints: lack of privacy, much further to walk to the fields, more disagreements over the ownership of livestock, and the nuisance of having neighbours inflicting themselves whenever a celebration is in evidence. As with resettlement, a great deal more could have been done to explain the policy to those whose lives were to be disrupted.

Research

In all areas so far mentioned there is a role of appropriately conceived research; in many areas research has been carried out but not applied; in some areas, for example, silviculture research still remains to be done. In most cases the institutions exist in which research can be carried out and personnel are already involved. It is important to establish where ongoing relevant research can be either extended or applied.

Training

In all areas mentioned there is a shortage of trained staff to extend the programmes and maximise their effectiveness. The existing vocational training structure cannot meet the increased demand for skills generated by the current rehabilitation programmes. These demands are arising partly because an increased level of mechanisation is required for a number of purposes; the operation of well-drilling rigs and water pumps to secure water; the use of sophisticated farm machinery to increase farm production, plus the use of bulldozers and other equipment to clear land; the use of road construction machinery and the ever-increasing use of trucks and other vehicles. Correspondingly, there is an increased need for repairs, servicing, electrical services, metal work and welding. In addition, training is required in many areas relating to agricultural and forestry development, including animal husbandry and horticulture. As mentioned above, plans for an extension of health care services will be constrained by the lack of trained personnel.

Accelerated vocational and in-service training at regional and community levels in many sectors has already been identified as a priority. In some cases schemes have been devised to meet immediate needs; the Agricultural Services Corporation of the Ministry of Agriculture, for example, is planning to set up regional workshops in which training will be given in the care, maintenance and overhaul of farm machinery.

The position of women

The health of women in Ethiopia has already been described. During the famine more women and children than men were found in the shelters and they were more malnourished. A greater number died but many also need to be rehabilitated. Many women sold all their meagre assets; household animals, cooking utensils and jewellery. Traditionally, women suffer from a low social status which deprives them of most opportunities for education and training and confines them to their roles as child-bearers and household workers. As more than 85 per cent of the female population of 21 million live in rural areas, they are also involved in the daily activities of subsistence agriculture.

The situation has changed since the revolution in that legislative measures to improve women's status were passed and women have been beneficiaries of the literacy campaigns. The national network of Women's Associations has been important in mobilising women. There is a political commitment to improve women's health and to provide family planning services. During public discussions on the new draft constitution the wording of the article relating to the equality of the sexes was changed from 'women have equal rights with men' to 'women and men have equal rights' at the insistence of women that there should be no suggestion that women were subordinate to men. Nevertheless, despite attempts to raise women's awareness, and despite the policy of encouraging the transition of the agrarian system towards socialist structures, the household is still the main unit of production and thus, in reality, the role and status of women is little changed. Most women are still faced with the wide range of essential tasks they have to perform in conditions of chronic food shortages, an insanitary environment and lack of basic facilities.

In urban areas a number of projects have attempted to assist certain categories of women, the unemployed, school drop-outs and unmarried mothers, to become involved in income-generating activities. In rural areas fewer programmes are in operation although many agencies are considering them. There is certainly a place for coordinated programmes to enhance the rural woman's life by involving her in income-generating activities and by assisting her to participate in activities which improve the standard of living for her and her family. These can be related to developing horticulture and animal husbandry; to the consideration of ways in which the time and energy consuming daily tasks (wood and water collection, grinding grain, and cooking) can be made more efficient. For example, there are various schemes which improve cooking methods by reducing the amount of fuel required, and to the development of traditional skills such as weaving and basket-making. Whereas there is awareness of these needs previous programmes have been fragmented and uncoordinated. Some have failed to have any longer term results as capital, market outlets etc were lacking. Few projects have taken the special needs of women in drought-affected areas into account.

Local participation

In the attempts to provide effective programmes the importance of involving those whom the programme is intended to benefit must always be stressed. In the identification, development and implementation of all effective projects, the active cooperation and participation of the local people is essential. There are now grassroot organisations through which programmes can be implemented: the PAs, producer's cooperatives, Women's Associations and Youth Associations. In many areas these organisations have been successfully mobilised, particularly in the provision of voluntary labour for community development schemes and the literacy campaigns. In some areas, however, their strengths have been under-utilised; with thoughtful preparation they could be drawn into a much wider range of production activities.

Famine prevention measures

The tone of the statements made at the RRC's Donors' meeting in January 1987 was a far cry from the inefficacious one of March 1984. The new Chief Commissioner of the RRC, Berhanu Jembere, put on record the deep gratitude of Socialist Ethiopia to the international donor community for its generous response. Michael Priestley spoke of the 'excellent relationship' he and the UN community enjoyed with their collaborators in the RRC. The difference in food requirements, as estimated by the FAO and the RRC, was not only accorded no importance but emphasis was put on the need to treat the RRC's appeal as the absolute minimum required rather than a target figure.

There is no doubt that attitudes have changed. But Ethiopia faces an endemic famine problem. Many of those still involved in both relief and development operations in Ethiopia reluctantly accept that another serious famine could occur within a few years. Is the changing of the climate of opinion enough? What are the substantive changes that will prevent a reoccurrence, if not of famine, of the delays in response that led to half a million deaths.

Monitoring and information

A Standing Emergency Prevention and Preparedness Group (EPPG), chaired by the UN Resident Coordinator and comprising working level representatives from UNDP, UNDRO, WFP, UNICEF, FAO, UNHER, WHO, the World Bank and other UN agencies involved in emergency relief prevention and preparedness, has been established in an attempt to ensure that the UN can act in a timely, effective and coordinated manner both to prevent future emergencies and to deal with them if they do occur. This new unit is earnestly seeking to cast off the bureaucratic image that bedevils many UN agencies and, by emphasising its links with the RRC and all bilateral and multilateral agencies and NGOs involved in Ethiopia, is attempting to provide an independent centre of information.

It is currently building up a new system of preparedness which will monitor and detail the flow of aid from all sources, maintain and continually update an inventory of all resources available and collate the data provided by various sources: the RRC, Ministry of Agriculture, Ministry of Health, and UNICEF early warning indicators. In addition, detailed background information on all areas of the country will be built up to form vulnerability profiles of all regions. The aim of this information gathering process will be to enable a continuous assessment of needs to be made which can then be linked to contingency plans.

The information is intended to be shared. An information sub-committee meets regularly under the chairmanship of the RRC; members include the World Bank, CRDA, and the office of the National Committee for Central Planning (ONCCP) and the EPPG. In addition, the RRC's own Early Warning System has been strengthened and a number of organisations involved in rural development contribute relevant data on rainfall, nutrition, etc. The Ethiopian Red Cross Society, which is still in the forefront of relief activities, has developed its own early warning system.

The mechanisms for collecting and collating the relevant data are, therefore, much improved. With reliable information on aid flows and resources within Ethiopia, misunderstandings as to availability of food reserves should be minimised. Will the availability of information alone be enough to trigger the response mechanism?

The National Food Security Reserve

With the assistance of the UN/WFP, a purely emergency reserve has been established. Over four years it is aimed to build up grain reserves of 180,000 tonnes which, stored in strategic locations, can be immediately released at times of emergency if there are delays in aid shipments. By the end of 1987 the present stock of 31,000 tonnes (donated by WFP, the Canadian, Indian and Dutch governments) is likely to be increased through further pledges to 53,000 tonnes. In January 1987 the RRC requested a further 47,000 tonnes to bring the total to 100,000.

Future response

Perhaps it is unreasonable to attach too much significance to the lack of enthusiasm for building up food reserves, but it was the lack of any coordinated response mechanism in 1984, rather than lack of information, which resulted in mass starvation. The provision of grain as a modest contingency measure is surely preferable to a repeat of the costly and belated exercise witnessed in late 1984 and 1985. As the problems of distribution were often greater than those of food availability, it is important that these emergency reserves are stored in suitable warehouses at strategic points.

All through the texts of the current reports and policy documents the efforts to overcome the largely bureaucratic problem of separating emergency and development needs can be detected. For budgetary, and sometimes overtly political, reasons donors need such a classification. But are tree-planting, or well-digging, relief measures or long-term development strategies? The new category suggested by Michael Priestley of 'emergency and famine prevention' may help circumvent political difficulties confronting some donors in their own countries, but the viewpoint of one experienced RRC official that this is merely semantics is understandable.

The fear is that the unprecedented level of solidarity and cooperation ultimately achieved in the crisis can be maintained only in an emergency. Once things stabilise, ideological lines sharpen again. There is evidence to suggest that the RRC, having suffered greatly from internal problems of leadership and direction after the defection of its Commissioner, Major Dawit, is now suffering from a move on the part of other Ministries directly involved with the long-term development strategies, to down-grade its status and reduce it to a relief agency. This may be part of the price it has to pay for being perceived as too close to Western donors.

Conceivably, in the event of another major famine the same delay in acknowledging its seriousness at the highest level may occur. Those in the lower levels of government may be no more willing to pass the bad news upwards than they were in the past. Whilst there is still an overlapping of personnel from the Office of Emergency Operations in Ethiopia in the new EPPG, the commitment to effective cooperation between all parties is not doubted. An element of doubt, however, does remain as to the lasting responsiveness of the institution. Personalities are perceived as important; institutional failure, especially the failure of international institutions, is only too common. In the opinion of some NGOs, the efforts going into the strengthening and computerisation of the information base should be centred not on the UN agencies but geared to the RRC.

Whereas the UN talks of an International Response System to parallel the improved information system, there are many who believe this to be unrealistic. Bob Geldof, on receipt of the Third World Prize in January 1987 said, 'The mass dying has been put off for a little while, so the screens went blank for a little while.' Many fear that a recurrence of famine in Ethiopia will not produce the spontaneous and generous response created in 1984 — or that again, only pictures of dying children will provoke the response. If that is so it will be because the cynicism of those who believe this to be so will have been matched by the cynicism of television producers with a built-in resistance to serious coverage of development issues, underestimating the genuine public concern and interest.

The next famine

Assuming that adequate information alerts the donor community in time and that massive mobilisation occurs to prevent starvation, will the lessons of famine 'management' have been digested?

The scale of the 1984 disaster affected the validity of many assumptions about effective policies in an emergency which had been held since the last famine. It is unlikely that many of those actively involved in the relief operations of 1984–86 will be in the same positions if a similar disaster occurs. Many organisations commissioned evaluations of their emergency activities. It is to be hoped that the most effective strategies will become incorporated into future policies in order to prevent the generals from fighting the last war.

15. Underlying Long-run Considerations: Climate and Population Growth

Climate

There are perhaps two aspects to the way in which the climate has affected the situation in Ethiopia. Firstly, is the much discussed question of whether the climate is changing and why. Secondly, is the wider question of the correlation of climate and poverty. Climate, as Robert Chambers and Gunnar Myrdal have pointed out, as an explanation of poverty is unfashionable. Mesfin Wolde Mariam in his book *Rural Vulnerability to Famine in Ethiopia* points out that vulnerability to famine is created by social forces and exacerbated by the 'intervening adverse effects of physical nature which, in turn, expose the failure of the social forces to act'.

I have attempted to show how, over a considerable time, certain sections of the population have become vulnerable to famine. Various policies are now being implemented in an attempt to reduce their vulnerability. But the seasonally adverse factors of Ethiopia's climate interact and reinforce each other in such a way that they cannot be ignored as a basic cause of the retardation of rural development. To be effective any measures aimed at the amelioration of the conditions in the drought-prone areas must take them into account.

There appears to be no consensus on whether recent African droughts are a 'natural fluctuation' or the harbingers of long-term climatic change. Because rainfall varies from year to year (and on longer time scales) drought must be a recurring phenomenon in any region where the average rainfall is close to the limit for prevailing agricultural activity. Thus, much of Africa is subject to recurrent drought interspersed with periods of adequate rainfall. Only a small change in overall rainfall can lead to drought.

As rainfall is seasonally highly concentrated, the distribution within the season and the timing of the start, are very important. The timing of the rainfall can result in the occurrence of an 'agricultural drought' even if the total rainfall is only little short of the norm. Whilst these small variations are significant in marginal areas, climatic conditions need several decades of close monitoring before any change is announced or agreed upon. It does seem agreed that there was above 'average' rainfall in the 1950s and a decline since then, with a slight recovery in 1974–75.

In scarcely any year since 1970 has the rainfall reached the mean values of 1954–70. During the early 1980s each year saw successively lower annual rainfall totals across the Sahel. The driest year was 1984, when rainfall appears to have been lower, taking the whole region into account, than any other year on record. A zone extending through northern Senegal, through central Sudan, and including the Tigray/Wollo region of Ethiopia and the Red Sea Hills, received less than 30 per cent of the 1931–60 mean rainfall. The climatic zones effectively shifted about 200–300 km south of their position in the 1950s.

River flows declined. The Nile discharge in northern Sudan for 1984–85 was reported to have been lower than 1913–14 — the lowest previously recorded. Significantly, the lowest previously recorded discharge at Aswan (July 1913 to June 1914), due to a 20–30 per cent deficiency in rainfall over the Ethiopian and Sudanese catchments of the Blue Nile at Atkbara, was estimated at that time to have been lower than at any time during the previous 200 years. Throughout the 1960s the Nile discharge was exceptionally high, the peak being in 1958–60.

Interpretations of these trends differ. Michael Dennet of the University of Reading states that the Sahel's rainfall from 1974 to 1983 was about 5 per cent less than in the 1931–60 period. If dry years were to continue, 'the possibility of this being due to chance is quite low'. Others go much further. E. P. Wright of the British Geological Survey notes that in the past 15 years average rainfall has been significantly lower than in the previous 60 — by as much as 50–60 per cent in the arid zone and 30–35 per cent in the semi-arid zone. Derek Winstanley, a meteorologist of the UN National Oceanic and Atmospheric Administration, points out that the present drought has lasted essentially for 17 years and that the odds against such a long succession of years of below-average rainfall are 125,000 to 1.

There is some historical evidence to suggest that past droughts have lasted a number of years and thus the present one is a natural, even though very unusual, event. However, the seasonal and spatial characteristics of the recent drought appear to differ from earlier droughts in this century (in the 1910s and 1940s). And evidence is accumulating of a very long-term downward trend in rainfall.

It is generally accepted that there is a marked element of persistence in departures from long-term mean conditions, with a clustering of dry years and wet years. This is not easily explainable, and whilst some observers regard it as likely that the present run of dry years will come to an end and wetter years return, others seek other indicators of longer-term change. At present there is still insufficient understanding of the climate to allow any reliable predictions to be made as to what can be expected of the rains over the next few decades, or even years or months. G. Farmer and T. K. L. Wigley in their comprehensive survey *Climatic Trends for Tropical Africa*, a research report for the Overseas Development Administration, go so far as to say, 'Put bluntly and in spite of occasional claims to the contrary our current long-term forecasting capability is close to zero.'

Confronted with the alarming evidence of the recent dry years, it is of little comfort to planners, politicians and the people most affected to be told this may be only a short-term phenomenon. Although there is as yet no conclusive evidence, some believe that since the decline in sub-Saharan rainfall north of the equator is unique in the period of reasonably accurate data, and that both seasonal and geographical patterns of rainfall deficits are changing, probably the drought reflects some entirely new intervening factor, possibly arising from man's influences on the environment.

Man's agricultural activities, particularly over-cultivation, overgrazing and deforestation, may have modifed the environment in such a way as to cause a prolongation and/or an intensification of naturally occurring drought. Bare soil and rock reflect more solar radiation back into the atmosphere than grass, shrubs and trees; this increased reflectivity (albedo) disperses cloud and reduces rain. A related hypothesis suggests that reduced soil moisture causes reduced evaporation which diminishes the contribution of latent heat, changing the radiation balance.

There are also theories of global climatic change relating to increasing concentrations of atmospheric carbon dioxide, which are the most likely cause of a consistent global warming. Although future climate cannot be forecast, there is some consensus that it is prudent to base planning decisions on the expectation that 'the rainfall regime of the last twenty years will be the norm'. In other words, recurring, serious droughts should be expected and policies aimed at diminishing the impact of the adverse weather must be adopted.

Bad land management reduces the use that can be made of rain that does fall. Policies have to take account of the nature of that rain; the main rainy season is associated with the Inter Tropical Convergence Zone (ITCZ), the meeting of the dry continental winds from the north and moist oceanic winds from the south. The convergence consists of separate weather disturbances which cause highly unpredictable storms. This randomness is the predominant feature and accounts for the pronounced differences in the rainfall experienced in adjacent areas. The intensity of the disturbances results in an abrupt transition from heavy rain to a clear sky which, since the rainy season is also warm, results in high evaporation levels and low soil penetration. As noted above, these heavy downfalls on inclines cause erosion and when occurring at inappropriate times can damage seedlings.

In early 1985 RRC Commissioner Dawit Wolde Ghiorgis said:

> We have to start again with the forestation programme, we have to start irrigation, soil and water conservation projects. If we had the know-how, the technology and the capability to properly utilise existing water we would not face shortages in coming years but we don't have the technology, the manpower, the money.

The main significance of climatic variability is that in large areas rainfall, a primary resource on which crop and animal production, electricity generation and industry depend, is inherently unreliable. Droughts that have afflicted several African countries in a crucial period for their development have contributed to their economic, political and social difficulties. There is evidence that peasant farmers in marginal areas adjust to living with the uncertainties created by unreliable rainfall, but this cannot be said of governments with wider responsibilities.

Whereas current research emphasises that climate is a variable, not a constant, the seasonality of the climate of such tropical areas as Ethiopia is a constant. In their book *Seasonal Dimensions to Rural Poverty*, Robert Chambers and others have demonstrated the impact of the seasonal factor on food production, nutrition and disease in a rural tropical environment. The case studies do not include Ethiopia but the overall framework and conclusions apply. Although, as Robert Chambers says, some points 'are almost embarrassingly obvious' they do need emphasising especially as it was 'embarrassingly obvious' from the failure of response to the recent famine that planners, policy makers and other urban-based professionals clearly do not understand the full implications of seasonality.

The start of the rains is when much work is required for planting new crops but at the same time food is short and food prices high (even in 'normal' years) and disease — malaria, diarrhoea, respiratory diseases, infectious skin conditions — more prevalent. The time of the year is known as 'the hungry season' or the 'lean period'. Success with the new crop may depend on prompt planting, yet, if there has been a succession of poor harvests, seeds and draught animals may be lacking; tools will have been sold to buy food. Because of a lack of these commodities or through illness or physical debilitation or because of late planting, the poorest farmers' harvest is often smaller than their richer neighbours. Women are often involved in the heavy agricultural work so that their other tasks, cooking, family hygiene and so on are neglected. They may also be pregnant as impregnation is likely to have occurred after the previous harvest. The period is marked by loss of body weight, low birth weight, high neonatal mortality, malnutrition, high incidence of disease and indebtedness.

Population growth

In his book *Africa in Crisis* Lloyd Timberlake quotes an Ethiopian relief worker as saying 'We are not over-populated, we are under-organised, under-funded and under-educated.' Many agencies have pointed out that Ethiopia, like other African countries, *could* feed itself; the fact that it cannot now do so does not prove it is overpopulated. It was partly the belief that the country had the agriculture potential to support more people that, in the past, prevented a coherent population policy from being seen as a necessity. The usefulness of the broad-brush approach, such as that used by the recent FAO Regional Agro–ecological Zone Study and Regional Potential Population Supporting Capacities Study, can, however, surely be questioned.

These studies took account of many variables: soil conditions, climatic conditions, level of inputs, types of crops, type of land management and level of conservation measures. A specially created climatic inventory, defining a growing period as the number of days when moisture and temperature are suitable for crop growth, was superimposed on a soil map of Africa resulting in a mosaic of the continent with tens of thousands of different land units. The basic data enable a calculation of basic food production to be made for every region and country and hence the potential population supporting capacity of each area, given a number of assumptions about the level of inputs. From this type of approach one can arrive at a wonderful vision of the future; given Africa is one entity with unrestricted movement of surplus products and labour, the continent has ample potentially cultivable land to feed future populations. If Africa could use all cultivable land for food production it could feed 1.5 times its projected population for the year 2000. If. . . . But Africa is *not* one entity.

The other end of the spectrum shows that, if the individual zones within a country attempt to attain self-sufficiency from their own land resources, then the situation is drastically different. It is this end of the spectrum, 'extreme' though it may be seen, that still describes many parts of Ethiopia; particularly the parts where those affected by famine live. The FAO studies show that these critical zones — those where land resources are already insufficient to meet the food needs of populations at present living in them — extend throughout the Sahel region into southern Sudan, Ethiopia, Somalia, Kenya, Tanzania, the highlands of Rwanda and Burundi. The 24 countries classified as being in a critical food situation in 1984 correspond almost exactly to the location of the critical zones.

Thus, in Ethiopia, one sees the problems of the whole continent in an acute form. Land resources and their potentials are very unevenly distributed within and between countries. In Ethiopia's case the drought affects the most densely populated, over-farmed areas. The concern over uneven distribution of population in relation to land resources has been expressed in all successive development plans and has been behind the PMAC's relocation policies. The resettlement, and more recent villagisation plans of the government, are discussed above but the rationale is that the 'long-term' is not available to Ethiopia and only bold policies can solve the problems of the over-populated highlands.

Do bold policies have a place, however, in the delicate area of family planning? Recently, concern has spread to the rate of population growth as well as to the issue of its distribution. The dangers arising when population increases faster than food production, and per capita food supplies therefore fall, have been realised. The 1984 census produced a shock for the Ethiopian government and all agencies involved in the planning of development programmes, for it revealed that population estimates had been about 10 million too low. With a population now estimated to be over 45 million, Ethiopia is the most populous African country after Nigeria and Egypt. High birth rates have to some extent been offset by the high mortality during the famine, and by some migration; the prevailing health conditions have been summarised above, but nevertheless the population growth rate is estimated to have risen from 1.5 per cent in 1950 to 2.5 per cent in 1982 and is currently 2.91 per cent.

From 1966 until 1984 the entire responsibility for the provision of family planning services fell upon the voluntary organisation, the Family Guidance Association of Ethiopia (FGAE). Initially, the organisation was up against the formidable combination of religious, cultural, social and political antagonism or indifference. Among orthodox Christians, parenthood is taken as a duty and children are regarded as God's blessings for whom He will provide. The impact of Islam on family planning in Ethiopia has not been closely studied, but even where vigorous religious teaching is not conducted, tradition tends to favour procreation. Of even more relevance, perhaps, is the traditional value attached to children in Ethiopia as in most of Africa, not only as additional labour in rural areas and as insurance against old age but also as a source of social prestige. Sterility is regarded as a disgrace; a barren woman is often threatened with divorce. The legal, economic and social status of women has been low, especially in rural areas, the issues of maternity receiving little attention. In a social system where children brought greater respect for a woman and were associated with the power and virility of a man, ideas of family limitation were not only unlikely to flourish, but tended also to carry some social stigma.

Through a cautious policy emphasising the value of child spacing and the welfare of the entire family, the FGAE has sensitised the government and religious authorities to the need for family planning, so that there is now a consensus on the need for the provision of education and information as well as practical services on all related issues.

In 1984 the Ministry of Health accepted that family planning services should be viewed as an important component of the Mother and Child Health Programmes. The movement has thus been legitimised, its link with the wider questions of food production, unemployment, shortage of housing provision, the inadequacy of health, education and recreational facilities recognised. But population policies alone do not increase the level of family planning practice.

The FGAE cannot meet the demand for its services, and family planning is reaching only approximately 2 per cent of the fertile women between the ages of 15 and 45 years. It has been proved in many situations that the extent to which family planning is accepted or rejected depends largely on how the message is put across to the individual. Within Ethiopia, teaching aids and films, promotional leaflets and hand-outs in different languages are used, but family planning information is given as far as possible through personal communication. In traditional societies the assumed credibility of the transmitter of the message is often as important as the message itself. The number of people reached in these ways has doubled from an estimated 120,608 in 1980 to 236,028 in 1986. The number of health institutions that offer an integrated family planning service including those administered by the

Ministry of Health and other Ministries and by state enterprises (including industries and state farms) has risen from 233 to 553 in the same period. The number of those accepting all types of contraceptives has risen from 49,228 to 171,813.

The training of health workers and others in family planning knowledge and service delivery is undertaken by the FGAE as there is no training provision in any professional, medical, nursing or health worker course of studies. The FGAE, in its headquarters in Addis Ababa, has so far trained 864 health workers, including Health Officers, Mother and Child Health/Family Planning Nurses, and Nurse/Midwives. In addition, they have provided training for non-medical workers employed by the Ministry of Agriculture —Rural Women Development Agents — working in rural areas to improve the lives of women in the countryside. They are trained to include guidance on methods of birth control and information on population issues, with education on nutrition, hygiene and child care.

As yet, however, the coverage by such trained workers can be only minimal in the countryside, where 88 per cent of the population still live. To extend the range of information, the mass organisations — The Revolutionary Ethiopian Youth Association, The Revolutionary Ethiopian Women's Association, The All-Ethiopian Peasants Association — as well as different religious groups, are participating in seminars and workshops in provincial towns in order to enlist the cooperation of men in the provision of family planning services.

Within the towns, especially Addis Ababa and Asmara, the acceptance of family planning is greater than even the fast-growing number of first-time visits to family planning clinics suggests. Recently a great surge in those requesting contraceptives of all types at the main clinics was found to be a result of a shortage of these goods in the pharmacies of Addis Ababa; clearly many people were buying them over the counter. The shortage was due to a lack of foreign exchange and, after consultations with the government, an allocation for such commodities was arranged. They are also exempt from import duties.

In the larger cities, and especially Addis Ababa, where housing is in acutely short supply, unemployment is high and low wages have been eroded by inflation, a young child is no longer seen as an extra pair of hands, unlike in the countryside, but as an economic liability. Economic considerations, therefore, reinforce the message received on television, over the radio and in the *kebeles*; men have clearly begun to accept it.

The rural population do not see television, few hear radio programmes. Despite a certain expansion since the revolution, less than 40 per cent are served by a clinic. With so few health workers trained in family planning procedures, even in existing clinics these services will not always be available or be seen as a priority. Ignorance is still considerable. Every nation embarking on a family planning programme has its share of setbacks, for each approach must be geared to local needs, conditions and attitudes.

In past years the FGAE devised a consent form for husbands to sign in order that their wives might be prescribed contraceptives; this was not entirely successful, its significance being misunderstood. Traditional methods of birth limitation are by no means unknown, breast-feeding is particularly important and in Ethiopia there are religious taboos against having intercourse on certain fast days and Saint's days. Approaches based on developing natural methods are favoured, but, again, they rely on trained personnel. In Jarso, a resettlement area where clinics staffed by Ethiopian Community Health Agents and the Irish voluntary organisation, 'Concern', have helped to improve the health of the highland settlers, a tremendous interest has been shown by the settlers, particularly the women, in family planning; most women, however, have no understanding of how pregnancy occurs.

Elsewhere, family planning workers have discovered in the process of encouraging women to use the rhythm method that most women believed themselves to be most fertile immediately after their menstrual period. Refraining from intercourse during the first week, they then resumed it when they were in fact entering the most fertile days of the cycle. A further constraint inherent in the provision of overstretched services is the difficulty of maintaining a woman's conviction that she should use some form of contraception throughout her fertile years. The task of family planning communication does not end once those who are willing to adopt family planning have been motivated. To ensure that they will sustain the practice over two decades involves an established service equal to the counter-campaigns that may arise to dissuade women from continuing to use some form of contraceptive.

We have a picture, therefore, of a growing number of dedicated professionals who have succeeded in persuading government and religious authorities that family planning is not synonymous with population control but is associated with responsible parenthood and family well-being. They have successfully sold the idea of child-spacing, believing any other approach to be counter-productive and contrary to the humanitarian consideration of the right of individuals to decide on how many children they should have. The growing awareness and acceptance of family planning measures in principle, which they have helped to create, now needs to be backed up by the provision of services; the infrastructure and resources need to be created to meet the demand. Realising this, the government has announced that a comprehensive population policy is being drawn up and intended to be put into effect in the course of the current Three-Year Plan.

But what are the realities of such a policy? Taking the 1984 census population figure of 42 million as a base and the population growth rate as 2.9 per cent, Ethiopia's population will be 66 million by the year 2000, double the 1984 figure by 2008, and 117 million by the year 2020.

The relief worker's opinion was just, and resentment at being told by outsiders that there are too many people is understandable, but at the same time it is hard to see how the country can cope with such high growth rates; it can be pointed out that many countries do not and are not expected to feed themselves by their own agricultural efforts — Switzerland, Britain, the Netherlands, Japan — but no European or North American country, and few parts of the Third World, have ever had to face such rapid increases. There is simply not enough time for self-sufficiency in food production to evolve, or diversification of trade with the possibility of increased food imports to become established.

In the provision of basic services rapid population growth obviously slows progress towards universal health care and education; in both these areas Ethiopia moves forward from a very narrow base. In terms of increasing literacy and primary education the rates are impressive but there is a long way to go. The 'demographic transition' by which modernisation brings a decline in fertility has often been described, but no country in sub-Saharan Africa is yet on that road. In the case of Ethiopia it is even likely that improved maternal health, better nutrition etc (if achieved) will lead to increased fertility levels unless the education campaign is unprecedentedly effective. Where campaigns have been successful in Asia, they have been preceded by two decades of experimentation, which Ethiopia has not had.

Ethiopia's main strength in the implementation of any new policy drawn up by the government will lie in the network of grassroots organisations which must be required to back up the work of the trained health workers. In particular, the public education aimed at improving the status of women, which is slowly having an impact, must be maintained.

Appendix

Basic Data:[1]
People's Democratic Republic of Ethiopia

Population	45.59 million	(1987)
Population growth (% p.a.)	2.91	(1987)
Life expectancy	46 years	(1984)

Age structure of population:

below 15 years	46.5%	(1984)
15–65 years	49.3%	,,
over 65 years	4.2%	,,
Urban population	11.3%	,,

Capital: Addis Ababa 1,412,575 million (1984)
Land Area: 1,222, 480 square kilometres

Source: Central Statistical Office

Gross Domestic Product
(Industrial Origin at Constant 1980/81 Factor Cost)
(In Ethiopian Birr millions)

	1983/84	*1984/85*	*1985/86*
Commodity Producing Sectors	5,229.2	4,616.1	5,355.5
Agricultural Sector	3,792.5	3,177.3	3,859.7
Industry	1,436.7	1,438.8	1,495.8
Services	3,085.9	3,149.4	3,285.6
GDP at Factor Cost	8,315.1	7,765.5	8,641.1
Growth Rate %	–3.7	–6.6	11.3

(*Source:* ONCCP)

GDP per capita (Birr)	241	217
(US$)	120	108

(*Source:* CSO/World Bank)

Exports: (Birr millions)

(Goods & non-financial services)	1,413.5	(1985/6)
Imports	2,176.1	(1985/6)

Production of Food Crops

	Average '000 Hectares	Output '000 Quintals	Yield per hectare	Average growth rate %
1979/80	6,056.9	74,955.8	12.4	–
1980/81	5,676.9	65,554.7	11.5	–12.5
1981/82	5,652.5	63,905.8	11.1	–4.0
1982/83	6,087.9	77,981.1	12.8	24.0
1983/84	5,646.3	63,563.2	11.2	–18.5
1984/85	5,613.0	47,309.5	8.4	–25.6
1985/86*	5,934.8	64,311.0	10.8	36.0

* Estimate:

Source: CSO

1. Statistical data for Ethiopia is difficult to obtain; these figures should, therefore, be taken as an approximation as near accuracy as could be obtained at this time.

Select bibliography

Chambers, Robert et al, *Seasonal Dimensions to Rural Poverty.*

Chambers, Robert, *The Crisis of Africa's Rural Poor: Perceptions and Priorities.* Brighton, Institute of Development Studies, 1985.

Donham, Donald L., James, Wendy, (eds.) *The Southern Marches of Imperial Ethiopia: Essays in History and Social Anthropology.* Cambridge: Cambridge University Press, 1986.

Halliday, Fred. & Molyneux, Maxine, *The Ethiopian Revolution,* London: Verso, 1981.

Foster, L. J., (ed.) *Agricultural Development in Drought-Prone Africa,* London: Overseas Development Institute/Tropical Agricultural Association.

Gilkes, Patrick, *The Dying Lion: Feudalism and Modernisation in Ethiopia,* London and New York: Julian Friedmann/St. Martin's Press, 1975.

Gill, Peter, *A Year in the Death of Africa: Politics, Bureaucracy and the Famine,* London: Paladin/Grafton Books, 1986.

Levine, Donald N., *Wax & Gold: Tradition and Innovation in Ethiopian Culture,* Chicago: University of Chicago Press, 1974.

Mesfin Wolde Mariam, *Rural Vulnerability to Famine in Ethiopia 1958–67,* London: Intermediate Technology Publications, 1986.

Ottaway, M. & Ottaway, D. *Ethiopia: Empire in Revolution,* New York: Africana, 1978.

Oxfam Publications:
    The Sahel: Why the Poor Suffer Most
    Ethiopia: Lessons to be Learned
    Food Emergencies in Sahelian Africa: Early Warning and Response
    Ethiopia: A Case for British Aid

Pankhurst, Richard, *The History of Famine and Epidemics in Ethiopia prior to the Twentieth Century,* Addis Ababa: Relief and Rehabilitation Commission, 1986.

Schwab, Peter, *Ethiopia: Politics, Economics and Society.* London: Frances Pinter, Ltd., 1985.

Sen, Amartya, *New Society,* October 1983, 'Poverty & Famines: an essay in entitlement & deprivation', Clarendon 1981.

Thompson, Blair, *Ethiopia: The Country that cut off its Head. The Diary of a Revolution,* London: Robson Books Ltd., 1975.

Timberlake, Lloyd, *Africa in Crisis.*

Articles

Farmer, G. & Wigley, T. M. L., Climatic Trends for Tropical Africa, Climatic Research Unit, University of East Anglia, 1985.

Grove, A. T. Desertification in the African Environment, *African Affairs,* Vol. 73, No. 291, April 1974. The Arid Environment, Royal Botanic Gardens, Kew, 1985

The State of Africa in the 1980s, *The Geographical Journal,* Vol. 152, No. 2, July 1986.

Korn, David A., Ethiopia: Dilemma for the West, *The World Today,* Institute of International Affairs, London, January 1986.

Vestal, Theodore M., Ethiopia's Famine: A Many Dimensioned Crisis, *The World Today,* Institute of International Affairs, London, July 1985.

Singer, Hans, Some Problems of Emergency Food Aid for Sub-Saharan Africa, *IDS Bulletin*, 1985, vol. 16 no. 3, Institute of Development Studies, Sussex.

Other sources & supporting documents

Bennett, Jon, John English, Bruce Dick, Tigray: An Investigation. Oxfam 1984.

Concern's Programme in Jarso & Ketto Settlements, Evaluation Team Report, Nov/Dec 1986.

Cutler, Peter & Rob Stephenson, 'State of Food Emergency Preparedness in Ethiopia', International Disaster Institute, November 1984.

Ethiopian Highlands Reclamation Study: Executive Summary, FAO, Rome, December 1985.

Family Guidance Association of Ethiopia, Facts and Figures, December 1986.

Government of Ethiopia: Three Year Development Plan 1986/87–1988/89, ONCCP November 1986.

Harris, Michael, *Ethiopia: Before & After*.

ICVA: Food, Famine & Service Delivery in times of Emergency.

North–South Round Table Conference Report: Beyond the Famine – New Directions in Development. Nairobi & Khartoum, 1986.

OEOA: Status Report on the Emergency Situation in Africa as of 1 September 1986; Issues of 'Africa Emergency'; reports issued by Information Service, United Nations Office for Emergency Operations in Africa.

Oxfam Reports, including Oxfam's Early Involvement & Ethiopian Monitoring Programme.

RRC, Various synoptic reports including Assistance Requirements, March 1984; Review & Assistance Requirements, 1986/87; Early Warning System Synoptic Report 1987.

UN General Assembly, 13th Special Session: Problems Facing African Countries, May 1986.

WHO: Health Conditions in the Ethiopian Drought Emergency, December 1984.

World Bank, Accelerated Development in Sub-Saharan Africa: An Agenda for Action, 1981; Financing Adjustment with Growth in Sub-Saharan Africa 1986–90, 1986.

Index